Coming to Terms with the Nation

D1291401

ASIA: LOCAL STUDIES/GLOBAL THEMES

Jeffrey N. Wasserstrom, Kären Wigen, and Hue-Tam Ho Tai, Editors

Coming to Terms with the Nation

Ethnic Classification in Modern China

——

Thomas S. Mullaney

With a Foreword by
Benedict Anderson

UNIVERSITY OF CALIFORNIA PRESS

Berkeley   Los Angeles   London

University of California Press, one of the most distinguished university presses in the United States, enriches lives around the world by advancing scholarship in the humanities, social sciences, and natural sciences. Its activities are supported by the UC Press Foundation and by philanthropic contributions from individuals and institutions. For more information, visit www.ucpress.edu.

University of California Press
Berkeley and Los Angeles, California

University of California Press, Ltd.
London, England

First paperback printing 2012

© 2011 by The Regents of the University of California

Library of Congress Cataloging-in-Publication Data

Mullaney, Thomas S. (Thomas Shawn).
  Coming to terms with the nation : ethnic classification in modern China / Thomas S. Mullaney ; with a foreword by Benedict Anderson.
    p. cm.—(Asia : local studies/global themes ; 18)
  Includes bibliographical references and index.
  ISBN 978-0-520-27274-3 (pbk.: alk. paper)
    1. Ethnology—China—History—20th century. 2. Ethnicity—China.
3. Minorities—Government policy—China. 4. China—Population.
I. Title.
  DS730.M85   2011
  305.800951—dc22   2010019209

19 18 17 16 15 14 13 12
10 9 8 7 6 5 4 3 2

This book is dedicated to my Parents,
Tom and Merri Mullaney,
to whom I owe everything.

[T]he written word is so intimately connected with the spoken word it represents that it manages to usurp the principal role. As much or even more importance is given to this representation of the vocal sign as to the vocal sign itself. It is rather as if people believed that in order to find out what a person looks like it is better to study his photograph than his face.

—FERDINAND DE SAUSSURE, COURSE IN GENERAL LINGUISTICS

CONTENTS

ILLUSTRATIONS

MAPS

FIGURE

TABLES

FOREWORD

When considering the fairly recent rise of "identity politics," in which one can easily get the impression that a person's "identity" has usurped his or her "soul," it is useful to recall that it is strictly laic and relational, rather than metaphysical and absolute. An identity is a naïve or strategic response to an external enquiry, and its content necessarily determined by who asks the questions, when and where, and what the answerer imagines he or she can guess about the kind of answer that is expected or demanded. Asked by a Bangkok interviewer "who" he is, a citizen of Thailand is unlikely to answer "a Thai." "A southerner" is much more likely. But "a Thai" would be the right answer to immigration officials in Tokyo. The same man, happening to spend time in Indiana, is likely to say "I'm an Asian," if he had reason to suppose that the local Indianans he meets have never heard of Thailand. He is in "their country," a very powerful one, and he feels he needs to adapt to their expectations. He will never speak of himself as an Asian in his own country.

. . .

The oncoming 220th anniversary of the institution of the census in 2010 is a good moment for reflecting on its checkered history and Janus-like character. One face, signifying human progress and the advance of democracy, was there at the start. In 1790, the infant American republic was the first state to experiment with it. It was understood as necessary for the republican project in which citizens, not monarchs, were to be sovereign, and their preferred leaders to be elected. The census was seen as essential for a fair electoral system, even if women were barred from voting for another almost 130 years, and till 1850 were not even tallied, since they could not be household heads, which was the target of the counting. To soothe the South, male black slaves were counted as three-fifths of a person; even if they could not vote, their numbers gave their masters a greater number of seats in the legislature. But the logic of the election-connected census pointed ahead to successive stages of emancipation, not completed till the 1960s. The American example was first copied in Europe (over the next decade) by the United Kingdom, the Netherlands, and France, all then run by oligarchies, but with political progress up ahead. It is significant of this electoral thrust that the American Bureau of the Census was not installed as a permanent, ceaselessly laboring arm of the state until 1902.

The other face of the census was its growing function as a crucial bureaucratic instrument for systematic policy-making. As time passed the questions asked by the census, which included many questions about identity, continued to expand, for reasons that had very little to do with democratization. Still, in North America and Western Europe, the census takers were dealing with populations that were familiar and of relatively small size. But this was by no means the case in the vast, populous zones acquired, from the 1860s onward, by industrial imperialisms. The British Empire led the way, followed in due course by the French, Dutch, American, and Japanese. These colonial censuses were instituted strictly for policy-making purposes, and were seen as the best basis on which colonial subjects could be identified, classified, and continuously surveilled. It was by no means an easy task.

The hardest part was devising a manageable classificatory system, though typically the coarsest base categories were simply race, religion, language-use, and ethnicity. In British India, however, the imperialists were fascinated by the deep roots and complexities of caste, and tried to rationalize it conceptually for census purposes. Unexpectedly, the policy of identifying cross-subcontinent castes had the long-term consequence of reifying these trans-Raj categories into competing political strata. Race was always tricky, especially after comparative philology showed that Sanskrit was a sort of ultimate ancestor to most European languages, allowing groups in both India and Ceylon to regard themselves as fellow Aryans, or quasi-whites. It was difficult to separate religion and race and ethnicity. If "Hindu" meant religious affiliation, then the dark-skinned Dravidians of the south were Hindu; but if Hindu was an ethnic marker they were to be excluded. The surveyors were befuddled by people who called themselves Hindu-Muslims or Muslim-Hindus, and it took time before this category, seen as impossibly illogical, disappeared from the census, if not from "real life." In British Malaya there was the bureaucratically anguished question of whether Jews and Arabs were white, or . . . ? But as time passed, the census takers learned some new lessons and later tricks. For example, the results of the 1921 census in British Burma showed that the people of Mergui district, on the colony's southeastern border with Siam, spoke "Burmese" to a man. But in the census of 1931, all of a sudden one hundred thousand people in the district said that they spoke "Mergui." Rangoon soon discovered that this eruption was caused by a casual change in the question asked. In 1921, as the nationalist movement was becoming a powerful political force, the question was "What is your maternal language?" To which "Burmese" was the logical answer. But in 1931, the question became: "What language do you use in everyday life?" To which "Mergui" was the obvious reply. The colonial authorities learned this way that they could manipulate identities by framing their questions in different ways.

An extraordinary and exemplary case is provided by the first two censuses (1911 and 1921) held in the remote Himalayan territory of predominantly Buddhist Ladakh, about which the British had so little knowledge that they decided in 1911 to let the population have full freedom to identify themselves as they pleased. Imagine the horror of the bureaucrat when the actual counting started to show that they had on their hands 5,934 "major groups" (castes, tribes, races, etc.) and 28,478 secondary identifications. This would never do. Hence in the 1921 census, Delhi arbitrarily decided on fifty-four categories, from which each subject had to take one pick.

A change of colonial masters could also have surprising effects. The Spanish Philippines got round to doing censuses very late, and the base categories were religion and race—from peninsular Spaniards, mestizos, and Chinese down to "natives." Ethnolinguistic groups simply did not appear. But the minute the Americans took over, they initiated a completely different system. The census managers drew on the experience of late nineteenth-century America, which had experienced an unprecedented flood of immigrants from Europe and elsewhere, and so worked up an elaborate specification of "savage" and "civilized" ethnicities, from which the population could take their pick. There was no space for "none of the above."

So far we have been considering only colonial bureaucrats in colonial capitals. But their efforts were substantially assisted by others. First were the Christian missionaries, Protestant (various sects) and Catholic, who obtained their converts substantially among remote, often upland, groups who were "still animist, or mainly so"—that is, not yet in the grip of Christianity's seasoned antagonists: Islam generally, and Hinduism and Buddhism more regionally. For the purposes of conversion, missionaries devoted years of their lives to mastering these peoples' languages, giving them Roman orthographies and compiling dictionaries. Second were young district officers and military men assigned to frontier zones. Unaware that radio and television awaited them in the not-too-distant future, they often fended off loneliness and boredom by amateur anthropology, archaeology, and books about travel and adventure. Last of all, chronologically, came professional social scientists, au courant with the methods of comparative linguistics, anthropological theory, and so forth. This historical progression can be seen as a parallel trajectory to the two Ladakh censuses discussed earlier.

. . .

Thomas Mullaney's wonderful book gives the reader a first-class account of the contemporary developments in China, which was too large and formidable for any single arrogant power to colonize—but a China whose borders abutted British India and Burma, French Indochina, and Russia-USSR. His aim is to show why and how the vast former Qing empire came to have, and officially celebrate, a limited number of mostly non-Han minorities under early Communist rule. One can see that the rulers nosed out British Delhi, given that the limited number of ethnic minorities in China was fifty-five, while the comparable figure for tiny Ladakh was merely fifty-four.

One could say the founding era for this story covers the second and third decades of the twentieth century. In 1911, the decaying Qing regime was overthrown and replaced by a republic. As we have seen, a republic, whatever its actual *in situ* deficiencies, draws its legitimacy and modernity out of a drastic shift of sovereignty from monarch to the national citizenry. Since the nationalist elites in China had no intention of relinquishing any part of the territorial legacy of the Manchus (though under pressure from the Soviet Union they lost "Outer Mongolia"—today's Mongolia—in 1921), it became necessary to start thinking about the non-Han portion of the imperial domain. The crucial outcome of a long debate among the literate Han was a fundamental shift in terminology, one centering on the concept of "minorities." The Manchu regime did not like to think in terms of "minorities," since they themselves were a tiny one. But minority, as a concept, was fundamentally tied to the idea of a citizenry and the logic of mathematics and voting. This goes back to Tocqueville—in America, not France—and his fear of a "tyranny of the majority," clearly born from censuses and popular elections. Minorities come into existence at the moment when electoral majorities can be counted. Though Chinese elites did not really think very much in an electoral vocabulary, they could not avoid a mathematical way of thinking about the citizenry of the Republic, which included everyone on a notionally equal basis. The traditional imperial Chinese notion of "barbarians" was no longer permissible: how could citizens be barbarian?

Meantime, Chinese social science was born, not least because significant numbers of Han academics were returning from tip-top training in Europe, America, and Japan. The anthropologists among them, caught up in the currents of the time, nonetheless saw it among their tasks to understand these minorities. That Yunnan should have been a favorite site for study is understandable in this context. Tibet was too cold and too difficult to reach and breathe in, and Xinjiang was too Muslim and too arid. Yunnan was fabulously beautiful, had a perfect climate, and, best of all for the romanticism of early anthropology, was a sort of Eden, full of sensuous, bare-breasted, innocent women who were a special attraction for puritan Confucian Han.

Alas, Generalissimo Chiang Kai-shek had no time for social scientists, especially those with romantic ideas, insisting that everyone in the Republic was simply Chinese: no minorities or majorities. On the other side of the 1930s political fence, the Communist Party, struggling to survive against Chiang's ferocious repression, retreated into the ex-empire's peripheries, and for progressive as well as strategic reasons committed itself to respect for the minorities and helping them as fellow citizens.

Within four years of coming to power in Peking, the new regime organized its first census, partly following the Soviet model, but also because, by the 1950s, censuses were globally understood as unavoidable instruments of modern government. (Only in the turbulent 1960s, and only in the Netherlands, was census-taking abolished.) It is at this point that Mullaney's core analysis begins.

In the flush of victory and still armed with the revolutionary spirit, the census organizers offered citizens a fairly free rein in self-identification. Peking, unaware of the example of Ladakh, was taken aback to find the census registers replete with the names of roughly four hundred would-be ethnic minorities, about two hundred of which were domiciled in Yunnan. This would never do—not merely because it anticipated serious bureaucratic problems, but also, as Mullaney wryly indicates, because minimal representation of these peoples in the national legislature would require bodies with many thousands of members from all over the country.

By luck, skill, and the passing of half a century, Mullaney was able to access almost all the secret documents, reports, anthropological notes, and field interviews that represent the story of how four hundred would-be *minzu* got squashed into the fifty-five official minorities accepted today (which, taken along with the majority Han, bring us to something of a magic number in contemporary China: fifty-six). Here is where the social scientists, whom the generalissimo had scorned, finally came into their own. They were the only group with the specialized skills required. Party cadres, no matter how loyal and energetic, could not easily manage conceptual abstractions and analytic tasks. Taking Yunnan as his example, Mullaney tells us how the government sent off teams of such social scientists, old and young, to spend six months of intensive research, to be followed immediately by a decisive report on which minority policy-making would thereafter be based.

The research had two components—scientific and political. It is with the first that Mullaney has uncovered a magnificent irony: namely, that the framing of the research was based on the writings of an adventurous military officer from the British Empire. Henry Rodolph Davies, born in 1865, and highly educated (Eton!), served in the imperial army first in the old Raj and later in newly conquered Burma (1886). He was a natural polyglot who mastered "Hindustani" and Persian, and over time made progress with Pashto, Chinese, and Burmese. He spent most of his thirties (1893–1903) traveling about Yunnan, surveying, mapping, interviewing, and comparing. He was fascinated by the diversity of the province, as previous travelers had been, and worked up the outline of what one could call a preliminary, quite personal, but scientific classificatory system for conceptually mastering this diversity. Drawing on the discipline of comparative linguistics, studying dozens of basic-word lists, he was able to divide into a relatively small number of language-families what contemporary Qing gazetteers described in terms of barbarian tribes numbering in the hundreds. Even if the communities concerned had little awareness of their affiliations (sometimes even with local enemies), science, with the help of imperialism, could see a logical and rational order. His book *Yün-nan: The Link Between India and the Yangtze* was published in 1909, just before the fall of the Manchus and the onset of the Republic, and it proved a life-long model for Chinese social scientists interested in the country's peripheries.

The political side of the research is, as Mullaney describes it, no less interesting. In this regard, the ghost of Mergui looms up. The social scientists might "know" the truth of Yunnan, but how were these new "minorities" to be persuaded of it? The author offers an instructive picture of how the researchers went about this task, in which a discreet coerciveness was sometimes necessary. They were helped by the concentrated and by then uncontested authority of the regime, and the local groups' still rather dim conceptions of what the practical policy outcomes of the research would mean for themselves.

What is moving in Mullaney's work is the wide range of his sympathies, for the social scientists (a number of whom he got to know personally), for the minority groups in Yunnan, for the local cadres, who were powerful but out of their depth (and sometimes suspicious), and for the regime in perhaps its best period. No one is denounced and the narrative is flavored with a gentle irony.

What we do not see, as it is out of his timeframe, are the long-term consequences of all this, perhaps because all the Yunnan groups were too small to cause any serious trouble. But China today faces its most visible troubles precisely in the big minority areas—Tibet and Xinjiang. It is quite possible that some of this unrest also emerges from the early 1950s. Were people living then in Tibet and Xinjiang thoroughly aware of themselves as "Tibetans/Uighurs, yes, all of us"? Or did this awareness gradually develop as the regime made policies in every field on the basis of the fifty-six, and the citizenry found themselves replying to the state's incessant "Who are you?" in new ways. Identity is never a one-way street.

Benedict Anderson

ACKNOWLEDGMENTS

This project has been my constant companion from the first year of graduate school in 2000 through my first three years at Stanford University. My only regret is that I lack a comparable amount of time to thank all of my friends, family members, and colleagues personally and extensively for their guidance and support over the course of these nine years. To borrow a verse from Neil Young: "One of these days, I'm gonna sit down and write a long letter . . . "

In the world of academia, my first and deepest gratitude goes to William Rowe and Madeleine Zelin. It was as an undergraduate at Johns Hopkins University where my interest in Chinese history was fostered by Professor Rowe. Thereafter, I had the tremendous fortune of spending six unforgettable years under the masterful guidance of Professor Zelin, my PhD advisor. I am grateful to Professor Zelin for never letting me lose sight of the "so what" question and, above all, for teaching me the importance of visualizing one's ideal historical sources before setting out to find them. It was this advice that, after a long and often frustrating search, led me to the archives that have opened up the history of the 1954 Ethnic Classification Project.

I am exceedingly grateful to all of my professors at Columbia. In my classes with Robert Hymes, I learned that the analysis of historiography could be brought to the level of an art form. Carol Gluck taught me resilience and the importance of constantly scaling "up and down the ladder." As Teaching Assistant to William Theodore de Bary, whose lectures merged magisterial scope and profound depth, I witnessed the pedagogical ideal. Barbara Fields was in many ways my first guide to graduate school, and refused to let me give up on the pursuit of capable, analytical writing. I am also grateful for the expert instruction of Partha Chatterjee, the late Wu Pei-fu, and Nadia Abu El-Haj, and for the guidance and support of Eugenia Lean, Adam

McKeown, Dorothy Ko, Chengzhi Wang, Amy Heinrich, and Dorothy Solinger. I would also like to thank Michael Tsin for navigating my altogether scattered graduate school application and finding hope in my candidacy. Although I did not get to work with him, nonetheless I consider Professor Tsin an important mentor to whom I owe a great deal.

My graduate school experience was profoundly influenced by my fellow students, and above all by my writing partner and beloved friend Alex Cook. I am also deeply grateful for the friendship and support of Dennis Frost, Kelly Frost, Nick Toloudis, Ted McCormick, Ben Martin, Chris Rea, Fabio Lanza, Bill Coleman, and Benno Weiner. I will always cherish the countless hours spent at Hungarian, the late-night dinners at Koronet, and the long afternoons at Labyrinth. I am also extremely grateful for the friendship of Andy Field, Lee Pennington, Nick Tackett, Nicole Cohen, Naomi Furusawa, Linda Feng, Sara Kile, Kerim Yasar, Martin Fromm, Se-Mi Oh, Matt Augustine, Satoko Shimazaki, Enhua Zhang, Jessamyn Abel, Lori Watt, Joy Kim, Steven Bryan, Torquil Duthie, Nina Sadd, and Ian Miller.

In addition to receiving the generous and selfless support of my professors and colleagues at Columbia, I have been incredibly fortunate to receive invaluable mentorship from a number of scholars at other institutions. My deepest gratitude goes to Stevan Harrell, Jeff Wasserstrom, Mark Elliott, Jonathan Lipman, Louisa Schein, Mette Hansen, Nicholas Tapp, and Frank Dikötter. Each of these scholars devoted an immense amount of care and time to my development, and my only hope of repaying them is by offering such assistance to their students in the future. I am also extremely grateful for the support and mentorship of Bryna Goodman, Gail Hershatter, Orville Schell, Tom Gold, Geof Bowker, Susan (Leigh) Star, Ben Elman, Pat Giersch, Emma Teng, Uradyn Bulag, Munkh-Erdene Lhamsuren, Jim Leibold, Charlotte Furth, Stéphane Gros, Don Sutton, Dru Gladney, Robert Culp, Madeleine Yue Dong, Janet Upton, Jamin Pelkey, and the editors at *China Information*. I am also grateful to Xiaoyuan Liu and John Torpey for commenting on my dissertation, and for the extensive comments and criticisms raised by two anonymous reviewers of my book manuscript.

Among my colleagues and friends in China, my deepest gratitude is extended to Yang Shengmin and Wang Xiaoyi. I met Professor Yang during his tenure as a Visiting Scholar at Columbia University. Despite a hectic work schedule, Professor Yang gave me ample opportunity to seek his advice on my project. In the following year, he sponsored my visit to the Central University for Nationalities, where I had the extreme fortune to meet Professor Wang Xiaoyi. Insofar as I explain Professor Wang's central role in this study in the introduction, suffice it to say that this book would scarcely have been possible without his guidance. I also wish to extend my heartfelt gratitude to Professor Wang's entire family, and especially Wang Shuang.

Among my associates, colleagues, and friends in China, I am also indebted to Shi Lianzhu, Yan Ruxian, the late Xu Lin, and Chang Hongen for agreeing to share their experiences from the Ethnic Classification Project of 1954. I also wish to thank Lang Weiwei, Li Shaoming, Bamo Ayi, Sun Hongkai, Qi Jinyu, Luo Huixuan, Peng Wenbin, Pan Jiao, Zhang Haiyang, Wang Jianmin, Cai Hua, Wang Mingming, and Lin Zongcheng. I am also exceedingly grateful to the directors and staff members at the Sichuan Provincial Archives, the Sichuan University Republican Era Periodicals Reading Room, and the Yunnan Provincial Archives. In the United Kingdom, my heartfelt thanks goes to Claire Haslam and her colleagues at the Worcester County Records Office.

In many ways, my life began anew in 2006. Having completed my dissertation and started my position at Stanford, my new colleagues transformed what could have been an overwhelming experience into an utter joy. I cannot adequately express my gratitude and fondness for my colleagues, each of whom I am inclined to cite by name and thank individually. Unable to do so, I will confine myself to those who played a direct role in this book, particularly Matt Sommer, Kären Wigen, Gordon Chang, Aron Rodrigue, Melissa Brown, Shao Dongfang, Jean Oi, Andy Walder, Jun Uchida, Yumi Moon, and all of the members of the Junior Faculty Reading Group. I would also like to thank all of my students—particularly Eric Vanden Bussche, Matthew Boswell, and Tony Wan—and the many members of the administrative staff whose support has been invaluable to me. Above all, I wish to thank Monica Wheeler, Linda Huynh, Shari Galliano, Julie Leong, Lydia Chen, Connie Chin, and Stephanie Lee.

There are many institutions whose generous financial support made this book possible. As a graduate student, I received the Social Science Research Council International Predissertation Fellowship, which enabled me to conduct archival research in Beijing, Sichuan, and Yunnan. At Stanford, grants from the Hewlett Fund, the Department of History, and the Center for East Asian Studies made it possible to conduct follow-up research and develop the manuscript in a timely fashion.

I am also grateful to each of the many institutions and associations that afforded me an opportunity to present early iterations of my work. These include the Association for Asian Studies, Bard College, Beijing Normal University, the University of California Irvine, the Central University for Nationalities, the Center for the Study of Ethnicity and Race at Columbia University, the Columbia University Department of History Graduate-Faculty Symposium, the Columbia University Graduate Student Conference on East Asia, Fudan University, the Johns Hopkins University Comparative and World History Seminar, the University of Oregon, the Southwest University for Nationalities, the Stanford University Center for East Asian Studies, and the University of Washington.

Last on this list, but first in my world, are my friends and family members. Among my friends, I extend my first and deepest gratitude to Andy Pels, Salley Pels, and Gregg Whitworth, my oldest, dearest, and most cherished friends. In my life before New York, I am also deeply grateful to Nadav Kurtz, Noah Donaldson, David

Herman, Emily Donahoe, the Key School, Jose Hagan, Serena Leung, Frances and Alex Kling, Valerie Nichols, and Harvey and Bea Dong. I wish to express love and gratitude to Joanne Chan Taylor and her entire family, to whom I wish all the happiness in the world. In New York, I am eternally grateful for the wonderful friends I made, above all Ruben Mercado and Nicole Hegeman. I am also grateful for the friendship of Emily Dinan, Ebru Yildiz, Naomi Watanabe, Claira Kim, Julia Hart, Louise Zervas, Jen Pomes, and Greg Franklin. Since coming west, my life has continued to be blessed. In particular, I wish to thank Matt Gleeson, my partner in all things creative, and Molly Nicholas, my teammate. I am also deeply grateful for the friendship and support of Amalia Miller, Stephanie Stolorow, my extended family at the Dolores Forest, Risa Wechsler, Sai Mayi Magram, and Amy Coleman.

My siblings and extended family supported, encouraged, and tolerated me throughout this entire process, and for that I am ineffably grateful. My love and thanks goes to Laura, Brian, Samantha, Scott, Mojgan, and Cameron. Most importantly, I wish to acknowledge the incalculable debt of gratitude I owe to my parents, Tom and Merri Mullaney, for whom the depth of my love cannot be fathomed. This book is for you both.

In closing, I wish to extend my deep appreciation to Reed Malcolm, Suzanne Knott, Kalicia Pivirotto, Chris Pitts, and their colleagues at the University of California Press. From start to finish, this entire process has been sheer joy. I also wish to thank the faculty board for the Local Studies/Global Themes series (Hue-Tam Ho Hai, Jeffrey Wasserstrom, and Kären Wigen), and Benedict Anderson for writing the foreword.

Introduction

Fifty-six stars
Fifty-six flowers
Fifty-six brothers and sisters together form one family
Fifty-six national languages together form one sentence:
I love my China, I love my China

—LOVE MY CHINA, LYRICS BY QIAO YU

User msohu: "Legally, how can I marry a girl from each of the fifty-six minzu?"
User qhfzfj: "Simple. First you marry someone from one minzu, then you get
   divorced. After that, switch minzu and get married again. Then get divorced,
   then get remarried, . . . and you've got it."

—EXCHANGE POSTED ON QIHOO, CHINESE ONLINE COMMUNITY SITE,
SEPTEMBER 23, 2007

From the sacred to the profane, the idea of China as a "unified, multinational country" *(tongyi de duo minzu guojia)* is a central, load-bearing concept within a wide and heterogeneous array of discourses and practices in the contemporary People's Republic. China is a plural singularity, this orthodoxy maintains, composed of exactly fifty-six ethnonational groups *(minzu)*: the Han ethnic majority, which constitutes over ninety percent of the population, and a long list of fifty-five minority nationalities who account for the rest.[1] Wherever the question of diversity is raised, this same taxonomic orthodoxy is reproduced, forming a carefully monitored orchestra of remarkable reach and consistency: anthropology museums with the requisite fifty-six displays, "nationalities doll sets" with the requisite fifty-six figurines, book series with the requisite fifty-six "brief histories" of each group, Olympic ceremonies with fifty-six delightfully costumed children, and the list goes on. Fifty-six stars, fifty-six flowers, fifty-six minzu, one China.

China has not always been home to fifty-six officially recognized groups, however. In the late Qing (1644–1911), gazetteerists reported to the imperial center about a wide variety of "barbarians" living in the frontier regions. For one province, Yunnan, such accounts portrayed the region as home to over one hundred

MAP 1. Yunnan Province

distinct peoples, with nearly one hundred more in the neighboring province of Guizhou. Only a few decades later, however, in the China of Chiang Kai-shek, the Nationalist regime vociferously argued that the country was home to only one people, "the Chinese people" *(Zhonghua minzu),* and that the supposedly distinct groups of the republic were merely subvarieties of a common stock. At the same time, a counterdiscourse emerged among Chinese scholars in the newly formed disciplines of ethnology and linguistics, a discourse in which China was reimagined as home to many dozens of unique ethnic groups—a newly imported concept also translated using the term *minzu.* Early Chinese Communists began mounting a comparable argument, railing against Chiang Kai-shek's vision of a mono-minzu China, and on behalf of one in which the country was seen as a composite of politically and economically equal ethnonational constituencies.

Following the revolution of 1949, this ethnotaxonomic volatility persisted. In the first census of the People's Republic of China (PRC), carried out in late 1953 and early 1954, officials tabulated over four hundred different responses to the question of minzu identity. This deluge came in response to the Communist Party's promise of ethnonational equality, which entailed a commitment to recognizing the existence of ethnonational diversity to a greater extent than their predecessors had ever been willing to do. Over the course of the subsequent three decades, however, only fifty-five of these were officially recognized, which entailed a remarkable level of categorical compression: from four hundred potential categories of minzu identity to under sixty. The most dramatic case, again, was that of Yunnan Province. Out of the four-hundred-plus names recorded in the 1953–54 census, more than half came from Yunnan alone. Over the following years, however, only twenty-five of these were ultimately recognized by the state.

How do we account for this polyphony of ethnotaxonomic theories? Were there in fact more distinct ethnocultural groups living in the territories of China during the Qing than in the early twentieth century? Had there been a mass exodus? On October 1, 1949, did these communities return, eager to be recognized by the new Communist regime? Clearly, this is not the case. These differences in ethnotaxonomy cannot be accounted for at the level of the categorized. Rather, what changed over the course of this period were the ethnopolitical worldviews of the different Chinese regimes, the modes and methods of categorization they employed, and the political commitments that guided their respective efforts to reconceptualize China in the postimperial era. There was no single "search for a nation in modern Chinese nationalism"—rather, there were searches, in the plural.[2] The Nationalists did not assimilate or expel hundreds of minority groups from the country following the 1911 Revolution. Rather, late republican Nationalists adopted and promoted an ethnotaxonomic worldview wherein the very meaning of the operative term, minzu, was defined in such a way so as to disallow the very possibility of a multi-minzu China. Like a "four-sided triangle," a multi-minzu China was for Chiang Kai-shek and others a logical impossibility, a contradiction in terms. Continuing into the Communist period, it is clear that the revolution of 1949 did not prompt an influx of minority communities. Rather, the emergence of the "unified multinational" People's Republic is understandable only when we take into account the radical changes in the very meaning of term minzu and the new regime's distinct approach to the "national question."

With these considerations in mind, then, the goal of this book is to move toward a deeper understanding of how the People's Republic came to be composed of fifty-six minzu by examining the history of ethnotaxonomic discourse and practice in the modern period. In other words, the present study will produce what Jane Caplan and John Torpey have described in a Western context as a "history of identification rather than of identities."[3] The centerpiece of this study is China's "Ethnic Classification Project," or minzu shibie, a collective term for a series of Communist-era expeditions wherein ethnologists and linguists set out to determine once and for all the precise ethnonational composition of the country, so that these different groups might be integrated into a centralized, territorially stable polity.

By means of the Ethnic Classification Project, the Communist state determined the number, names, and internal compositions of China's officially recognized ethnonational groups. As such, I argue that the project stands at the center of practically all questions of ethnicity in contemporary China, being itself part of the history of each of the minzu categories to which it gave shape and, in some cases, existence. Despite its centrality, however, the details of the project have remained virtually unknown, clouded in a great deal of confusion. When the project is directly addressed in English-language scholarship, which is rarely, it is caught between starkly different interpretations. By some it has been summarily dismissed as "arbitrary"[4] and "procrustean,"[5] and by others vaunted as "ethnographic inquiry into the minutiae of everyday life and local custom"[6] and "perhaps the most extensive series of fieldwork projects ever conducted anywhere on earth."[7] The project, as we will see, was neither of these things—neither a Communist-imposed scheme whose ethnological dimensions can be dismissed as pseudoscience, nor a purely social scientific endeavor that can be treated apart from the broader history of modern Chinese ethnopolitics.

In 1995, the first (and until now, only) dedicated analysis of the Classification was published in the PRC by Shi Lianzhu.[8] For the first time, some of the most basic questions about the project were finally answered: the names of the researchers involved, the timeframes in which they conducted their field research, the ethnonyms of those investigated, and so on. However, the study cautiously and uncritically portrayed the Classification as little more than a process of discovery. Candidate by candidate, phase by phase, the researchers who carried out the project are portrayed as systematically excavating true, preexisting identities of China's minority peoples. The identities of China's non-Han minority groups, it would seem, were carefully unearthed from beneath accumulated layers of misunderstanding.

The tone and analytical approach of the book was a direct reflection of its authorship and the ethnopolitical environment in which it was published. Although written by Shi Lianzhu, a researcher in the Ethnic Classification Project, it was published under the name of Huang Guangxue, a government official in the Nationalities Affairs Commission. Having no interest in raising questions about the accuracy of the project or its taxonomic conclusions—and even less so in revealing that the Chinese state played a significant role in the construction of the country's officially recognized minzu—the text treats the Classification as having played absolutely no role in the ethnogenesis of China's non-Han peoples, an argument that the present study will refute. China's fifty-six-minzu model was not, as Shi and Huang's study suggests, an immaculate conception.

Having announced my central focus as the history of ethnotaxonomic discourse and practice in modern China, and the role of the Classification in the development of the fifty-six-minzu model, I should state clearly that this is in no way meant to suggest that we can discount the findings of historians who have examined the *longue durée* histories of China's non-Han peoples. One simply cannot understand ethnic diversity in Yunnan, for example, without taking into account the topography of the province. Cut up by complex river systems and marked by rapid fluctuations in elevation, Yunnan's geography doubtless has contributed to the splintering of communities and linguistic diversification. Likewise, another key factor has been the province's location at the crossroads of migration and cultural exchange emanating from the civilizational centers of modern-day Southeast Asia, Tibet, and China. This complex and layered history of migration is undoubtedly constitutive of modern Yunnan and its resident communities. The fifty-six-minzu model was not produced by way of discourse alone.

As vitally important as these factors are in the production and enactment of identity, however, an approach based entirely on geography, migration, and deep history ignores the significant role played by taxonomy, and treats categorization unproblematically as the passive description of "pre-existing properties of the world."[9] In doing so, we fail to distinguish between two related but very different histories: the history of *diversification* and the history of *categorization*—that is, between the history of how and why human communities undergo differentiation and/or amalgamation along linguistic, cultural, religious, physical, and other trajectories; and the history of how and why, at different moments in time, specific types of difference are privileged over all others as the organizing criteria of taxonomic work and state infrastructure. The first of these issues is undoubtedly a historical one requiring a *longue durée* perspective that takes into account migration, geography, cultural interaction, and so forth. On its own, however, such a perspective helps us understand only the present-day "plurality" of the region in an overall and nonspecific sense of variation, and not how these communities have come to be categorized into the specific number of minzu recognized today. In order for us to move from the unbounded and ever-shifting plurality of the region to the bounded and fixed "diversity" of the PRC, these *longue durée* histories must be considered in relation to the Ethnic Classification Project, which crafted the prism through which the modern Chinese state, and increasingly the people of China and the world at large, have come to view and understand non-Han Chinese identity. In other words, to explain the present-day diversity of Yunnan, I argue that we must adopt a bifocal view that takes into account both long-term, on-the-ground processes of differentiation and amalgamation, and what Lorraine Daston has described as "salience," a term she employs as "shorthand for the multifarious ways in which previously unprepossessing phenomena come to rivet scientific attention" and thereby "coalesce into domains of inquiry."[10] Only then can we understand how and why contemporary China is understood to be home to fifty-six distinct peoples, as opposed to many hundreds (as in the late Qing imaginary) or one (in the eyes of Guomindang authorities during the first half of the twentieth century).

REVISITING THE CLASSIFICATION:
NEW SOURCES, NEW INSIGHTS

Our limited knowledge of the Classification derives in large part from the long-standing absence of primary source materials. Until very recently, firsthand reports from the project had been off-limits, greatly limiting our understanding of even the most basic facts about the project: who was involved, when it was undertaken, which ethnonymic groups were investigated, and so on. Fortunately, in reconstructing the history of the 1954 Ethnic Classification Project, I have benefited immensely from five new bodies of sources, compiled from archives, libraries, institutions, and private collections in Beijing, Kunming, Chengdu, London, and Worcester, England.[11]

First, this book constitutes the only study to date to draw upon the actual text of the 1953–54 census registers. I cannot emphasize enough the importance of this source. For the first time, rather than simply recapitulating the oft-cited fact concerning Yunnan Province—namely, that it accounted for more than half of the four-hundred-plus minzu names registered in the inaugural census of the PRC—we will finally be able to see these names, the specific counties from which they hailed, and the populations of each. Rather than starting in the present day and trying to reverse engineer the logic and practice of the Classification, then, we will now be able to understand both the impetus for the project and the specific problems that the team, and the Chinese state, were attempting to resolve. To my way of thinking, this text offers us a vantage point that, although not standing outside of taxonomy in general, does stand outside the "black box" of the fifty-six-minzu paradigm.

A second set of documents, and the one on which the majority of this study is based, is a remarkable collection of recently declassified reports from the 1954 Ethnic Classification itself. These are firsthand (and mainly handwritten) reports from the project that contain unprecedented detail regarding groups who, in terms of the official discourse of the PRC, no longer exist as minzu. As with the census materials, these reports allow us to witness taxonomy in action, rather than trying to reconstruct the logic of Classification based on evidence from the post-Classification world. A sample of the titles of these documents bespeak the vast differences between pre- and post-Classification sources:

"The Languages of the Shuitian, Luoluo, Zhili, Ziyi, Lang'e, and Talu Minzu of Yongsheng County"
"Report on the Investigation into the Situation of the 'Liming' Minzu of Yongsheng County"
"Transcript of the Visitation with the 'Liude' Minzu of Lude Village in the Second Area of Yongsheng County"
"Materials from the Investigation of the 'Mili' Minzu of Xinping County"[12]

Anyone familiar with the fifty-six minzu model will know that *none* of the minzu listed here—the Liming, Liude, Mili, and others—officially exist in the contemporary PRC. There is no Liming display at the ethnological museum in Beijing, no Liude figurine in the minority doll set, and no "Brief History of the Mili." But owing to the unique historical context of these documents—after the Communist revolution, yet before the stabilization of a standardized ethnotaxonomic orthodoxy— we will finally be able to follow the classification process when the future was still "to be determined," at a time when there could have been a Shuitian minzu, a Liude minzu, a Mili minzu, and so forth. What is more, these reports enable us to hear something we have never been able to hear before: the voices of Classification interviewees whose self-reported ethnonyms circa 1954 have, by the present day, all but disappeared, unknown even to seasoned Chinese ethnologists. We will hear from those who opposed the Classification team's taxonomic hypotheses, those who supported them and, most intriguingly, those whose opinions and worldviews changed *during the course of the Classification itself.*

Third, my analysis of Chinese ethnotaxonomy in the first half of the twentieth century has benefited greatly from the Republican Era Periodicals Reading Room at Sichuan University. Thanks to this first-class collection of original edition academic, professional, and regional newspapers, magazines, journals, and short-run series, I was able to investigate the development of early Chinese ethnology in its original context, rather than through the lens of "collected volumes" that have since been republished for each of China's foremost anthropologists, linguists, sociologists, and ethnologists. These latter collections, while doing a wonderful service to scholarship by preserving and republishing the seminal works of key scholars, cut out of the picture those scholars not considered worthy of republication and those articles not deemed essential to an understanding of each given scholar's overall contribution. The first editorial process canonizes ethnology on a scholar-by-scholar basis, and the second process canonizes the individuals themselves on an article-by-article basis. At each step, the historical context of early Chinese ethnology disappears from view, particularly the work of ethnotaxonomy, considered as merely the "means" to the more significant "ends" of ethnological research.

Fourth, this is the first study to draw upon the unpublished materials of Henry Rodolph Davies, the turn-of-the-century British military officer who, as we will see, is responsible for developing an ethnic taxonomy of Yunnan that was later adopted by early twentieth-century Chinese ethnologists and linguists and, ultimately, by the Ethnic Classification team in 1954. Read in collaboration with his book *Yünnan: The Link Between India and the Yangtze,* published in 1909, these unpublished journals offer unprecedented insight into the early taxonomic work of this practically unknown figure.

Finally, I was immensely fortunate to be able to conduct oral history interviews with five of the members of the 1954 Yunnan Province Ethnic Classification research team: Shi Lianzhu, Xu Lin, Zhou Yaowen, Yan Ruxian, and Wang Xiaoyi. Surprised to find a foreign researcher interested in, and even cognizant of, a project that has been all but forgotten in China, each of these scholars went out of his or her way to provide assistance, information, and encouragement. In particular, I am indebted to Professor Wang Xiaoyi, whose centrality to this story deserves a special introduction.

I met Professor Wang in the winter of 2003 at the Central University for Nationalities. During our initial interviews in his Beijing apartment, I could sense that his memories of the early 1950s were remarkably vivid. Most stirring was the account of his 1951 trip to Tibet with the Eighteenth Army and his professor Lin Yaohua. The experience started rather precipitously for Wang, who was still a nineteen-year-old student of sociology at Yanjing University when he was approached by his professor. Lin, the esteemed anthropologist and ethnologist who had come of age professionally in the latter half of the Republican period (1911–49), asked Wang if he would be interested in joining the expedition. Wang agreed without hesitation, with the exuberance and impetuousness befitting a young man his age. Lin Yaohua sought out Wang's other professors and negotiated on his student's behalf: Wang rushed to complete his remaining graduation requirements and set out for Lhasa with Lin in June.

Professor Wang recounted to me the severity of the mountain ascent, the oxygen-depleted atmosphere, and an audioscape punctuated by the heaving breaths of the team's pack animals. The yaks respired with the struggling cadence of a steam locomotive, Wang recalled, a sound that he reproduced for me in the form of three exaggerated expulsions of breath. The last stretch of the journey was particularly unforgettable: a two-month march from Chamdo—the site of a devastating battle for Tibetan forces just months earlier—to Lhasa, during which the terrain had grown so steep and the air so thin that the team could sometimes manage only a dozen or so yards each hour. From Chamdo onward, moreover, Wang began nursing a dull but persistent pain in his jaw. Over the next sixty days, as the team forded a series of mountain peaks, the toothache grew worse. Naïvely, I remarked, "So you had to wait until Lhasa to have your tooth taken care of?" He chuckled courteously and responded, as if recalling the sensation: "I had to wait until I got back to Beijing, two years later."

The conversation turned then to the Ethnic Classification Project of 1954. "What month was the team formed?" I inquired, aware that this was a rather specific question to ask of events which took place nearly one half-century ago. Wang's eyes reoriented upwards and paused for five long seconds. Just as I began to resign to what was clearly a reasonable lacuna in his otherwise formidable recall, Wang exited the room for a few brief moments, and returned holding a plainly bound book. "1954," he repeated, and began to leaf through the pages. "February . . . March . . . April . . . " he spoke in the muted, elongated syllables of one reflecting out loud. It was then that I realized what he was holding: this book was Wang Xiaoyi's diary from 1954, a diary that, as I would soon learn, he updated in detail on a daily basis throughout the Classification project. He took precise notes on each meeting, each lecture, each preparation session, and each interview. Just as importantly, he kept close tabs on the quotidian rhythms of the expedition: haircuts, visits to the bookstore, laundry, visits to the infirmary, and even nights at the opera.

Over the course of our meetings, Wang led me through the expedition on a day-by-day basis. As I shuttled back and forth between Beijing and the archives in southwest China, moreover, I had the unique pleasure of comparing and corroborating Wang's diary accounts against those of the original Classification reports, and also of re-presenting both Professor Wang and other members of the team with photocopied versions of the 1954 documents. Looking over the pages of the reports, some of which were written by his own hand, Wang was caught off guard. I received a similar reaction from Shi Lianzhu. When presenting him with his writings from the project, the tempo and cadence of Shi's normally robust and commanding temperament subsided noticeably. In an uncharacteristically subdued and self-reflective moment, he remarked: "I haven't seen these since I submitted them to Professor Lin in 1954."

Together, these new sources unveiled to this student of twentieth-century Chinese state formation, ethnicity, social science, and taxonomy a window of unprecedented clarity through which I was able to observe the very earliest stages of perhaps the largest social engineering project in human history: the construction of the "unified, multinational People's Republic of China."

STRUCTURE AND METHODOLOGY

The creation, animation, and maintenance of the fifty-six-minzu model is a topic whose scope far exceeds the bounds of any single volume. The goal of this study is more circumscribed, but at the same time ambitious in its own right. Here we will investigate the 1954 Yunnan Province Ethnic Classification Project, the single most complex piece within China's ethnonational puzzle. Chapter 1 opens with a close analysis of the reasons for the expedition, with particular attention paid to the inaugural census of the People's Republic of China. When designing the census schedule, Communist authorities decided to break with convention and pose the question of ethnonational identity as an open-ended, fill-in-the-blank inquiry. Quite unlike most modern censuses, there were no predetermined ethnonyms from which to choose and no check boxes—just a blank in which registrars were instructed to record faithfully whatever answer was provided by the registrant. As we will see, this led to the creation of one of the most intriguing registration documents in the history of the modern state, one in which no less than twenty of the resulting "nationalities" in Yunnan Province were registered with populations of *one person each*, and many others with populations of two, five, ten, and so forth. More importantly, we will see how the Communist state's initial approach to the question of categorization—one in which each registrant was permitted to self-identify at will—resulted in failure and prompted the formation of the Yunnan Province Ethnic Classification Research Team. To undertake a highly objectivist categorization of the peoples of Yunnan was the state's second choice, a "Plan B" prompted by a political crisis.

More broadly, chapter 1 places the early Communist period in a framework with which it is still not commonly associated, China's postimperial transition and the tortuous history of transformation from empire to nation-state. As James Townshend, Pamela Crossley, Magnus Fiskesjö, and others have argued, the Communists were attempting to resolve a problem that, in effect, was left over from the collapse of the multiethnic Qing empire, and that subsequent regimes had failed to answer.[13] By carrying out the systematic recognition of minority populations, particularly in the distant western borderlands, the Communists were attempting to reintegrate the former Qing territories into a unified polity, left in pieces after the revolutionaries of 1911 initially rejected those Qing discourses and practices designed to legitimate Manchu rule over non-Manchu subjects. I see the endeavors of early Communist state officials, and their social scientific advisors, as an attempt to reestablish territorial integrity and to legitimate a state in which a predominantly Han Chinese regime would govern a highly diverse polity encompassing peoples of strikingly different linguistic, cultural, religious, and social backgrounds. In our ongoing attempt to understand "how the Qing became China," I argue that we must include the early Communist period, and the Ethnic Classification Project more specifically, in our narratives.[14]

Chapter 2 takes us to the opening weeks of the project where we find a small group of Beijing scholars attempting to make sense of the overwhelming task confronting them: to categorize the minorities of Yunnan Province, one of the most ethnically variegated on earth, *in less than six months*. Under these draconian time constraints, this group of ethnologists and linguists had no chance to develop an ethnotaxonomic framework *de novo*. Rather, as we will see, they came to rely on an existing framework, one whose genealogy traces back through the Republican period and, ultimately, to the work of an obscure, turn-of-the-century British colonial officer by the name of Henry Rodolph Davies. The Davies model, as we will see, came to define the ethnotaxonomic worldview of Republican-era Chinese ethnologists and, incredibly, the work of the Classification team in 1954.

By delineating this relationship, my objective is to demonstrate that the epistemological and methodological foundations of the Classification trace their genealogies, first, beyond the "1949 divide," and second, outside of the political circles in which scholars often ground their studies of contemporary Chinese ethnopolitics.[15] It was not the leadership of the Chinese Communist Party, nor even its team of experts at the Nationalities Affairs Commission, that first decided that Yunnan was home to roughly two dozen minzu. Instead, this decision was reached by Chinese ethnologists and linguists in the 1930s and 1940s, well before the Ethnic Classification ever existed, and before anyone knew that the Chinese Communists would proclaim victory on October 1, 1949. And when the Classification was undertaken in 1954, my research shows that Chinese ethnologists and linguists were at the helm of the project, not the limited number of Communist cadres who took part. Rather than caricaturizing twentieth-century Chinese taxonomists as handmaidens of the state, then, I pay close attention to the ways in which these "establishment intellectuals" articulated, defended, and ultimately attained paradigmatic status on behalf of their epistemological, ontological, and methodological approaches to minzu and minzu taxonomy.[16] It was they who designed the blueprints of ethnic diversity in Yunnan; they who, to answer Partha Chatterjee's question to Benedict Anderson in a contemporary Chinese context, first imagined these communities.[17] To adopt a broader, more comparative perspective, then, the objective of this chapter is to place the Classification within the larger, transnational history of the modern social sciences (ethnology and linguistics, in particular), modern governmentality, and the intimate relationship that has long existed between the two.[18]

In chapter 3, we follow these Beijing scholars to the capital of Yunnan Province, where they convened with the other half of the Ethnic Classification team. The Yunnan contingent, which comprised the team's only state and party representatives, attempted to enforce its epistemic authority over the project, particularly over the team's academic contingent whose metropolitan and "ivory tower" backgrounds made them somewhat suspect in the eyes of local Communist leaders. In particular, the political directors of the Classification instructed the team's ethnologists and linguists to assess the claims of local minority communities in accordance with the Soviet definition of nationality (natsia) as articulated by Joseph Stalin. According to Stalin's criteria, a natsia—which Chinese Communist authorities took as the Russian equivalent of the Chinese term minzu—could only exist in the capitalist mode of production, for only in the capitalist stage could a community come to share the four "commonalities" that Stalin regarded as the essential ingredients of nationhood: common territory, common language, common economic mode of production, and common psychology or culture.[19] For groups who had yet to enter the capitalist stage, they were to be classified not as full-fledged minzu, but as one of the three other forms of human organization: clans, tribes, or tribal federations.

The research contingent did not accept this mandate, as we will see, and instead undertook a sophisticated reconceptualization of minzu that departed from the one prescribed by Communist state authorities. Based on a dynamic concept I call "ethnic potential," team leader Lin Yaohua developed an enlarged definition of minzu that encompassed not only fully realized national minority groups, but also embryonic or inchoate assemblages that, while lacking the four commonalities outlined in the Stalinist definition, demonstrated the "potential" of achieving such commonalities in the future. This definition of minzu had the dual effect of liberating the team's social scientific contingent from the dictates of the Stalinist model, while also opening up a wide space into which the Chinese state would be free, and indeed required, to intervene and oversee the actualization of these "potential" minzu in the post-Classification period.

These findings require us to revisit our prevailing assumptions about the Classification, the most persistent of which has been that the project was undertaken in slavish obedience to Soviet theories. It was not. And for those scholars of Chinese ethnicity who have long doubted this oversimplified view, but who have been unable to provide empirical corroboration, chapter 3 confirms their suspicions. In his pioneering work of over a decade ago, for example, Dru Gladney delineated how the Hui were able to achieve official minzu status despite their failure to comply with Stalin's definition.[20] Louisa Schein has since brought to light similar contradictions vis-à-vis the Miao, as has Ralph Litzinger for the Yao.[21] James Millward has speculated that, "in the days when Marxist-Leninist approaches were still de rigueur, many Chinese historians often simply book-ended their articles with boiler-plate recitations of Marxist themes and then went about their own business in the central sections."[22] Through an analysis of recently declassified sources from the Classification, this chapter finally provides evidence for what these scholars have long suspected.[23]

Chapter 4 accompanies the Classification team into the field, observing taxonomy in action. Here, the researchers' categorical models began to buckle under the pressure of a new set of requirements that Chinese ethnologists and linguists in the past had never had to deal with: the consent of the categorized. To secure such consent, which was a crucial factor in determining the ethnic potential of a proposed minzu grouping, researchers came to rely on methods developed by Communist organizers, strategies designed to transform the worldviews of their minority informants *during the interview process itself.* As we will see, these strategies varied greatly, depending on the extent to which interviewees either agreed or disagreed with the team's taxonomic hypotheses. At one end of the spectrum, scholars carefully orchestrated the interview process, gathering together representatives of those candidate groups that it intended to merge and then, through a set of techniques I term "participant transformation," setting the conditions under which these candidates came to "realize" (seemingly on their own) the bonds they shared with one another. On the other end of the spectrum, entrenched opposition prompted the team to draw upon an even more complex, covert, and epistemically violent repertoire, including what the team called "persuasion work" *(shuofu gongzuo).*

More broadly, this chapter enables us to see more clearly how Lin Yaohua's concept of "ethnic potential" played a central role in the taxonomic practice of the team. Researchers based their taxonomic recommendations on an estimation of whether or not, based on both objective linguistic data and more affective interview data, a given cluster of applicants could reasonably be merged and transformed into a cohesive minzu unit by the state *after* the Classification was over. In one example from the chapter, that of the Achang, we will see that the team based their proposed merger of three applicant communities according to their hypothesis that such communities would be susceptible to a process we might call "Achangization." Insofar as their languages were similar enough, and owing to the malleability of self-consciousness, these communities demonstrated enough potential for unification, the team felt. The same was true for the category "Yi," which, by the close of the project, would inherit more than three dozen new "branches." As with the Achang and "Achangization," each of the subordinated groups would, the team advised, need to undergo a process we might call (somewhat clumsily) "Yi-ization." Non-Han citizens in the post-Classification period have thus been the subject of two state-led programs of nationalization: one geared toward "becoming Chinese," and the other toward becoming Achang, Bai, Lisu, Wa, Yi, Zhuang, and so forth.[24]

Chapter 5 expands our temporal purview and reviews the wide and seemingly disparate array of discourses and practices in the post-Classification era that have contributed to the Achangization of the Achang, the Lisu-ization of the Lisu, and so forth. Whereas I will not claim that such projects have been completely successful, or that every individual in China categorized as Lisu, Miao, Yi, or otherwise everywhere and always self-identifies with the official designations, nevertheless I do contend that the post-Classification period has witnessed the development of an immense, robust, and virtually ubiquitous infrastructure whose objective is to bring the quotidian, on-the-ground experience of ethnicity into ever-closer concordance with the fifty-six-minzu model. Whatever the private sentiments of party cadres, state authorities, ethnologists, linguists, publishers, filmmakers, choreographers, musicians, tour guides, museum curators, toy manufacturers, clothing designers, or otherwise, the development and dissemination of policies, knowledge, cultural artifacts, and artistic productions must necessarily abide by the country's ethnotaxonomic orthodoxy. And whatever the sentiments of average non-Han citizens, all but those willing to adopt openly confrontational postures vis-à-vis the state and the party must interface with the political and economic infrastructure as a member of the Lisu, Miao, Yi, Zhuang, or one of the other official minorities.

At the same time, chapter 5 poses the inverse yet intimately related question: as the fifty-six officially recognized categories have become increasingly reified and ubiquitous, where have the unrecognized categories gone? Where are the hundreds of ethnonyms that refer to communities not recognized as minzu by the state? As we will see, many remain accessible, although they are dispersed in some unlikely places. Others, however, are probably lost for good. I argue that by fostering these simultaneous processes of emergence and disappearance, the Chinese state has been remarkably successful in bringing about a "convergence" between ethnotaxonomic theory and practice, a term Geoffrey Bowker and Susan Leigh Star describe as the purposive act of changing the world "such that the system's description of reality becomes true."[25]

Having outlined the structure of the book, a few further words are necessary regarding certain methodological issues. Much like the 1954 Ethnic Classification research team, the reader will encounter a bewildering array of ethnonyms all from a large, landlocked province of southwest China slightly smaller than California. Some of the historical figures we will meet regarded Yunnan as home to over two hundred distinct groups, whereas others saw it as home to one hundred, two dozen, or only one. Each of these competing taxonomies, moreover, contain names that differ, not only from the official ethnic taxonomy of the PRC today, but also from one another. This is all to say: Yunnan in the early 1950s was not merely "illegible," to borrow from the terminology of James Scott.[26] It was a taxonomic labyrinth.

This poses a distinct challenge to both the reader and the author. Confronted with this confusing array of names, the initial temptation is to begin by sorting everybody out, outlining their ethnic names, their customs, the languages they speak, and the parts of Yunnan they inhabit. Ideally, we might start with a distribution map, thereby anchoring our analysis in a clear sense of the provincial ethnoscape. We might also provide an overview of Yunnan's history, showing where each of these contemporary groups originated and how they came to reside in their current locations. To make sense of the province's hopelessly complex mosaic of ethnic names, we might also provide a concordance detailing the relationships of taxonomic synonymy that connect Shan and Dai, Yi and Lolo, Miao and Hmong, or Hani and Woni, to name just three common commensurations.[27] Another set of "a.k.a." commensurations could be used to link contemporary ethnonyms with historical categories, tracing lines from the minzu of today to various "barbarians" inscribed in imperial Chinese texts. Furthermore, we might rehearse the etymological history of the term *minzu*, that notoriously contested word that, since its importation to China from Japan in the late nineteenth century, has been used by widely different communities of practice to translate no fewer than four politically charged concepts: race, nation, nationality *(natsia),* and ethnic group. In other words, the editorial inclination is to *classify* the peoples of Yunnan in advance, so that we would know about whom we are talking.

At first glance, the benefits of disambiguation seem readily apparent. By providing a "starter classification" of the ethnic groups of Yunnan, we would be able to study the Classification in two discrete steps: first, by identifying who the people of Yunnan *really* are, and second, by figuring out how various taxonomists in Chinese history categorized them (and by extension, how well or poorly they performed their tasks). The reader could use this author's taxonomy to assess the integrity of the one formulated in 1954, akin to a gemological test in which the hardness of one stone is assayed by scratching it against another. As a study of taxonomy and identification, however, I have decided that each of these inclinations needs be to resisted and, in both the analysis performed and the narrative produced, replaced with an approach that leaves unresolved the very taxonomic ambiguities and complexities that our historical agents were attempting to disambiguate and simplify. When confronted with scholars and politicians who were, through the formulation of a variety of classificatory schema, trying to "combine likes" and reduce complexity, my analysis of their actions will not be predicated on the goal of evaluating their conclusions or attempting to replace them with my own. Phrased more broadly, my contention is that one cannot examine taxonomy by assuming the role of taxonomist. What I am interested in understanding is, as Alain Desrosières has described it in a Western context, the "social history of the creation of equivalence."[28] In this respect, my study resonates with the insights of Nelson Goodman, Mary Douglas, Paul Feyerabend, Bruno Latour, Ian Hacking, Geoffrey Bowker, Susan Leigh Star, and others whose scholarship has inspired us to look more deeply into "how classification works."[29]

With this in mind, my study observes a set of principles that, insofar as they are rarely cited explicitly in the course of the book, merit outlining here. First, following Bowker and Star, I will assume that, if a category "did not exist contemporaneously, it should not be retroactively applied."[30] As such, I have opted not to examine the Classification through the lens of one or another of China's fifty-six recognized minzu. Whereas this approach is virtually axiomatic among scholars who investigate ethnicity in China, and has undoubtedly advanced our understanding of the Chinese ethnosphere to an unprecedented degree, it has also produced unintended side effects, particularly with regards to the Classification. First and foremost, since the groups officially recognized now were not recognized at the time of the Classification, the use of any one contemporary group as an optic through which to study the Classification confines us to a teleological reading. Moreover, a single-minzu approach pushes from view one of the fundamental characteristics of the project, namely, the sheer number of applicants groups between which researchers had to adjudicate. The Classification in Yunnan was not carried out on a candidate-by-candidate basis, but was rather a differential process wherein the categorical fate of each community was highly dependent upon its relationship to other communities in the region. To work on any one group in particular would render these relationships invisible.

Second, I will not attempt to fix the definition of *minzu* in advance, nor will I pit my own definition thereof against the historical agents in my book. Unlike Walker Connor and others who lament the "terminological chaos" that surrounds concepts such as nation, ethnic group, and so forth—and who have made clear their desire to demarcate such concepts so as to facilitate more rigorous, cross-comparative work—I consider the ambiguity of these terms, as well as ongoing efforts to standardize them, to be a fundamental part of the history of the social sciences, the modern state, and the ongoing collaboration there-between.[31] For Chiang Kai-shek, for example, his objective vis-à-vis the term *minzu* was to link it inextricably to the ideas of singularity and indivisibility, and thereby advance a concept of a unitary "Zhong-hua minzu" within which no divisions could be recognized. Opposing him were not only the Chinese Communists, but also Chinese ethnologists, both of whom advocated (in different ways) a concept of minzu grounded firmly in notions of plu-rality and diversity. Thus, the reason that minzu, circa 1954, is inextricably tied to the concept of diversity has less to do with the etymology of the term than with the particular history of this ethnopolitical debate and, to put it crudely, the fact that the Communists won. Rather than providing one consistent translation of minzu, then, I do my best to adjust my translations to match the particular worldview of the writer in question. For Chiang Kai-shek, the *Zhonghua minzu* signified a broad, indivisible totality—as such, I have decided to translate his minzu as "Chinese people" and/or "Chinese nation." For Chinese Communists operating within a de-cidedly Marxist-Leninist nomenclature, the translation of choice is "nationality." For Chinese ethnologists, by contrast, the concept of minzu was set equal to the En-glish-language terms "ethnicity" and "ethnic group" (as evidenced by their choice of "minzuxue," or "the study of minzu," as the standard translation of the discipli-nary title "ethnology"). At the same time, because ethnologists also found them-selves operating within the ethnopolitical terrain of the era, there are multiple oc-casions in which I translate minzu as "nation," "nationality," or "people," even when issuing forth from the pens of Chinese social scientists.

There is only one major exception to this otherwise flexible approach, and that pertains to my translation of the most important term in my study, *minzu shibie*. Despite the fact that this term can be translated as a "Nationalities" Classification Project, thereby privileging Chinese Communist nomenclature, I am committed to "Ethnic Classification" for one very simple reason: whereas there has been a long-standing assumption that the project was a Communist-directed enterprise, and that the participating social scientists played a minor role, my study demonstrates that the Classification was primarily the work of ethnologists and linguists.

In one final point, I should note from the outset that this study makes no at-tempt to falsify the findings of the 1954 Classification or the broader fifty-six-minzu model to which it contributed. I do this not because they are nonfalsifiable—they most certainly are—but because such an approach actually prevents us from un-derstanding the logic according to which the project was undertaken, and the logic according to which "nationality work" has been carried out in the post-Classifica-tion period. As we will see, those who helped build the fifty-six-minzu model, and those who help maintain it today, did and do not think of it as a high-fidelity rep-resentation of presently existing realities, but rather as a semidescriptive, semi-prescriptive blueprint of what could exist in the future with the help of state inter-vention. The objective of the team in 1954 was never strictly that of describing already existing, already stable "imagined communities," but rather that of outlining a set of plausible, or "imaginable" minzu categories that it would be feasible for the state to actualize in the post-Classification world—categories that would be "good enough for government use," we might say. Thus, for those who would attempt to disprove the fifty-six-minzu model by citing contradictory fieldwork findings, the architects of the model need only respond that the framework is still under construction, and that the realization of these categories is still a work-in-progress. This actualization, I argue, has been one of the fundamental objectives of the coordinated set of projects and enterprises collectively referred to as "nationality work" *(minzu gongzuo).*

With this structure and method in mind, we now travel to Beijing circa 1952, where we find a fledgling Communist regime attempting to consolidate its political control and establish a stable government on the mainland. In doing so, one of the primary challenges they faced was the so-called nationality question.

1
—

Identity Crisis in
Postimperial China

We say China is a country vast in territory, rich in resources and large in population; as a matter of fact, it is the Han nationality whose population is large and the minority nationalities whose territory is vast and whose resources are rich.

—MAO ZEDONG, "ON THE TEN MAJOR RELATIONSHIPS"

In 1952, the newly established Communist regime in Beijing announced plans to convene the inaugural session of the National People's Congress (NPC). The congress was scheduled for autumn 1954, in time for the fifth anniversary of the founding of the People's Republic of China (PRC), and would herald the Chinese Communist Party's (CCP) transition from a revolutionary force to the legitimate government of mainland China. Here, the party would promulgate the first state constitution and implement a national system of representative government, which thus far had only been undertaken at the local level.[1] The CCP began laying the groundwork for this political debut in February 1953 with the ratification of a unified Election Law. The law standardized electoral procedures and detailed the calculus of congressional representation at the county, provincial, and national levels.

As Deng Xiaoping outlined in a speech delivered on February 11, 1953, the Election Law also contained certain preferential policies toward national minorities. For one, the law guaranteed a minimum of 150 minority delegates in the first NPC. Authors of the law expected even more than this number, however, anticipating that approximately 170 of the scheduled twelve hundred representatives—or, one in seven—would hail from one of the country's non-Han minority communities. Whereas this exceeded the actual relative population of minorities, estimated at the time to constitute somewhere in the range of one in ten, Deng defended the preferential multiplier. "We feel that this number is reasonable," he explained, "because there are many nationalities in China, distributed over a wide area, and they need this sort of treatment. This is the only way we can get a considerable number of delegates of the minority nationalities at the National People's Congress."[2]

More importantly, the 1953 Election Law promised that at least one representative seat would be awarded to each minority group regardless of population size. This was designed to safeguard smaller minorities who might fall under the political influence of larger groups should congressional representation be based strictly on proportionality. To protect these smaller groups, defined as those whose populations fell below 10 percent of the total population of a given administrative unit, the ratio of representation was calculated preferentially. At the county level, for example, where each Han delegate represented one thousand Han individuals, each minority delegate represented as few as five hundred, provided that the total population of that minority was less than 10 percent of the total population of the county.[3]

One major obstacle stood in the way of this otherwise sound policy: before minority representatives could be apportioned, it remained to be determined *who the minorities of China were*, in terms of their names, their populations, and their geographical distributions. Focusing on Yunnan, one finds a number of answers to these questions, none of them consistent. In a report dating to 1951, published for internal circulation, the Central Nationalities Affairs Commission in Beijing listed 107 groups in the province.[4] While many of the minzu names listed therein are familiar to us today—such as the Hui, Lisu, Nu, Yao, and Yi—far more correlate in no way to those minorities now understood as populating the province—such as the Axi, Chashan, Heihua, Mingji, Nazha, and so forth. At the provincial level, the figures were different still. In a distribution map published in 1951 for internal circulation, the Yunnan Province Nationalities Affairs Commission listed 132 groups.[5] In 1953, the commission revised this map somewhat, reducing the total number of groups to 125.[6] The groups listed in this document exhibit a remarkable range in terms of population size. Five groups were listed with populations of less than one hundred people; twenty-nine groups with populations between one hundred and one thousand; fifty groups with populations between one and ten thousand; twenty-three groups with populations between ten and one hundred thousand; eleven with populations between one hundred thousand and one million; and one with a population greater than one million.[7] This largest group (the Yi, with a population of 1,145,840 people) was thirty-one thousand times larger than the smallest (the Alu, with a population of thirty-seven). The map itself showed how this long tail of miniscule groups posed a challenge to the provincial Nationalities Affairs Commission (NAC). Out of necessity, the map was immense, for any smaller size would have rendered it impossible to represent these small minzu to scale. The profusion of groups also rendered simple color-coding insufficient. In addition to coding the distribution of groups using solid colors, the mapmakers had to design a series of finely variegated hash-mark patterns in order to accommodate all the different groups.

As evidenced by these official sources from the early PRC, no consensus existed as to the precise number of groups in Yunnan. With an eye to this question, the Communists launched a nationwide census and voter registration campaign in the summer of 1953. Between July 1953 and May 1954, two and a half million census takers were enrolled throughout the country to undertake an enumeration of the mainland population.[8] Because of the colossal scope of the registration campaign, Communist authorities were parsimonious when it came to the design of the census schedule. After debating which questions should be posed to their nearly six hundred million respondents, officials ultimately decided upon only five. The first four of these involved the most basic of demographic information, including name, age, gender, and relationship to the head of one's household. The selection of a fifth question was a more complicated issue, however. Certain dimensions of identity, such as occupation, literacy, and place of work were considered but dismissed, deemed impertinent to the forthcoming NPC. Interestingly, one of the possibilities that was ultimately excluded was that of economic class, an axis of identity that seemingly would have been preserved, given the party's revolutionary ethos and the land reform process. Instead of class, occupation, literacy, or place of work, authorities ultimately settled upon a question that no modern Chinese census had ever posed before: that of nationality or minzu.[9]

The outcome of the census, as we will soon see, proved shocking to Communist authorities and ultimately precipitated the Ethnic Classification Project that constitutes the focus of this book. Before examining the census results, it is necessary to pause for a moment and understand why the Communists wished to include minzu on the census schedule in the first place. As Walker Connor has noted, Marxist writings tell us that nationalities are parts of the superstructure, ideational manifestations of underlying economic relationships and processes that are destined to wither away once the inherent contradictions within the economic structure resolve themselves dialectically. Why, then, go about categorically recognizing that which is going to disappear in time?

This chapter argues that there were three reasons for the Communist's recognition of minzu within its new political structure, and thus, for their inclusion of minzu identity on the first national census. The first reason is the deeply historical problem of maintaining the territorial integrity of a highly diverse empire. Well before the Communist revolution, regimes based in the northeast of China had struggled to incorporate the diverse peoples of the west into a stable and unified polity. One method for doing so had been to interface with these peoples through a carefully constructed network of policies and modes that in one way or another drew upon and carefully manipulated the practices of those peoples being ruled. In this respect, the Classification needs to be situated within the broader history of China's postimperial transition.

The second problem is more proximate, and originates in the ongoing rivalry between the Communists and the Nationalists during the first half of the twentieth century. Starting in the 1930s, the Chinese Communists began to develop an ethnopolitical platform that set them apart in many regards from their Nationalist rivals. They argued that in contrast to the Nationalists' growing commitment to the concept of a mono-minzu China, China was in fact a composite of a multiplicity of distinct minzu communities, and that the territorial integrity of the country depended upon the recognition and political integration of such communities.

Third, with regards to categorization, the advent of the Classification is attributable to a political crisis prompted by the failure of the state's initial experiment with a highly noninterventionist policy of self-categorization. In their inaugural census of 1953–54, the Communists' initial policy with regards to ethnic categorization was to permit individuals to determine their own ethnonyms, a policy that resulted in an astonishing proliferation of minzu categories and threatened to render impossible the state's promise of proportional representation for non-Han communities in the first National People's Congress.

To understand each of these questions, we must explore the history of the term *minzu* itself, one of those most controversial and pivotal concepts in modern Chinese history. As we will see, the very inclusion of minzu in the 1953–54 census schedule was itself the culmination of a complex history dating back to the fall of the Qing dynasty (1644–1911) and the formation of the first Chinese republic.

PLURALITY AND UNITY IN YUNNAN

Scholars have long debated the applicability of the terms *ethnicity* and *nationality* to the premodern period, with some scholars advocating its extension into the distant past, and others regarding it as a concept unique to the modern nation-state.[10] Fortunately, we do not require either of these terms to note that the region in question—Yunnan—has long encompassed a wide plurality of languages, cultural traditions, religions, and peoples. This plurality, moreover, has proven to be a perennial problem for empires in their efforts to incorporate the territory and its people more fully into their domains.

The region was first brought into the eastern imperial orbit when the kingdom of Dali was overtaken by the Mongols in 1253 and incorporated into the Chinese administered area that would become known as the Yuan dynasty (1271–1368). The Yuan garrisoned multiple towns in the newly formed province of Yunnan, which thereafter became magnets for Chinese merchants. In those areas where opposition was strongest, the court developed relationships with powerful local leaders and shored up a system of indirect rule. Under the subsequent Chinese Ming dynasty (1368–1644), this embryonic system of indirect rule was systematized further, as the central court bestowed official titles upon native chieftains in return for their loyalty and maintenance of regional order.[11]

The Manchu Qing dynasty (1644–1911) addressed the problem of diversity with a much more complex system than that of the Yuan or Ming, while at the same time drawing on dimensions of each. Referred to by Mark Elliott as "Qing Universalism," the Manchu system of rule was maintained through the balance of three interrelated components. The first was Manchu military prowess, through which the Qing was able to extend its imperial boundaries far beyond the Great Wall to the distant territories of the present-day Chinese interior.[12] Martial expertise alone could not insure territorial integrity, however. Thus, a second vital component of Qing universalism was the Eight Banner System, a sophisticated political and demographic framework that incorporated each of the Qing's potential rivals within a centralized, bureaucratic hierarchy, and helped to dismantle existing power structures. Third, in order to preserve boundaries between the Manchu elite and the numerically superior non-Manchu subject population, the Qing undertook a series of long-term social engineering projects designed to develop and fortify a uniquely Manchu identity among members of the imperial court. These included the development of a written Manchu language and the promotion of a basket of sociocultural practices that together came to be reified as the "Manchu way" (involving martial skill, equestrianism, and frugality, among other characteristics).[13]

What is striking for our purposes, however, is the extent to which "Qing Universalism" was not universalist at all, at least not with regards to the empire's southwestern frontier regions. The "barbarians" of Yunnan, for example, did not constitute a category within the Banner System, nor were they the focus of the court's elaborate system of "simultaneous" emperorship.[14] Unlike the famous portrait of the Qianlong emperor in which he is presented to a Tibetan audience as an emanation of the bodhisattva Manjusri, we have no evidence of parallel efforts by Qing emperors to present themselves as, for example, descendants of a Miao or "Lolo" line.[15] The reasons for this have been amply demonstrated by Nicola Di Cosmo, James Millward, Peter Perdue, and others. As a conquest alliance that emerged in the north, the Manchus would not easily abandon this regional focus, particularly in the face of powerful Mongolian, and later Russian, rivals.[16] Furthermore, the system of governance in Yunnan remained, with few exceptions, largely indirect during not only the Qing, but also the Yuan and Ming dynasties. Following Ming precedent, the Kangxi emperor (1662–1723) bestowed official titles upon a select group of native rulers in the southwest, entrusting them with the preservation of order, the submission of tribute, and the provision of troops in support of imperial campaigns. Starting in 1659, the court further systematized this mode of indirect rule by reorganizing the inheritance laws of native officials. Moving away from customary systems of inheritance, native rule would now descend along strict, patrilineal lines, with inheritors required to submit family genealogies as verification.[17]

Efforts to enforce a more direct form of rule were largely disruptive and short-lived.[18] The reign of the Yongzheng emperor (r. 1723–35), for example, witnessed a departure from the indirect rule of the Qianlong period and the initiation of what C. Patterson Giersch has referred to as "new frontier militarism."[19] With the successive appointment of three aggressive provincial and regional administrators— Li Wei, Gao Qizhuo, and E'ertai (Ortai)—the Qing court removed powerful native rulers from multiple cities, wrested control of key industries, and established powerbases in key locales throughout the province.[20] This expansion of power was not met unchecked however, as the court's intrusion into the complex and long-standing system of local rule resulted in frequent and bloody uprisings. Consequently, Yongzheng's aggressive policy of frontier activism was in large part repealed by his son, the Qianlong emperor (r. 1736–95).[21] Yinjishan, appointed to succeed E'ertai, set about reestablishing stable relations with local powerholders and repairing the system of indirect rule of the pre-Yongzheng period. Once again, the Qing court became concerned with policing in-migration and intermarriage, so as to prevent local level processes of acculturation from obscuring the lines that divided the different constituents of the multiethnic empire. The court wished to maintain its ability to "distinguish the barbarians from the Chinese."[22]

Toward the middle of the nineteenth century, continued Han Chinese expansion into the southwest placed increasing strain on the delicate ethnic balance that the Qing had struggled to maintain. In the summer of 1839, as David Atwill and others have outlined, the town of Mianning witnessed the outbreak of widespread Han-Hui violence, culminating in pogroms that left mosques in ruins and nearly two thousand Muslim Yunnanese dead.[23] A second massacre took place in the spring of 1845, when simmering Han-Hui hostilities came to a boil in Baoshan, Yunnan. On October 2, 1845, a Han militia entered the town and carried out the systematic murder of an estimated eight thousand Hui.[24]

The regime's delicate ethnic balance was further upset in the east where, in the late nineteenth century, antidynastic revolutionaries were themselves seizing upon notions of Manchu difference to delineate battle lines between the imperial elite and their subjects. Within this emergent revolutionary movement, a new term emerged that played a central, discursive role: that of minzu.[25] Introduced into Chinese by way of the Japanese neologism minzoku, the concept proved a useful tool for anti-Qing activists who were otherwise hard-pressed to portray as alien a court that had successfully postured itself as a patron of Confucian ritual practice, the civil service exam, Chinese language scholarship, and a host of other institutions central to traditional Chinese civilization.[26] Searching for conceptual grounds upon which to articulate their anti-Manchu stance, and influenced by Social Darwinist concepts recently introduced to China, nationalists such as Zhang Binglin (1868–1936), Liang Qichao (1873–1929), Zou Rong (1885–1905), and others began to promote the concepts of "Hanzu" and "Manzu."[27] These categories, although articulated along lines of cultural difference, marked a departure from traditional cultural conceptualizations of identity. Zhang's categories of Hanzu and Manzu, although designed according to cultural criteria, exhibited a level of essentialism and mutual exclusivity characteristic of racial categories. This hybridized, cultural-cum-racial conceptualization of minzu resulted in what Kai-wing Chow has termed a form of "Han racism,"[28] a system of culturalist differentiation designed to "undermine the reformists' ground for continual support for the Manchu regime."[29] Outfitted with this amalgamated idea of culture-race, Liang Qichao and others were able to articulate their opposition to Manchu rule as the cultural equivalent of racial struggle.[30]

In 1911 the Qing ultimately collapsed. Of course, we should not overstate the ethnic origins of the 1911 Revolution, which was the culmination of a complex set of factors that informed and intersected with anti-Manchuism: the secular devolution of centralized state power to the provinces in the wake of the Taiping Rebellion and its suppression, the erosion of support for conservative reform following the Sino-French War (1883–85) and the Sino-Japanese War (1894–95), the acerbic response to the court's invasive and destabilizing "new policies," and the dramatic shift in state-intellectual relations following the abolition of the civil service examination system in 1905. Which is to say: Zou Rong's rabidly anti-Manchu racism did not depose Puyi by force of its rhetoric. Nevertheless, anti-Manchu revolutionaries gave a distinct shape and tone to late imperial radicalism and, as Edward Rhoads has shown, to the nature and severity of violence that was sometimes unleashed on Manchu peoples during the revolution.[31] In essence, anti-Manchu revolutionaries had achieved their stated objective: the restoration of Han control over a country that was itself predominantly Han Chinese. The flag of the Wuhan revolutionaries captured this concept visually, with eighteen stars symbolizing the eighteen historic provinces of "China proper"—a geographic formulation that, by excluding the territories of Xinjiang and Tibet, among others, imagined the boundaries of China as being coterminous with that of its predominant ethnonational group.[32] At the same time, the disintegration of the Manchu regime was a mixed blessing, being accompanied by a disintegration of the very "Qing universalism" that had kept intact a diverse empire for more than two centuries.[33] With the collapse of Manchu rule, Chinese leaders in the new era would have to develop their own means of reconciling the binaries of diversity and unity, plurality and singularity.[34] Should they fail, they stood to lose vast expanses of territory.

As Joseph Esherick has outlined, there was at this time a minority of political elites who welcomed this territorial reduction and its attendant idea of a China whose international borders coincided with the distribution of the Han. This position, which Esherick identifies as the "China proper" position, was overshadowed however by the countervailing position of "Greater China-ism" (da Zhongguo zhuyi). Exponents of the Greater China position argued for the need to maintain border provinces as buffer regions against foreign aggressors. Likewise, they argued for the need to prevent imperial forces from infiltrating these regions and mobilizing local national sentiments against the Chinese regime. More pragmatically, insofar as the postimperial Chinese regime inherited a body of international treaties based upon the preexisting territorial boundaries of the Qing, they argued that it would prove too costly and complicated to redesign them along the contours of China proper.[35]

Ultimately, the "Greater China" position prevailed and Republican leaders committed themselves to restoring control over the territories of the former Qing. This would have to be accomplished quickly, however, as the ethnopolitical and territorial repercussions of the 1911 Revolution were already becoming manifest, as demonstrated by Xiaoyuan Liu, Hsiao-ting Lin, and others. On November 3, 1912, Outer Mongolia was recognized as autonomous under the Russo-Mongolian Treaty.[36] In 1913, the Simla Conference initiated a twenty-year period in which no Chinese military or civilian authorities were permitted to hold residence in Tibet.[37] In Southwest China, and particularly in Yunnan, local warlords exercised de facto political control over the region. This disintegration, which came as the result primarily of the weakness of the Republican authority, was reflective of the collapse of postimperial legitimacy as well: by waging their revolution as a pro-Han, anti-Manchu enterprise, Republican nationalists unwittingly alienated the rest of non-Han China as well. In building a China for the Chinese (read Han), they had made no place for Tibetans, Mongolians, and so forth.

Confronted with catastrophic territorial failure, much of which was taking place along the country's borders, a faction within the new Republican regime began advocating greater inclusionism, tempering the party's revolutionary rhetoric and replacing it within a more catholic discourse. They harkened back to the Qing model, reconceptualizing Chinese nationhood as a "Republic of Five Peoples" *(wuzu gonghe)* comprising the Han, Tibetans, Mongolians, Manchus, and Hui (a formulation embodied in the regime's new five-color flag).[38] Unlike the concept of minzu deployed by Zhang Binglin and others, the *wuzu gonghe* conception no longer portrayed Tibetans, Mongolians, and others as essentially and irrevocably different, but rather emphasized both the possibility of and necessity for assimilating such groups into the Han majority. As James Leibold has shown, Sun Yat-sen (1866–1925) initially balked at this notion, but his counterproposal was overruled by the provisional assembly in early 1912.[39]

For all this symbolism, the Republican regime did not make the concept of a multi-minzu China a central facet of its state practice, as seen in the absence of all minzu-related questions in their census of 1912. The census schedule, which was to be carried out on a county-by-county basis, contained seventeen questions, none of which pertained to linguistic or ethnic diversity. The census questions revealed the regime's overarching concern with birth and death rates, gender ratios, the sizes and distributions of professional occupations, and the disposition of foreign communities. Further instructions by the census bureau reveal the regime's parallel con-

cern with criminal elements. The "Regulations for the Enumeration and Recording of Populations in the Counties" instructed registrars to take note of householders
with histories of imprisonment, those with suspicious reputations, and those who
lived in groups with individuals with whom they shared no kinship connection.
The Republican state wanted to know a great deal about the population of China,
but nothing about ethnonational difference.[40]

It was within this ethnopolitical context that the CCP was founded and began
articulating its own approach to the "nationality question." Early Communist policies toward minzu were largely abstract and untested, derived from the vicissi-
tudes of their trilateral relationship with the Guomindang (GMD) and the Soviet
Union. During the 1920s, Soviet authorities maintained strategic relations with
both Leninist parties in China, ideologically gravitating toward the CCP, while
pragmatically recognizing the Guomindang as the party most capable of unifying China and resisting foreign aggression. Within this complex geopolitical equation, minzu was an important, although not particularly visible, strategic variable.
At most, it provided an ideological and geopolitical wedge that both the Soviets
and the Chinese Communists used to their own political advantage vis-à-vis the
Guomindang.[41]

This period of strategic, hybridized CCP-GMD-Soviet minority policy formulation came to an end starting in 1925, following the death of Sun Yat-sen. After
the ascendancy of Chiang Kai-shek (1887–1975), the Guomindang discarded the
idea of a multinational China, a shift symbolized once again by a change in the nation's flag: this time with the abolition of the five-color Republican flag in 1928 and
its replacement with one demonstrating the homogeneity and indivisibility of the
Chinese nation, the singular Zhonghua Minzu.[42] Unlike Sun, whose ethnopolitical platform was influenced by Soviet advisors and served as a bridge between the
GMD and the CCP during the First United Front (1924–27), Chiang was vociferously opposed to the Communist discourse of national self-determination as it related to the non-Han peoples of China. Following the sharp polarization of the two
parties, most violently demonstrated in the "White Terror" of 1927, Chiang committed his newly formed Nanjing Government to what Xiaoyuan Liu has described
as a "single-race republic"[43] and what Frank Dikkötter has termed the "nation-race"
(guozu).[44]

Beleaguered, the CCP eventually retreated from the cities and began to establish itself in the countryside.[45] At first, the rural reincarnation of the Communist
Party had little contact with minority groups, and thus little reason to concern itself with the issue of minzu.[46] Nevertheless, even as they operated in the Jiangxi Soviet in southeastern China, established in 1931, the party began to fold certain minzu
policies into its official platform, particularly the idea of "national self-determination" (minzu zijue). In the Constitution of the Soviet Republic, promulgated on November 7, 1931, CCP authorities proclaimed that "the Chinese Soviet Republic cat-

egorically and unconditionally recognizes the right of national minorities to self-determination."[47] More specifically, the national minorities of Mongolia, Tibet, Xinjiang, Yunnan, and Guizhou would be afforded one of three options were the CCP to gain power over the mainland: first, to "separate from the Chinese Soviet Republic and establish their own state"; second, to "join the [Chinese] Soviet federation" or third, to "establish autonomous regions within the Chinese Soviet Republic."[48] More concretely, the 1931 congress committed the regime to the development of minority-language education, minority-language publishing houses, the use of local languages in the execution of government in minority areas, and the training of minority cadres.

In 1934, the nationality question became a practical rather than purely theoretical part of Communist politics. In that year, the fifth in a series of extermination campaigns waged by the GMD prompted the Communist leadership to abandon its base in Jiangxi and set off on what later came to be known as the Long March. During their journey, Communist leaders, troops, and followers were exposed for the first time to the ethnically diverse and impoverished areas of the southwest. When the Red Army entered the largely Miao area of Guizhou, for example, Communists witnessed firsthand the region's acute destitution: villagers walking naked through the streets, widespread opium addiction, and severe oppression at the hands of local warlords. Following his passage through Guizhou Province, Zhu De recorded terse impressions of the scene: "Corn with bits of cabbage, chief food of people. Peasants too poor to eat rice. . . . Peasants call selves 'dry men'—sucked dry of everything. . . . Poor hovels with black rotting thatched roofs everywhere."[49]

Here, on the Long March, the issue of national minorities took on strategic, real-world consequences. During their travels, the Communists began to propagandize their policies of national equality and self-determination, employing it, as Dru Gladney has argued, "for the strategic purpose of enlisting the support of the peoples disgruntled by Qing rule and Chiang Kai-shek's nationality policy."[50] For their survival, the Communists improvised a discourse of recognition and self-determination in order to establish "an intimate relationship with the upper-stratum representatives of the non-Han peoples."[51] They incorporated it in their emerging state program, integrating it more fully into their vision of a socialist China.

The outbreak of full-scale war with Japan placed severe strains on the ethnopolitical stance of the GMD. On the one hand, the threat of national subjugation prompted Chiang Kai-shek to redouble his commitment to the idea of a singular and homogenous China, conceptualized in terms of the nation-race.[52] The clearest statement of Chiang's ethnopolitical platform was his treatise *China's Destiny,* published first in 1943 and revised in 1947. In this text, Chiang was clear in his anti-recognitionist stance. "The fact that [the Chinese nation] comprises five stocks," he argued, "is due not to diversity in race or blood but to dissimilarity in creed and geographical environment." "In a word," he continued, "the distinction between the five stocks is territorial as well as religious, but not ethnological."[53] Chiang was con-vinced that the fate of China depended upon an unwavering opposition to any and all policies that would officially recognize such distinctions or imbue them with political significance. Reflecting on the Qing, he portrayed the Banner System—the very institution that has been identified as the backbone of Qing universalism and the Manchu's ability to rule over a diverse empire—as the cause of its down-fall.[54] "The magnificent state organization and excellent political institutions and laws of the Manchu Dynasty," Chiang lauded, "compared favorably with those of the Han and Tang Dynasties, surpassed those of the Sung and Ming Dynasties and were far superior to those of the Yuan Dynasty." He continued, however. "If the Manchu emperors had not attempted to draw distinctions between the Han, Manchu, Mongolian, Mohammedan, and Tibetan stocks and, instead, had treated them all on a footing of equality irrespective of religion, occupation, social status, and sex, in recognition of the fact that these five stocks are essentially integral parts of one nation . . . China would surely have kept pace with the European and Amer-ican nations in attaining strength and prosperity."[55]

Like Sun Yat-sen before him, Chiang portrayed himself as an advocate, not tech-nically of assimilationism, but of *reassimilationism:* the reconstitution of a people purported to share a common progenitor. In the 1947 edition of *China's Destiny,* Chiang argued that each of the "five stocks," whereas they were commonly believed to have descended from either the Xiongnu or the Xianbei (both non-Chinese tribes), were in fact descendants of common ancestors: the ruling house of the Yin (i.e., Shang) dynasty and the mythical Yellow Emperor *(Huangdi).* By linking the Mongols, Jurchens, Turfans, Tibetans, Manchus, and Mohammedans to these ori-gins—particularly the Yellow Emperor—he attempted to portray assimilationist policies as a process of *reunion.*[56]

At the same time, the Japanese threat forced the Nationalists to reconsider their policy of nonrecognition, insofar as the blanket denial of ethnonational diversity afforded Japanese propagandists the opportunity to manipulate the very desires for self-determination and political recognition that were left unfulfilled by the exist-ing political framework. And if Japanese infiltrators failed to take advantage of this opportunity, the Communists surely would. Under these countervailing pressures, the Nationalist regime attempted to reconcile their ethnopolitical stance by argu-ing for the postponement of the resolution of the "national question" until after the war. In 1938, the GMD congress took steps in this direction through its reaffirma-tion of the GMD Manifesto of 1923, the document wherein the Nationalists first articulated their support for the concept of a multi-minzu China. The promise of the manifesto, however, would have to wait until after victory, as any discussion of diversity within a wartime context would facilitate the Japanese plot to divide and conquer the Chinese mainland.[57]

For the Chinese Communists, the war prompted precisely the opposite response:

a redoubled commitment to the *immediate* recognition of national minorities and opposition to the monogenic argument being advanced by GMD conservatives. In a series of treatises written in the late 1930s, the CCP further emphasized its dedication to recognizing the existence of non-Han nationalities. Most well known among these was *The Question of the Huihui Nationality*, a succinct study that criticized the minority policies of imperial and Republican era China, and mounted a case arguing that the Hui constituted a distinct minzu rather than a religious subset of the Han.[58] GMD policies, the authors of *Huihui* contended, were designed to "paralyze . . . the national movement and national awakening" *(minzu juexing).*[59] By portraying the Hui as merely a Chinese varietal, the GMD was sidestepping the issue of political representation and equality. As evidence, the authors of *Huihui* pointed to the Republican constitution, wherein the political position of the Hui-as-such was not stipulated, and Republican legislative bodies such as the National Assembly and the National Consultative Political Assembly, in which no Hui representatives were to be found.[60]

Equally energetic arguments were made in the course of other contemporaneous writings, including *Outline of the Question of the Mongolian Nationality in Wartime, The Question of the Mongolian Nationality,* and *The National Question in Wartime China.*[61] Chen Lianzhen and Huang Caoliang, authors of *The National Question,* placed the GMD's nationality policy at the heart of the country's geopolitical crisis. The loss of Manchuria to the Japanese, they argued, was the "insidious consequence of the fact that China had not reached a correct and reasonable resolution to the problem of domestic nationalities."[62] By failing to address the boiling issue of domestic diversity, Chinese authorities had opened the door to Japanese infiltration, allowing foreign aggressors to use the minzu question to pit China's minorities off against the Han. The GMD's nonrecognitionist stance enabled the Japanese to "use China to control China" *(yihua zhihua)*—ironically echoing the timeworn imperial Chinese strategy of using the barbarians to control the barbarians.[63]

By the 1940s, then, Communist and Guomindang strategies toward national unity were becoming increasingly polarized. For the GMD, all questions of the political recognition of Chinese diversity would have to wait until after the war. Until that time, minzu was to be understood strictly in terms of a monogenic singularity. There was one minzu in China and it was coextensive with the Chinese polity. This definition undergirded, and was itself perpetuated by, the party's avowedly nonrecognitionist stance. For the Communists, the concept of minzu was inseparable from that of diversity and polygenism. The Chinese state and its minzu were not one and the same—instead, the former was composed of the latter, thereby making the political recognition of diversity essential to state legitimacy and anticolonial resistance. For the Guomindang, the recognition of ethnic difference within China was seen as serving the interests of the Japanese, for whom such cleavages created conditions of possibility for division and conquest. To the Communists, such division and conquest was avoidable, not by denying the existence of independent Chinese minority nationalities, but by conveying to these groups that it would be possible for them to exist *both* as Chinese *and* as Hui, Mongolian, Tibetan, and so on. In counterintuitive fashion, the recognition of particularity was, in the Communist way of thinking, the path to a new unity.[64] Chen and Huang addressed the problem by citing Lenin, who used the metaphor of marriage and divorce to frame the issue: "If we advocate national self-determination, will not our country, once unified, fall into pieces? Particularly as we all battle to the death against the Japanese pirates, wouldn't supporting national self-determination be the same as serving as their lackeys in shattering our united front? With regards to this sort of opinion, Ilyich [i.e., Lenin] responded using a vivid metaphor. He asked: 'If a country has a law [securing] the right to divorce, will that send a happily married couple running to court to request a separation?'"[65]

There is some evidence that, with the end of the war in 1945, the Nationalist regime was preparing to fulfill its promise of a new ethnopolitical policy. In Nanjing in November 1946, the National Assembly of the GMD convened to develop a new state constitution. Adopted on Christmas Day, 1946, the new constitution formally guaranteed all nationalities equality before the law and representation in the Legislative Yuan. Moreover, in a bold departure from the longstanding northern, large-nationality orientation of the Qing and the early Republican concept of *wuzu gonghe*, this promise was to be extended not only to Tibetans, Mongolians, Uighurs, Hui, and Manchu, but also to the "various nationalities in the frontier regions."[66] At the same time, other evidence points in the opposite direction. For example, the postwar census, scheduled to begin July 1, 1948 and conclude December 31, 1953, once again did not include any questions pertaining to minzu identity. If the GMD was in fact committed to the formation of a legislature in which were represented the different nationalities of China, it seems that this system was not to be based on proportionality.

Whatever the ultimate intentions of the Nationalist regime, GMD authorities never found the time to make good on their commitments. By summer 1946, the unstable peace with the Communists collapsed and the mainland once again descended into full-scale war. Within two years, moreover, the military advantage fell to Communist forces, which, in a series of campaigns, took control of key urban areas in 1948 and 1949. Beijing fell to the Communists in January 1949, Taiyuan in March, Nanjing in April, and Wuhan and Shanghai in May. The Nationalists ultimately lost the mainland, and with it any possibility of reinventing themselves as the legitimate regime at the head of a multinational polity. Following the Communists' military victory in late 1949, the ethnopolitical debate over recognition came to an end. If China had been a single-minzu polity under the Guomindang, under the Communists it was reconfigured as a "unified, multinational" republic composed of a diverse assemblage of minzu.

The Communists immediately folded this policy into their statecraft. On September 29, 1949, two days prior to the official founding of the People's Republic, the CCP promulgated the "Common Program of the Chinese People's Political Consultative Congress." The document would serve as the political guidelines for the PRC until a formal constitution could be created. *The Common Program* also outlined the new government's policies toward national minorities. On the broadest level, the document declared the inherent equality of all nationalities (Article 9) and pledged to protect minorities from the dual threats of Han nationalism and divisive ethnonationalistic chauvinism (Article 50).[67] More concretely, Article 51 of *The Common Program* outlined novel policies regarding autonomous minority areas. In particular, the document outlined a theory of "regional autonomy" to be "exercised in areas where national minorities are concentrated and various kinds of autonomy organizations of the different nationalities shall be set up according to the size of the respective populations and regions." In areas where there coexisted more than one minority group, *The Common Program* pledged that "the different nationalities shall each have an appropriate number of representatives in the local organs of political power."[68]

Starting in 1950, Communist authorities began to propagandize their new nationalities policies among local minority elites in key minority regions, to enlist their support as intermediaries between the state and the local populations. In June 1950, the Central People's Government dispatched Minority Visitation Teams (*minzu fangwentuan*) to border regions throughout the country. The first of these teams, the Southwest Minority Visitation Team, departed Beijing on July 2, 1950, and traveled to Yunnan under the direction of ethnologist Xia Kangnong, who had established himself in the Republican period as one of the foremost minority researchers.[69] In all, the team spent approximately one year in the province, gathering information on local conditions, disseminating news about the Communist government's new policies toward national minorities, and administering care, such as veterinary services and inoculation against disease.[70]

At the same time, provincial authorities began to form autonomous region governments and democratic coalition governments throughout Yunnan. Further corroborating John Herman's argument about the persistence of indirect rule in the southwest, the leaders of these local governments were typically those known as "Elite Personages" (*shangceng renshi*) and many, in fact, were relatives of the families that imperial Chinese authorities had long employed to manage local affairs.[71] The goal was to enroll non-Han groups in all levels of government, as a means of legitimating their rule, fulfilling their longstanding promise of ethnonational equality, and securing the territorial integrity of their multinational polity.

Having committed themselves to a concept of China as a multi-minzu country, however, the Communists unwittingly stumbled upon a remarkably complex problem: if China was home to multiple minzu, who were they? How many minzu were there, what were their names, where did they reside, and how many of each were there? This new set of questions went far beyond the rather simple and ideological issue of recognition and ventured into the much more complex realm of categorization. With this, we resume our discussion of the inaugural census and the early Communist approach to this question of ethnotaxonomy.

THE 1953 EXPERIMENT WITH SELF-CATEGORIZATION

Unlike the Soviet census upon which the inaugural PRC registration campaign was loosely based, one which presented respondents with a predetermined set of nationality categories from which to choose, the Chinese census of 1953–54 posed the question of minzu as an unbounded, fill-in-the-blank query wherein a registrant dictated his or her minzu name to the census taker, who then transcribed it into Chinese characters.[72] This policy was known colloquially as "names are to be chosen by the bearers," or *ming cong zhuren*.[73] The underlying principle of this policy was a commitment to self-categorization: a political ideal that granted citizens the unfettered right to select their own minzu designations. More specifically, it specified that any individual over the age of eighteen would be free to select his or her own minzu status, which would then be officially recognized by the state.[74] Whatever people called themselves, so too would the government.

The remarkably open nature of the minzu question is most readily appreciated when one compares it against the other questions posed during the registration campaign. When it came to documenting personal names, for example, census takers received instructions on how to sift through the multiple appellations that the average person in China adopted and carried at different stages of life. In certain cases, respondents lacked names altogether, particularly in the recently banned but still persistent practice of betrothal adoption.[75] In such instances, census takers were instructed to assign the person with a name for the sake of documentation.

Age was also a complex issue. According to local custom, an infant in China was considered one year old at birth, and then one year older at the passage of the child's first Lunar New Year. An infant born shortly before the New Year, therefore, would be quickly be counted as two years old in China, whereas in other contexts the same child would not yet be considered one.[76] To assist census officials in translating between customary modes of chronology and the Gregorian calendar upon which the census was based, participants were outfitted with conversion charts listing dates from 1853 to 1953 in terms of the Western calendar, the lunar calendar, and imperial reign dates.[77]

Place of residence was an especially complicated issue, insofar as the double-counting of absent family members could lead to vast overestimations of the country's population. Customary practice rendered the issue quite sensitive, however, since it was common for family members to refer to their kin as "temporarily absent" even when they had been away for extended periods of time or had established lives elsewhere. Realizing that it would be an affront not to count these "temporarily absent" individuals, census officials developed a face-saving way of procuring the desired data without bruising the sensibilities of their respondents. The census form was divided into two sections: the right-hand side would include information on permanent residents and those who had been absent for less than six months; the left-hand side would include information about "temporarily absent" family members who had been away for more than six months (and thus, according to census procedures, would ultimately be counted as residents of another location). After recording both, the census office would use the right half and discard the left.[78]

In contrast to the care and attention that the architects of the census paid to the questions of personal names, age, and residency, almost no effort was made to anticipate or neutralize ambiguities associated with the fifth question, that of nationality or minzu. Not only was the question left wide open, but in the event that one's respondent did not understand the question being posed, census takers were not allowed to assign a minzu designation on the person's behalf. Rather, they were instructed to approach the issue indirectly, with leading questions such as "Are you Hui or are you Han?" *(Huimin haishi Hanmin?)* or perhaps "Are you a bannerman or are you Han?" *(Zaiqi haishi Hanmin?).*[79] By invoking such well-known groups, and contrasting them against the Han majority, these auxiliary questions were designed to induce a corresponding response from the interviewee. Once an answer was provided, however, no further provisions were made to insure commensurability or comparability among the names being procured. Census takers were not provided with any standardized list of nationalities, nor any conversion charts with which they could translate between customary and official modes of identification. No official ethnotaxonomy existed, after all. Thus, whatever a person called him- or herself, so too would the state.

When considered in light of the Communist Party's development in the late Republican period, this policy was not unreasonable. As we have seen, the Communists had developed their ethnopolitical platform in dialogue with the minorities of north China who, as Katherine Kaup has observed, possessed centralized religious and leadership structures and were, relative to those in the southwest, "more clearly demarcated and separated geographically from the Han."[80] Moreover, with the exception of the Chinese-speaking Hui, the languages of the northern groups were more unified, unlike the predominantly nonliterate, "dialect-fractured southern languages."[81] Based on their experience in the north with the Hui and the Mongols, the Communists perhaps assumed that the nationalities of China at large would exhibit a comparably robust sense of self-identity, making self-categorization a viable alternative to state-led categorization.

As census research neared the halfway mark, however, problems began to surface that called into question this unbounded approach to minzu registration. The problems surfaced, not in the north, where the Communists had developed their ethnopolitical platform, but in the southwestern province of Yunnan where the CCP had virtually no experience with the question of cultural and linguistic diversity. In the county of Yunlong, local census officials reported the discovery of ten additional groups, or at the very least, ten ethnonyms that had never before been recorded by authorities.[82] In Yongsheng County, the situation was identical. Prior to the inaugural census, county officials had recorded the names of some twenty-eight minority groups. During the 1953–54 registration, this number had grown to thirty-eight.[83] In Yuanmou County, local officials reported to the provincial government that many of their respondents did not know how to answer the question of minzu. Even with the auxiliary prompts, many locals simply did not know what the term meant.

In addition to those who did not understand the question being asked, there was an even larger number of people who, from the perspective of state authorities, posed an even bigger problem: those who understood minzu in ways that diverged from the official interpretation. In their report on registration work in Kunming, census takers described two "chaotic" taxonomic phenomena: "single minzu with multiple names" *(yi zhong minzu ji zhong mingcheng)* and "single names with multiple ways of writing them" *(yi zhong mingcheng ji zhong xiefa).*[84]

In early 1954, as the tabulation of census data neared completion, it quickly became apparent that local reports such as these, at first seemingly isolated and anecdotal, were signs of a much broader crisis. Back in Beijing, the scope of the problem soon became evident: nationwide, over four hundred distinct entries appeared in the census registers in response to the question of minzu identity. Among these, roughly two hundred of them were recorded in one province alone: China's southwesternmost province of Yunnan (see table 1).[85]

Because of the highly unorthodox conditions under which it was produced, the inaugural census resulted in a chaotic body of data, a fractured mosaic in which the largest pieces dwarfed the smallest by many orders of magnitude. Despite this, however, certain facets and characteristics of the province could be gleaned. First, the central and provincial governments had now quantified a fact that both already knew, namely that Yunnan was home to a large number of ethnic minorities. According to the census results, roughly one-third of the province (32.6 percent) self-identified as non-Han. Among these, fourteen groups appeared in the census registers with populations in excess of one hundred thousand people: the Bai, Benren, Dai, Hani, Hui, Jingpo, Kawa, Lahu, Lisu, Miao, Naxi, Pula, Yi, and Zhuang. Second, within the over five million non-Han residents, there were thirteen medium-sized groups with populations of between ten and one hundred thousand, scattered throughout the province: the Achang, Azhe, Bulang, Huayao, Kucong, Muji, Nu, Tu, Xiangtang, Xie, Xifan, Yao, and Zang. In line with the Communists' expecta-

Ethnonym	Population	Ethnonym	Population	Ethnonym	Population
Achang	19,621	Fuduo	1	Lemo	4,807
Ahei	246	Funi	18	Li	350
Ake	1,002	Gaoli	5	Li (alternate	1
Akuo	2	Gaomian	60	character)	
Aluo	1	Gaoshan	6	Lie	6
Ani	18	Gelao	50	Limin	1
Ao	58	Gesi	260	Lishi	1
Azhe	37	Gucong	1	Lisu	249,467
Azhe (alternative	15,928	Gui	5	Longren	8
character)		Guola	63	Lude	105
Bai	658,172	Han	11,632,155	Lulu	676
Baijia	602	Hanhui	2	Luoyi	1
Bairen	n/a	Hani	441,085	Lüxi	281
Baiyi	4	Hei	243	Mahei	1,260
Bajia	1,782	Heipu	118	Malimasha	2
Banxi	295	Heisu	2,975	Man	954
Banyi	3	Hong	8	Manzi	2
Ben	6,415	Huahong	2	Masha	8
Bendizu	7	Huasu	845	Mata	56
Benglong	3,126	Huayao	16,719	Meng	3,507
Benren	120,564	Hui	216,454	Meng (alternate	1
Boluo	1	Jia	5	character)	
Bujiao	176	Jiangxi	4	Mengwu	1,243
Bulang	32,148	Jiazhou	475	Mengyong	10
Buwa	42	Jingdong	36	Mianren	1
Buxia	216	Jingpo	106,803	Miao	360,468
Cang	1	Kabie	421	Micha	8
Canyi	720	Kang	18	Mili	5,047
Chaman	900	Kawa	158,842	Mingji	n/a
Chaoxian	7	Keji	23	Misi	3
Dai	483,347	Kejia	2	Moluo	1
Daisi	369	Kela	393	Mosu	96
Dalao	1,970	Kucong	10,457	Muji	10,085
Danren	1,054	La	1	Nahua	1
Dazhuba	9	Laba	1	Nama	1
Deng	47	Lahu	134,854	Nanjing	46
Diga	261	Lalu	7,040	Nanni	38
Dingge	399	Laluo	8	Naxi	141,727
Dongchuan	4	Lama	800	Naxi (alternate	5
Donglan	4	Lami	2,644	character)	
Douyi	2	Lang'e	1,223	Naxiang	n/a
Douyun	697	Lao	5,595	Nayi	1
Douyundou	2,327	Laowu	3	Naza	430
Du	2,413	Laxi	62	Nibo'er	1
Fan	5	Lazi	24	Nu	13,003

(continued)

TABLE 1 *(continued)*

Ethnonym	Population	Ethnonym	Population	Ethnonym	Population
Paijiao	63	Shuitian	2,172	Yongbai	104
Pin	50	Tagu	1,207	Yuenan	45
Pula	103,620	Talu	723	Zang	66,816
Punan	4	Tamiao	2,178	Zeheng	4
Qiang	1	Tanglang	586	Zhili	428
Qijia	18	Tu	42,729	Zhong	65
Qing	161	Tu (alternate	2	Zhuang	477,160
Qiu	n/a	character)		Zhuohe	22
Qu	88	Tu'e	12	Zi	113
Riben	1	Tujia	1,188	Zijun	1,637
Ri'erman	1	Tulao	493	Zong	39
Ruanke	425	Tusi	134	"Other minzu"	38,148
Sa	1,443	Wu	5	(qita minzu)	
Sanda	459	Wu'ersiwei	1	"Unclear minzu"	
Sanni	1	Xiang	1	(buming minzu)	3
Shan	1	Xiangtang	11,888	Illegible	n/a
Shang	5	Xie	10,067	Illegible (alternate	119
Shanhou	1,240	Xifan	16,091	character)	
Shanyihong	1	Ximoluo	993	Minorities	5,625,082
Shi	1	Yang	284		
Shoutou	4	Yao	72,184	Total	17,257,237
Shu	1	Yi	1,493,347	population	
Shui	1,960	Yishan	1		
Shuihu	2,025	Yishi	1		

SOURCE: Yunnan sheng renmin zhengfu minzu shiwu weiyuanhui yanjiushi [Yunnan Province People's Government Nationalities Affairs Commission Research Office], *"Yunnan shaoshu minzu renkou tongjibiao—xuanweihui cailiao* [Chart of the Total Populations of Minority Nationalities in Yunnan—Election Affairs Commission Materials]," YNPA, Quanzong 2152, Index 1, File 48 (August 25, 1954).

NOTE: See Appendix C for a reprint of this chart, sorted by population size.

tions, therefore, there were indeed many sizeable groups in the region who knew *exactly* who they were and what their name was.

Beyond these twenty-seven large and medium-sized groups, however, the ethnographic picture started to get very hazy. Thirty-eight registrants appeared in the census with populations of between one hundred and one thousand: the Ahei, Baijia, Banxi, Bujiao, Buxia, Canyi, Chaman, Daisi, Diga, Dingge, Douyun, Gesi, Hei, Heipu, Huasu, Jiazhou, Kabie, Kela, Lama, Li, Lude, Lulu, Lüxi, Man, Naza, Qing, Ruanke, Sanda, Talu, Tanglang, Tulao, Tusi, Ximoluo, Yang, Yongbai, Zhili, Zi, and one registrant whose name was illegible in the census report. At the far end of the population range was a long tail of ninety-two registrants with populations of less than one hundred people, twenty of which were recorded with "populations" of only one.

These included the Aluo, Akuo, Ani, Ao, Azhe, Baiyi, Banyi, Bendizu, Boluo, Buwa, Cang, Chaoxian, Dazhuba, Deng, Dongchuan, Donglan, Douyi, Fan, Fuduo, Funi, Gaoli, Gaomian, Gaoshan, Gucong, Gui, Guola, Hanhui, Hong, Huahong, Jia, Jiang-xi, Jingdong, Kang, Keji, Kejia, La, Laba, Laluo, Laowu, Laxi, Lazi, Li, Lie, Limin, Lishi, Longren, Luoyi, Malimasha, Manzi, Masha, Mata, Meng, Mengyong, Mian-ren, Micha, Misi, Moluo, Mosu, Nahua, Nama, Nanjing, Nanni, Naxi, Nayi, Niboér, Paijiao, Pin, Punan, Qiang, Qijia, Qu, Riben, Riérman, Sanni, Shan, Shang, Shan-yihong, Shi, Shoutou, Shu, Tu, Tué, Wu, Wuérsiwei, Xiang, Yishan, Yishi, Yuenan, Zeheng, Zhong, Zhuohe, and Zong.[86]

For state authorities, the 1953–54 census data was befuddling. To call it "illegi-ble," in the James Scott sense, would be a vast understatement.[87] Indeed, to read the list of self-registered minzu in the inaugural census is primarily an exercise in foren-sic reconstruction, not categorization. The case of one entry, the Xiang, is particu-larly illustrative. Based on the census results, what could and could not be inferred about this "group," one whose "population" equaled one? First and most basically, the appearance of the commonplace Chinese character *xiang* (elephant) tells us al-most nothing about the encounter that took place between the registrant and the census worker. We do not and cannot know what the individual said, only what one particular Chinese-speaking census taker considered to be a reasonable approxi-mation of the individual's declaration of self. Due to vast dialectical variations within Chinese, moreover, the character inscription and the original response are doubly mediated, first from the respondent's language into the census taker's Chinese, and from there to state authorities elsewhere in China speaking different dialects. As the Xiang, the nineteen other isolates, and many of the other single-digit entries demonstrate, the fill-in-the-blank census exposed the fact that in contrast to large self-identified groups such as the Lemo and the Jingpo, there were at the same time many people and communities whose understanding of minzu departed radically from that of the state. Because each respondent was permitted to answer the ques-tion of minzu improvisationally—not guided by various options that might have provided the person hints as to the specific type of answer sought by the census-taker—it left the door wide open for people to answer, in essence, *their own ver-sions of the minzu question.* Faced with the radically open-ended nature of the cen-sus data, then, central and provincial authorities were presented with one "Xiang," one "Fuduo," four "Donglan," and yet absolutely no way to know what a Xiang, Fuduo, or Donglan was. Were they ethnonyms, patronyms, pseudonyms, toponyms, eponyms, or perhaps something else still?[88] The fact is that when confronted with the radical uncertainty of the entry, one has little choice but to acknowledge this uncertainty and recognize: Xiang, Fuduo, Donglan, and many of the other entries in the inaugural census were simply *nyms*, floating taxa whose classificatory frame-works are lost to us.

Whereas the case of the Xiang and other microscopic entries are rather dramatic, the same question of taxonomic ambiguity applies to numerous groups which appeared in the census with populations of less than one hundred people. For example, what *kind of category* was Buwa (population forty-two), Dazhuba (population nine), Kang (population eighteen), Dingge (population 399), and so forth? When asked their minzu status, what exactly did they think this word meant? Whereas this question cannot be answered, what becomes evident is this: when we talk about the inaugural census of the PRC, we are not in fact talking about an inventory of ethnonational groups, but rather a list of *versions* of minzu where each version depended upon the respondents' interpretation of the question. It is this type of improvisation and interpretation that is not possible when confronted with a pregiven list of minzu options, and a battalion of census takers trained in helping their respondents select an acceptable answer. The Communists had expected the people of Yunnan not only to know their own minzu identities, but also to know them in a way that was commensurable with the concept of minzu as understood by state authorities. The sheer chaos of the census data revealed to Communist authorities just how naïve this expectation had been, and that the only means of commensurating the worldviews of the six hundred million citizens of "New China" would be to standardize and delimit the concept.

Heuristics aside, there were more unvarnished facts that authorities derived from the data and that concern us most here: the number of self-reported names far outstripped all official estimates of ethnic diversity in the province; there were simply too many for the state to handle and their numbers had to be reduced. As explained by Deng Xiaoping in his exegesis of the Election Law, the state guaranteed at least one representative to each officially recognized national minority regardless of population size—just one of the many promises to national minorities that had been widely propagandized in the early years of the PRC.[89] Based on this provision, then, the Communist leadership was faced with the prospect of at least 190 national delegates hailing from Yunnan province alone, and at least four hundred minority delegates nationwide. With only twelve hundred seats in the forthcoming NPC, minority nationalities hailing from just Yunnan would have accounted for over one-sixth of the entire parliament—a staggering number when one considers that they constituted less than 1 percent of the population of the country.[90] In addition to these mandated seats, as we saw, the 1953 Law made additional provisions based on proportionality, designed to insure that larger minorities would receive a level of representation reflective of their size. If we make a conservative estimate regarding the number of additional minority representatives, hypothesizing somewhere between fifty and one hundred supplemental delegates countrywide, we are left with a National People's Congress in which 40 percent of the legislative body would hail from a non-Han minority nationality—an overwhelmingly large percentage when we consider that the combined population of these minority nationalities constituted only 6 percent of the total population of China circa 1953.[91] And as for those groups with populations of one, they confronted officials with the absurd prospect of minority delegates literally standing in on behalf of themselves—ones of a kind, the loneliest "nations" on earth.

This bewildering mosaic posed a host of problems for the state beyond the immediate question of congressional representation. Were they to recognize each of these self-identified names, Communist authorities would then be compelled to implement an array of administrative, legal, and cultural projects. For each authenticated minority, the state would have to address the potential creation of autonomous administrative units, the development of minority language scripts, and the training of minority cadres, among other cultural policies outlined in Article 53 of *The Common Program*.[92] To recognize diversity at such a level would have paralyzed the government.

Confronted with this dire political crisis, Communist authorities realized that if minzu was going to serve as one of the axes of Chinese citizenship, it could not be left to the people to determine at will. If the People's Republic was going to be home to a bounded set of imagined communities, then the state would need to intervene and discipline the imaginations of its people. It was with this realization that the Communist state turned to the two communities in China with the expertise and experience necessary to resolve this taxonomic crisis: Chinese ethnologists and linguists, on the one hand, and local provincial authorities, on the other. In early 1954, with time running out before the upcoming congressional elections, they decided to tackle the most complex region first: the province of Yunnan, which alone accounted for more than half of all the entries in the inaugural census. In the middle of April 1954, the Yunnan Province Ethnic Classification team was established.[93]

CONCLUSION

The Ethnic Classification Project was not undertaken as part of a preexisting or even premeditated Communist goal of taxonomic reductionism. To the contrary, it was carried out in response to a political crisis that had emerged precisely because of the party's radically liberal experiment with practically unfettered self-categorization. Had the PRC carried out its inaugural census according to conventional governmentalist models, using existing models in circulation at both the central and provincial level Nationalities Affairs Commissions, it is highly likely that there would now be far more officially recognized minzu in Yunnan, and nationwide, than there are today.

This raises a second key point. Whereas current accounts of the Classification attribute the radical reduction of ethnic categories to Communist prerogative, what the following chapters will demonstrate is that the remarkably synthetic categorization of minorities in China was in fact the result of the influence from the Chinese social sciences, especially ethnology and linguistics. To understand and explain the methodological and epistemological framework that subtended the Classification project of 1954, it is not upon the Communist state that we should train our focus, but rather upon the state's social scientific advisors.

Third, the taxonomic crisis that resulted from the fill-in-the-blank census of 1953 sheds light on a gaping hole in the Chinese Communist approach to the "nationality question." Whereas Communist theorists had spilled a great deal of ink over abstract topics such as equality, self-determination, and regional autonomy, they had not dealt whatsoever with the problem of minzu categorization. The CCP approach to the nationality question simply failed to appreciate the central importance of taxonomy within the broader question of self-determination, representation, and political equality. They falsely assumed that the problem of categorization could be circumvented simply by affording everyone in the country the right to determine their own identity. The outcome of the first census, however, was a stark lesson for the CCP, revealing the naïvety of this ideal. The price of recognition was categorization, for it was only through categorization that a multitude of people could be recast as a singular, corporate person, and only through category that a variety of conceptions of minzu could be brought into congress with one another, both literally and figuratively. Inseparable from any mature understanding of self-determination is the determination of selves.

Fourth, as evidenced by the remarkable text of the inaugural census, a polysemous document containing much more and much less than simply "ethnonyms," this chapter brings to the surface a host of ambiguities which are normally overlooked by existing accounts of the Classification. There has long been an altogether uncritical and inaccurate tendency among scholars—both inside and outside China, both internal to and critical of the Classification—to refer to the census entries as "ethnic groups."[94] By assuming that each of the census entries refers to a self-aware group, we cannot help but cast the entire story of the Classification as a political allegory featuring four-hundred-plus self-aware minority communities yearning, and in large part failing, to achieve political recognition. Whereas there were clearly groups for whom the census did in fact constitute a moment of politically self-aware assertion, the remainder appear instead to have been individuals who were simply improvising responses to a question they had never heard or considered before. With these considerations in mind, then, the inaugural census and the Ethnic Classification cannot be understood as projects which acted upon a previously existing set of non-Han communities. The census and the Classification were both *constitutive* of the minzu they ended up categorizing, in part because both enterprises were part of the larger process by which the Chinese state began to standardize the definition of minzu on a mass level.

Fifth, in this chapter we have examined Chinese Communist governmentality in its early years, at a time before state authorities knew how to see ethnic identity like a state, in the sense meant by James Scott. A bit like Hollywood action films in which leading men are never seen asking for directions, the literature on govern-mentality disproportionately features state authorities that possess what seems like a preternatural sense of where they are going and how to get there (even when they never arrive). Whereas their projects often fail, it is not because of any inability on their part to administer national censuses, to construct vast bureaucratic record-keeping infrastructures, or, in any number of ways, to conceptualize the populations and societies under their administrative control in a fashion we have come to expect of modern state and its putatively coherent epistemic framework *govern-mentality*. Such skills, it would seem, come naturally to states.

Whereas we have come to think of states as behaving in certain fundamental ways—one of the most basic being the administration of censuses that reduce the complexities of their populations into abstractions that facilitate both political representation and social control—the case of China circa 1953 provides a vivid counterexample. Here we find a government that had no experience in how to use even one of the most basic technologies of statecraft. The fledgling Communist state reminds us that governmentality should not be thought of as a basket of traits, skills, technologies, and epistemological commitments that modern states come into possession of simply by virtue of being modern states. Rather, before a state can see like a state, it must *need* to do so and it must *learn* to do so. This holds true, not only during the emergence of the modern nation-state as a novel form of political organization, but also in postrevolutionary contexts in which an ascendant party suddenly finds itself the new regime. As the rest of this study will bear out, the Chinese Communists did not teach themselves how to see like a state, at least not when it came to the fundamentally important problem of ethnic categorization. To the contrary, the history of the Classification project is one of an inexperienced Chinese state that was able to orient itself only by observing the world through the eyes of its social scientific advisors. Simply put, the following chapters will make the case that the "mentality" of "governmentality" was, in the case of the 1954 Ethnic Classification, in large part the mentality of the comparative social sciences. Social science served as the eyes of the modern Chinese nation-state, and in doing so, taught the state how to see ethnicity *categorically*.

With these considerations in mind, we travel now to the campus of the Central Institute for Nationalities in Beijing. There, an elite team of ethnologists and linguists was gathering in late April 1954 to make sense of what at first must have seemed like an impossible mission: to provide the central state with definitive taxonomic recommendations regarding the most ethnically diverse province in China, and one of the most diverse regions on earth, in less than six months.

Ethnicity as Language

Among those who research ethnic groups in the southwest, there is no one who does not take H. R. Davies' taxonomy as his starting point.

—DING SU, 1941

In the closing weeks of April 1954, a small group of scholars in Beijing began to discuss the Herculean task that awaited them in Yunnan. The Classification team would have less than six months to prosecute a coordinated, multisite investigation and produce a series of definitive taxonomic recommendations about the province's minority groups. Their findings would result in a complete reassessment of the country's ethnonational demography, moreover, and not simply in the development of ethnological knowledge. They would influence not merely the direction of their discipline, but also China's administrative geography, the allocation of economic and political resources, and entire domains of cultural production. In this chapter we will examine how the team was able to fulfill this immense task in the time allotted. In particular, we will examine the criteria and methodology they adopted in response to the census and the chaotic and confusing body of demographic data contained therein.

The Beijing group was led by Lin Yaohua, who had been appointed vice-director of the Ethnic Classification research team. Lin was a native of Fujian Province, having received his master's degree in 1935 from the Department of Sociology at Yanjing University. As one of the star pupils of the renowned Wu Wenzao, he went on to Harvard University in 1937, where he completed his doctoral work over the next few years. Upon graduating, Lin immediately made a name for himself, garnering praise for his first two books, *The Golden Wing: A Sociological Study of Chinese Family* and *The Lolo of Liangshan*.[1] Following 1949, Lin went on to conduct ethnological field research in Inner Mongolia (1950), Tibet (1951), and Inner Mongolia once again (1953). During the first of his trips, Lin was accompanied by many of the scholars who were now part of the Classification team, including Shi Lianzhu, Wang Furen, Huang Shuping, and Wang Xiaoyi.[2]

TABLE 2 Yunnanese Groups Outlined by Luo Jiguang

Achang	Minjia
Benglong	Naxi
Burmese	Nong
Chashan	Nu
Dai	Puman
Hani	Qiu
Jingpo	Sha
Kawa	Tibetan
Lahu	Xifan
Langsu	Yao
Lisu	Yi
Miao	Zaiwa

On April 26, during a late afternoon session, the team met to tackle the problem of taxonomic criteria. Lin, who had departed for Kunming that morning, was not present at the meeting, inviting Luo Jiguang to address the team in his absence. Luo (1914–78) was a specialist in the minority languages of the southwest, trained at Peking University under Luo Changpei, one of the most influential linguists in modern Chinese history. He graduated in 1936 and went on to teach at National Yunnan University and at the Linguistic Research Institute of the Chinese Academy of Social Sciences. Along with his colleague Fu Maoji, he became increasingly involved in minority language script development, one of the major priorities of the early PRC period for the Communist state.[3]

During that late April session, Luo argued that the profusion of ethnonyms confronting the Classification team could be reduced at the outset to just over twenty discrete groups. There was only one proviso: the team would need to treat language as a surrogate for minzu identity, in essence ceding the question of ethnic taxonomy to the discipline of linguistics.[4] Luo outlined twenty-four groups in all (see table 2).

Luo Jiguang was not the sole exponent of this position. Three days later, on the afternoon of April 29, the Classification team invited linguist Ma Xueliang (1913–99), also a Republican-era graduate of Peking University. Ma's lecture, entitled "The Utility of Language in the Course of Investigations," elaborated upon Luo's point and rephrased it with even greater simplicity and precision: before conducting ethnological investigations in Yunnan, linguistic categorization should be carried out first. Once language-based comparisons and classification had yielded the basic contours of identity in the province, researchers could follow up with studies of local culture, customs, and so forth.[5]

In addition to these advisors, the Ethnic Classification team also comprised a group of linguists who shared an identical outlook. The most important was Fu Maoji, a specialist in the minority languages of the southwest and prize student of

TABLE 3   Yunnanese Groups Outlined by Luo Changpei and Fu Maoji in 1954

Achang	Naxi
Benglong	Nong
Burmese	Nu
Buyi	Puman
Chashan	Qiang
Dai	Qiu
Hani	Sha
Jiarong	Tibetan
Jingpo	Wa
Lahu	Xifan
Langsu	Yao
Lisu	Yi
Miao	Zaiwa
Minjia	Zhuang

SOURCE: Luo Changpei and Fu Maoji, "*Guonei shaoshuminzu yuyan wenzi de qingkuang* [The Situation of Linguistic Scripts for Domestic Minority Nationalities]," *Zhongguo yuwen* (1954).

Luo Changpei. Fu Maoji was appointed to work alongside Lin Yaohua as vice-director of the Yunnan Province Ethnic Classification research team, and to oversee the team's corps of language specialists. In collaboration with Luo Changpei, Fu had published a largely identical taxonomy even before the advent of Classification, proposing the very same argument that their colleagues were now presenting to the Classification team. In a March 1954 article published in *Chinese Philology*, Luo and Fu contended that "among the approximately 140 ethnonyms in Yunnan, many are the same in reality and different in name alone. If one treats the possession of an independent language as our criterion, then these ethnonyms could be merged into twenty-five or so groups."[6] In that article, Luo Changpei and Fu Maoji produced a taxonomy that included the groups shown in table 3.

With the exception of the Buyi, Jiarong, Qiang, and Zhuang, the pair's taxonomy was identical to the one proposed by Luo Jiguang to the Classification team. The similarity of their taxonomies is even more pronounced when contrasted against those of the central and provincial Nationalities Affairs Commissions seen in chapter 1, as well as the inaugural census of the PRC. Whereas these texts listed hundreds of minzu, leading Chinese linguists regarded Yunnan as home to roughly two dozen.

As we will see in this chapter and the next, the Classification team ultimately did accept this commensuration, adopting language-based categorization as the taxonomic foundation of the project. Where, however, did this paradigm come from? How did language become an accepted surrogate for ethnic identity? More broadly, where did the taxonomic and epistemological foundations of the Classification come from, most notably its commitment to the formulation of a highly limited and mutually exclusive set of identity categories? Traditionally, the answer to this question has been to treat the Ethnic Classification Project as a uniquely Communist affair, one in which CCP officials at the central and provincial levels more or less indiscriminately created such categories and imposed them upon both ethnic minorities and ethnologists. To the extent that scholars have pointed to pre-1949 antecedents, or deeper historical continuities, attention has been paid in large part to a presumed Sino-Soviet connection—the idea being, once again, that the Chinese Communists undertook this categorical imposition in lock step with the dictates of Soviet precedent and Soviet advisors.

In this chapter we will see that the origins of this taxonomic worldview fall well before the 1949 divide and bear the imprint, not of Soviet colonial practices, but of those emanating from the British Empire and its loose, transnational network of amateur ethnologists and linguists. This story takes us back to the waning years of the Qing dynasty and to an unlikely starting point: the work of an obscure British military officer by the name of Henry Rodolph Davies. It was his 1909 work, championed and only partly modified by Republican era Chinese social scientists, that became the foundation of Chinese ethnological studies of the southwest, the 1954 Ethnic Classification Project and, indeed, the present-day classification of ethnic groups in Yunnan. In the ongoing story of colonial anthropological practice in Africa, South Asia, North America, Taiwan, and so forth, we must now include southwest China.

H. R. DAVIES AS THE LINK BETWEEN INDIA AND THE YANGZI

Henry Rodolph Davies was born on September 28, 1865, the second son of Henry Fanshawe Davies and Ellen Christopher Alexander Hankey. Centered in Worcestershire, the Davies family was steeped in a long tradition of military service to the British empire. Davies' grandfather and great uncle were both veterans of the Peninsular War. Davies' father had become a "young gentleman" in the British Navy at the age of twelve, and at age fifteen was dispatched to South Asia to serve in the Second Anglo-Burmese War. By the time his son Henry Rodolph was born, he had acceded to the rank of lieutenant colonel, and was later promoted to lieutenant general.[7]

Davies received his education at Eton and excelled at the study of languages. In addition to French, "Hindustani," and Persian, in which his school records listed him as being highly proficient, he had also reached intermediate levels in Burmese, Pushtu (Pashto), and Chinese.[8] As evidenced by this assemblage of languages, Davies had his eyes trained on Britain's colonial sphere of influence in Asia. Cartographically, his linguistic schooling traced a long crescent, originating in Afghanistan and sweeping through northern India, Burma, and the Sino-Burmese border region of southwest Yunnan.[9]

Having obtained his commission in August of 1884, Davies was dispatched first to British-controlled Burma in October 1887, and then to Siam in November of 1892.[10] Davies' experience in China began in 1893, when he was enlisted to serve on the Burmese boundary commission alongside William Warry, the British government's advisor to the government of Burma; the district superintendent of police; fifty men from the Nineteenth Yorkshire Regiment; and two Chinese delegates. Starting on November 17, the team set out for Yunnan from the Burmese side, traveling through the Kachin Hills and the Northern Shan states. Their goal was to find the Chinese passes or "gates" that demarcated the border between Burma and the Qing imperial domain.[11] Over the course of late fall and early winter, the team located three such gates—the Huju Guan (Crouching Tiger Pass), Tianma Guan (Heavenly Horse Pass), and Hanlong Guan (Han Dragon Pass)—fulfilling their objective by January 7, 1894.

Upon completion of their official business, the Chinese deputies invited Davies to stay behind and travel through the province. Davies agreed, and spent the subsequent months sojourning and collecting piecemeal observations of the terrain and the people. On April 3, 1895, he arrived in Simao, only to learn that the local elites were expecting a visit from French travelers in a few days. The local "mandarin" only knew the Frenchman's Chinese name, and so Davies was unable to decipher who it might be. As he discovered later, the traveler was none other than Prince Henri d'Orléans, en route from Tongking. Davies would later read this sojourner's account and find out that d'Orléans and his companions "must have reached Ssumao [Simao] the day after I left it."[12]

For Davies, one of the most arresting features of the region was its cultural and racial diversity. During this excursion through southwest China, Davies had his first encounter with a group he recorded as "Nga-ch'ang," whom he described as a "distinct race who do not exist anywhere else."[13] The "Mohammedans," or Hui, also caught his attention, in particular their relationship with the local Chinese. "The two races naturally hate each other and always will do so," he later noted, "but there is no enmity on the outside."[14]

Davies was not alone in his fascination with the non-Chinese peoples of Yunnan. Numerous sojourners, missionaries, and colonial officers found themselves intrigued by the people of the region and the seemingly irreducible complexity of the cultural, linguistic, and social mosaic they formed. Constituting the Other to the Chinese, which in turn constituted a global Other in the minds Euro-American observers, these groups appeared to colonial onlookers in the context of a double, nested alterity. A. R. Colquhoun recounted his journeys through the region, published in the form of meandering travelogues as well as brief articles.[15] In 1911, Samuel Clarke published *Among the Tribes in South-west China* in which he outlined Protestant missionary penetration into the local non-Chinese communities. "There is no family of the human race," he lamented, "of which so little is accurately known as of the non-Chinese races of Southern China. This is in great measure due

to the perfect maze of senseless names, taken from the Chinese, in which the subject is involved."[16] In 1913, French physician A. F. Legendre published *Au Yunnan,*
documenting his travels through China's distant frontier regions.[17] One decade later,
and perhaps most famously, the Austrian-American polymath Joseph Rock began
writing prolifically about the Naxi.[18] For Clarke, Davies, and others, the "perfect
maze of senseless names" referred to prevailing conceptualizations of southwest
China as a place inhabited by hundreds of groups. In late imperial writings such as
the *Yunnan Gazetteer (Yunnan tongzhi), Record of Guizhou (Qianji),* and other texts,
southwest China was presented as a phenomenally complex region where groups
were not so much categorized as cataloged.[19]

For European and American observers, such compendia were anathema to the
increasingly comparativist and reductive mindset of the social sciences and modern governmentality. Centered in Western Europe and North America, political and
academic elites were undergoing a fundamental transformation in the way they went
about "knowing" their populations and research subjects. As Alain Desrosières has
summarized it, "between 1895 and 1935 the norms presiding over legitimate de-
scriptions of the social world were completely changed."[20] This transformation began in the late nineteenth century, when the development of the comparative social
sciences, coupled with the demands of direct political control, prompted state authorities in Europe and elsewhere to abandon existing modes of demographic
knowledge and deploy a repertoire of new technologies in their stead. Designed to
tame the heterogeneity of their populations and to render them "legible"[21] and "open
to the scrutiny of officialdom,"[22] these included national identification cards, pass-
ports, birth certificates, composite portraiture, and other forms of demographic
technologies. Nicholas Dirks has outlined similar trends in late nineteenth-century
India, where state representatives began to criticize earlier demographic manuals
and gazetteers as "prolix and insufficiently statistical" and replace them with a highly
systematic and comparative form of anthropology.[23] Only generalizable data lent
itself to the sort of extrapolation required by modern state bureaucracy.

Davies returned to England where he was honored with the McGregor Award,
and where he soon caught the attention of British authorities and business magnates
interested in the region.[24] One entrepreneur in particular, John Halliday of the newly
formed Yunnan Company, invited Davies to lead an expedition in 1898 to investigate a potential railway route linking India and the Yangzi River by way of Yunnan
Province.[25] The British were in competition with the French, their colonial neighbors to the east who, like them, were eager to be the first to develop shorter trade
routes into the Qing empire. Were the empire to disintegrate—a geopolitical potentiality never far from the minds of either power—whoever developed this rail link
would become the new center of economic gravity for China's resource-rich central
and southern provinces, the new magnet toward which the Chinese needle would
reorient.[26] Davies would be dispatched to take precise notes on the topography of

northern Burma and southern Yunnan, information critical to the British government and the newly established Yunnan Company in their deliberations over whether to invest in railway development in the region. Davies agreed to the request and was assigned to lead the Burma division of the expedition, along with Lieutenant W. A. Watts-Jones, Captain C. M. D. Ryder, and two engineers from the Yunnan Company. They would be accompanied by the Shanghai group, led by Captain E. Pottinger and Lieutenant C. G. W. Hunter, who would ascend the Yangzi from the east.[27]

In November 1898, Davies arrived in Burma, equipped with a plane-table, a prismatic compass, two aneroid barometers, a boiling-point thermometer, a six-inch sextant, and sketch books.[28] With these instruments, the thirty-four-year-old officer took almost daily measurements of longitude, latitude, altitude, and temperature, maintaining all of these notes in a register he updated methodically. In addition to this information, Davies' register detailed the names of the towns through which they passed, the mileages separating different locales, the directions traveled, and the total distance traversed.[29] Between the start of his journey on November 15, 1899, and the close of his travels on June 29, 1900, Davies crossed 2,442.5 miles of terrain, for a daily average of 10.8 miles during those 226 days.[30]

At the same time, Davies expanded upon the budding ethnographic interests that had begun to take shape three years earlier. Upon encountering different tribes in the region, Davies turned his attention away from his cartographic work and toward the collection of vocabularies, inquiring after local language translations of a long series of words. To each respondent Davies posed a list of over one hundred words:

> Man (human being), man (male), woman, child, father, mother, son, daughter, elder brother, younger brother, elder sister, younger sister, husband, wife, head, body, face, nose, mouth, ear, eye, hair, tooth, tongue, back, stomach, leg, arm, hat, turban, coat, trousers, shoe, bag, sword, spear, gun, bow, arrow, stick, house, door, hatch, floor, post, plank, horse, buffalo, cow, pig, goat, dog, cat, chicken, chicken's egg, bird, fish, tiger, gold, silver, copper, iron, village, road, river, hill, field, paddy, rice, cooked rice, tree, leaf, flower, fruit, grass, boat, day, night, fire, water, wind, earth, sand, stone, sky, sun, moon, star, good, big, small, long, short, tall, short or low, broad, narrow, hot, cold, heavy, light, many, few, near, far, thick, thin, wet, dry, old (men), old (things), new, red, yellow, black, white, I, thou, one, two, three, four, five, six, seven, eight, nine, ten, one hundred, one thousand, ten thousand, three men, two houses, white house, good man, pound, cook, grind, hold, cut, pierce, shoot, spoil, hurt (transitive), a Chinaman, Lolo, Hsi-fan, Miao-tzu, Tibetan, Lo'p'u, Ku-tsung.[31]

Through the collection, transcription, and comparison of this sample set of vocables, or "specimens" as he referred to them, Davies was drawing upon and placing himself within a long tradition. He was engaging in the collection of what is known as "core" or "basic vocabulary," a practice dating back to the seventeenth century. In 1642 Johannes de Laet defined his sample as "the names of those things which are domestic and most common to that nation."[32] Eventually reified as the

"Swadesh list" after the American linguist Morris Swadesh (1909–67), the basic vocabulary contained only those words that pertain to the basic aspects of daily life,
are learned early in childhood, and appear frequently in speech, qualities which render them comparatively resistant to replacement by foreign loanwords, making them
particularly useful to those engaged in comparative philology.[33] The practice of collecting basic vocabulary developed over the course of the late seventeenth to eighteenth centuries, in the works of Olaus Rudbeck (1675), Gottfried Leibniz (1698),
Hiob Ludolf (1702), Rasmus Rask, Johanns Friedrich Fritz (1748), Iwarus Abel
(1782), W. Carey (1816), David Bailie Warden (1825, 1834), Jules Sébastien César
Dumont d'Urville (1833), Arthur James Johnes (1846), Robert Gordon Latham,
S. W. Koelle (1854), and Daniel G. Brinton (1891), among many others.[34]

In southwest China specifically, the collection of vocabulary had become standard practice for sojourners like Davies. In 1872, Abbé Desgodin collected a series of linguistic "specimens" from the "Lu-tzu" and "Mo-so" peoples, publishing
his findings in the *Bulletin de la Société de Géographie* in the following year.[35] Others
who published or who reported collecting vocabularies in the region included Holt
S. Hallett (1886), Paul Vial (1890), Prince Henri d'Orléans (1896), and R. F. Johnson (1908).[36] To supplement his own collections, Davies drew on Desgodins, as
well as the collections of E. C. Young and Edward Colborne Baber. Davies organized his "specimens" into a single table, listing the names of the groups he encountered along the top axis, the English terms along the vertical axis, and then
transcriptions of local equivalents in the body of the table. Comparative lexical tables of this sort date back to the mid-eighteenth century, seen in the work of Dumont d'Urville, Robert Gordon Latham, and others.[37] Scanning over the transliterations, Davies then set about discerning patterns, which he notated to himself
with small checkmarks and marginal codes. For the Hsi-fan and Pru-mi Hsi-fan,
he annotated certain vocables with the letter L to indicate their similarity to corresponding terms in his Lolo sample. By comparison, a marginal note T indicated
equivalence with Tibetan, LT a more pronounced correlation to Lolo than Tibetan,
and TL the opposite. For those terms that observed no similarity to others, Davies
made no annotation.

Through this method, and in consultation with the vocabulary lists of Desgodin,
Davies began to work out a theory of equivalence between the languages of the tribes
he encountered in the region.[38] "The Munia Sifan vocabulary and the Sifan vocabulary given by Baber seem nearer Lolo than Tibetan," he noted in his journal. "The
P'rü-mi Sifan seems nearer Tibetan than Lolo." "Moso appears rather nearer Munia Sifan than Lolo." In a practice that would later come to be called "lexicostatis-
tics," Davies tabulated rough percentages of similarity, as we see in his comparison
of "Lu-tzu," "Lo-Lo," and "Tibetan": "Of 61 Lu-tzu words," Davies noted in the margins of the table, "35 appear closely connected with Tibetan and 6 connected with
Lo-Lo where the Lo-Lo words differ from Tibetan."[39]

From these classes of linguistic equivalence, Davies also began to postulate classes of ethnic equivalence. "Lisu near P'u-tu-ho and the Lolos near them call themselves Lei-su," he wrote, "but they are not Lisu. Lei-su are probably the same as Nesu." Further on he noted: "Wo-ni is a general name for the three tribes called Pu-tu, Pi-o, and K'a-tu (or K'a-to as it is pronounced in some districts). These three tribes speak dialects which differ so little that they are mutually intelligible."[40]

Through his postulation of ethnic classes of equivalence by way of linguistic classes of equivalence—particularly a nested set of relationships in which certain dialect subsets were understood to belong to parent categories—Davies was drawing upon the highly influential *stammbaum* or "family tree" theory of language and linguistic reconstruction as first articulated by August Schleicher in the 1860s. Influenced heavily by Charles Darwin, Schleicher's method of genealogical reconstruction relied upon the comparison of grammars and word lists to infer the existence of a common ancestry between seemingly disparate groups.[41] As Bernard Cohn has explained, "the theory of language implicit in the comparative method is that there are 'genetic' or 'genealogical' relations among languages that have been determined to belong to a 'family.' "[42] "As with genealogies," Cohn explains, "which could represent all the members of a family or descent group visually as a tree with a root, trunk, branches, and even twigs, so could dialects and languages be similarly represented."[43] Schleicher's views on language were even more explicit than those suggested here by Cohn. He saw in linguistics the capacity to lend empirical support for Darwin's theory of evolution, perhaps to an even greater extent than could naturalists. With that in mind, he regarded the categories of linguistic taxonomy and those of the natural sciences as correlated: the naturalist's genus *(gattung)* corresponded to linguist's family *(sprachfamilie)*, and species *(arten)* to language *(sprachen)*.[44] In this way, language provided a window into the ethnic and racial structure of humanity, a structure which could be revealed through the comparison of grammars and vocabularies.

By the nineteenth century, the allure of "ethnological philology" was widespread in Europe and the United States. As one scholar has argued, it was "the maturest and apparently most precise of the disciplines by which . . . men were attempting to trace modern phenomena in an unbroken line to a remote or historical past."[45] Its popularity can be witnessed in the wide array of ethnological and racial treatises whose taxonomies were based on linguistic division. In 1883, for example, Robert Needham Cust (1821–1909) published his highly influential *Modern Languages of Africa,* which subsequently played a central role in the categorization of African ethnicities and tribes.[46] In the United States, one finds the taxonomic work of Swiss philologist and ethnologist Albert Gallatin (1761–1849), who helped to found the American Ethnological Society and later undertook an extensive categorization of Native American languages.[47] Carrying on this tradition and applying it to the classification of Native American identity was Major John Wesley Powell (1834–1902), who served as director of the Bureau of Ethnology from 1879 until his death, publishing his immensely influential "Indian Linguistic Families North of Mexico" in 1891.[48] Powell's language-based taxonomy would later form the basis for the *Handbook of American Indians* published in 1907 and 1911 by the Bureau of American Ethnology.[49] A. L. Kroeber, who would later critique his taxonomy, nevertheless had to acknowledge "the extent and depth of influence which the Powell classification of linguistic stocks has from the day of its promulgation exercised on every aspect of American ethnology."[50] In 1892, Horatio Hale proclaimed this nascent view perhaps most forcefully. "Solely by their languages," Hale contended, "can the tribes of men be scientifically classified." "Linguistic anthropology," he continued," is the only true science of man."[51]

In 1909, Cambridge University Press published Davies' *Yün-nan: The Link Between India and the Yangtze*, a travelogue intended for a more general audience. Accompanied by glossy black-and-white photos of the region and a map of the terrain, the manuscript recounted the warp and weft of his daily travels, tickling readers with tales of the exotic quotidian, complete with accounts of local tribal chieftains, near-death experiences, and the local environment. Whereas the text meanders somewhat disjointedly, reflective of the genre of travel writing popular in the era, one dimension of the province had clearly made an enduring impression on the author: namely, the province's non-Chinese ethnic groups. On the opening page of *Yün-nan*, Davies proclaimed, "It is not only to the statesman and the merchant that Yün-nan will appeal. For the geographer and the explorer there are still many blank spaces on the map. To the geologist and the mining engineer its great mountain ranges must contain much of interest. For the ethnologist, above all, it is a wide field of research in which he might work for a lifetime and still leave much to be done by his successors."[52]

With regards to the ethnic groups of Yunnan, Davies summarized his taxonomic work in the appendix of his manuscript. In the course of roughly forty pages—in every sense the afterthought of an amateur linguist and ethnologist—Davies put forth a revolutionary claim about the demography of Yunnan Province and of southwest China more generally. Whereas imperial gazetteers, local provincial authorities, and popular lore portrayed Yunnan as home to dozens or even hundreds of disparate non-Chinese groups, Davies proposed an ethnic taxonomy which contained only twenty-two (see table 4).

Davies organized Yunnan's non-Chinese population into three broad stocks: Mon-Khmer, Shan-Dai, and Sino-Tibetan. According to his working theory, these original stocks had dispersed across Yunnan and, due to the mountainous terrain, had disintegrated into small enclaves that underwent subsequent processes of estrangement and divergence. Over the course of this history, these three original stocks

TABLE 4 Yunnanese Groups Outlined by Davies*

A-ch'ang (aka Nga-ch'ang)	Miao (aka Mhong)
Hsi-fan	Min-chia (aka Pe-tsö)
Kachin (aka Ching-p'aw)	Mo-so (aka Na-shi)
K'a-mu	Palaung
La	P'u-man
La-hu (aka Lo-hei)	Shan (aka Tai)
La-shi	Tibetan (aka Pê or Pö)
Li-so (aka Li-su)	Wa
Lo-lo (aka Nei-su or Ngo-su)	Wo-ni
Lu-tzŭ (aka A-Nung)	Yao
Ma-ru	Zi (aka A-si or Tsai-wa)

*All "aka's" are those indicated by H. R. Davies in the course of his text.

splintered into twenty-two, whose boundaries could be discerned with the aid of comparative linguistics. Structurally, his taxonomy appeared as shown in table 5.

By his own admission, Davies' taxonomy was based on a very limited number of factors, all of which were linguistic. "I have not as a rule," Davies explained, "attempted to give much detail about the customs and beliefs of these tribes, as it is difficult to get information of this sort of sufficient accuracy to be of value."[53] He went on to acknowledge the limits of his methodology, but nevertheless defended its legitimacy. "That resemblance of language is not necessarily a proof of the relationship of two races is undoubtedly true. Conquest or other causes may have introduced an alien tongue. But if supported by probability and if not contradicted by historical facts or great physical diversity, connection of language may be accepted as affording a *prima facie* case for connection of race."[54]

Davies' self-imposed limitation is reminiscent of observations made by Michel Foucault regarding the efficacy of modern forms of knowledge production. Modern scientific practice derives its power not by expanding the taxonomist's range of observation, but conversely by "limiting and filtering the visible."[55] Depending upon the "systematically negative conditions"[56] one establishes, one is able to model the social world in multifarious ways by canceling out entire fields of potential data.[57] Having chosen this particular form of limited observation, Davies transformed Yunnan and its people into a practically boundless source of readily available data. Every person he met during his travels was a viable research subject.

THE DAVIES MODEL IN REPUBLICAN CHINA

When *Yün-nan* was published in 1909, H. R. Davies was in China celebrating his marriage to Isabel Warwick, daughter of the late Major-General D. K. Evans. The ceremony was conducted in Shanhaiguan, the eastern terminus of the Great Wall

TABLE 5 The Davies Model (groups are in italics)

1.	Sinitic Languages of Yün-nan and Western Ssŭ-ch'uan	1.3.1.1	*Tibetan or Pê or Pö, including probably some Hsi-fan dialects*
1.1	Mon-Khmer Family	1.3.2	Hsi-fan group
1.1.1	Miao-Yao Group	1.3.2.1	*Hsi-fan*
1.1.1.1	*Miao or Mhong*	1.3.2.2	*Mo-so or Na-shi*
1.1.1.2	*Yao*	1.3.2.3	*Lu-tzŭ or A-Nung*
1.1.2	Min-chia Group	1.3.3	Lo-lo group
1.1.2.1	*Min-chia or Pe-tsö*	1.3.3.1	*Lo-lo or Nei-su or Ngo-su*
1.1.2.1.1	Lama-jên[1]	1.3.3.2	*Li-so or Li-su*
1.1.3	Wa-Palaung Group	1.3.3.3	*La-hu or Lo-hei*
1.1.3.1	*Wa*	1.3.3.4	*Wo-ni*
1.1.3.2	*La*	1.3.3.4.1	Ma-hei
1.1.3.3	*P'u-man*	1.3.3.4.2	K'a-to
1.1.3.4	*Palaung*	1.3.3.4.3	Pu-tu
1.1.3.5	*K'a-mu*	1.3.3.4.4	Pi-o
1.2	Shan Family	1.3.3.4.5	A-k'a
1.2.1	[No third order of classification]	1.3.3.4.6	San-su
1.2.1.1	*Shan or Tai and its dialects*	1.3.3.4.7	K'u-ts'ung
1.2.1.1.1	Lü or Shui Pai-yi	1.3.3.4.8	P'u-la
1.2.1.1.2	Sha-jên	1.3.3.4.9	Lo-pi
1.2.1.1.3	Lung-jên	1.3.4	Burmese group
1.2.1.1.4	Tai Che or Tai Hke	1.3.4.1	*A-ch'ang or Nga-ch'ang*
1.2.1.1.5	Tai Nö	1.3.4.2	*Ma-ru*
1.2.1.1.6	Tai Long or Tai Taü	1.3.4.3	*La-shi*
1.2.1.1.7	Tai Lem[2]	1.3.4.4	*Zi or A-si or Tsai-wa*
1.3	Tibeto-Burman Family	1.3.5	Kachin group
1.3.1	Tibetan group	1.3.5.1	*Kachin or Ching-p'aw*

[1]Davies, *Yün-nan*, 372. Davies does not include the Lama-jên in his chart, but does expressly outline them in the text of his study.

[2]Davies, *Yün-nan*, 380–81. As with the Lama-jên, Davies outlines his opinions regarding the Tai Che, Tai Nö, Tai Long, and Tai Lem, but does not include them in his chart.

in Hebei Province.[58] This would be the last time that Davies would spend any extended period of time in the country that had served as his temporary home for much of the preceding decade. In 1911, as the Qing empire was disintegrating, he was dispatched to the European theater, succeeding Brevet-Colonel Fanshawe as head of the Second Battalion of the Oxfordshire and Buckinghamshire Light Infantry. In the early 1920s, Davies contributed infrequent reviews of books relating to southwestern China, but never again returned to the region.[59] With this, Davies' relationship with China came to an end.

Unbeknownst to Davies, his work began to receive attention in China in the early 1920s, discussed among a small coterie of broadly read and Western-trained scholars. Mention of Davies first appeared in the work of the eminent polymath Ding

Wenjiang, whose university lecture titled "On the Tribes of Yunnan" was based on the British officer's taxonomy.[60] In 1925, the esteemed anthropologist and archaeologist Li Ji based considerable portions of his influential study *The Formation of the Chinese People* on Davies' classification, praising it as a "great advance."[61]

More focused attention began to develop shortly thereafter, particularly following the establishment of the first division of Chinese ethnology in 1928. Upon the foundation of the new discipline, the first and most pressing challenge its practitioners faced was the creation of a rational and reductive ethnic taxonomy—a shared standard by which to categorize their objects of study, the minzu of China. These early Chinese ethnologists were dissatisfied with imperial texts such as the *Yunnan Gazetteer,* disparaging them as unsystematic and unscientific. Texts such as the *Record of Guizhou* and the *Yunnan Gazetteer,* they argued, idiosyncratically divided non-Han groups into an excessive number of categories according to a mixed bag of taxonomic criteria: geographical origins, cultural practices, and sartorial habits, among others. The classificatory schema found in these texts were simply not viable candidates for becoming the ontological foundation of the new discipline.

Cen Jiawu (1912–66), a young researcher of southwestern ethnicity (and, later, professor at Zhongshan University and Lingnan University) took aim at *Record of Guizhou,* arguing that, from the perspective of new and more scientific methods, imperial scholarship such as this was simply incorrect.[62] What the discipline required, scholars agreed, was a systematic means of overcoming these myriad particularities and arriving at a reductive portrait of China's minority populations— a "standardized gaze," in modern parlance.[63] In 1932, Rui Yifu set out to tackle the problem of ethnonymic rationalization on a global scale, with plans to develop standardized Chinese transliterations for all of the world's ethnic groups. Rui compiled a list of more than four thousand names and began work on northeast China. The project was slated to finish in April 1934, but Rui was sidetracked by a trip to the Miao areas of western Guangxi Province.[64] He never fulfilled his objective. Ling Chunsheng (1902–81), a Miao expert who held a PhD from the University of Paris, shared Cen's and Rui's concerns, arguing against the classificatory schema found in late imperial materials. There was a deeper architecture to the ethnic world of southwest China, he and his colleagues believed, which earlier research had failed to uncover. At best, earlier modes of ethnic taxonomy produced "enumerative" compendia of ethnonyms that, as Ling phrased it, were mired in particulars and "could not be synthesized."[65] Ling and others believed that most of the groups in Yunnan were in fact of "the same stock, just with different names" *(tongzhong er yiming).*

In many respects, this emerging critique was a valorization of the British colonial episteme and a simultaneous downgrading of Ming and Qing colonial worldviews. Indeed, if Laura Hostetler's comparison and interpretation of Ming and Qing gazetteers is correct—and that the secular increase in the quantity and descriptive breadth of southwestern barbarian categories signified "increased familiarity on the part of Qing officialdom with the region, and with the distinctions (or similarities) among the peoples dwelling there"—then it is all the more striking that Chinese ethnologists in the 1930s and 1940s should have pointed to these very same texts as proof of the dynasty's unscientific appreciation of the region and its ability to perceive the true, underlying order that structured ethnicity. Whereas Hostetler sees continuity between the Qing, Republican, and PRC ethnotaxonomies, Chinese ethnologists vociferously rejected it.[66]

For Republican era scholars, the problem became one of seeing past or through this confusion of names to the order that lay beneath. As they searched for a new form of X-ray vision, scholars soon discovered that the most effective means of seeing the minzu of southwest China might in fact be to *stop looking and start listening*. They began to pay close attention to the neighboring anthropological discipline of linguistics—and, in particular, the language-based ethnic taxonomy articulated by one "Dai Weisi," one of the four Chinese names by which Davies would come to be known.[67]

Davies' linguistic model attracted attention for two primary reasons. First, compared to late imperial texts such as the *Yunnan Gazetteer*, it facilitated the creation of at-a-glance models that were incomparably more economical. To borrow from the language of the information theorist Edward Tufte, Davies' model came closer to a design strategy that was "transparent and self-effacing," "giving the focus over to data rather than data-containers."[68] What imperial sources presented baroquely in dozens of elaborate woodblock prints and page upon page of exegetical prose, Davies could present in a single diagram.

One look at Davies' diagram could provide a sense of both Yunnan's ethnological present and well as its ethnic past, facilitating both synchronic and diachronic readings. Originating at the first order of classification, the first three orders of Davies' diagram represented historical time, showing how the protolanguages and speakers of southwestern China branched outward and gave rise to ever wider and more abundant differences. Moving from the third to the fourth order, the diagram moved from history to the present, to the realm of groups existing in the ethnographic present. The taxonomy diverged further at the fifth order, arriving at an outermost stratum of dialects and ethnic subgroups, also called "branches." The structure can be summarized as follows:

First Order:	The Sinitic languages
Second Order:	Language families
Third Order:	Language groups
Fourth Order:	Languages/Ethnic groups (i.e., speakers of said languages)
Fifth Order:	Dialects/Ethnic branches (i.e., speakers of said dialects)

For Chinese ethnologists concerned with the professionalization of their fledgling discipline, the interplay between the fourth and fifth orders of classification was critical. The fourth order of classification, simply put, was perfectly suited to serve as the discipline's ontology: an economical, agreed upon space of attribution that could determine the vital infrastructural question of "what will be visible or invisible within the system."[69] In defining the ethnic ontology of the region, this collection of minzu would thereby also serve as the boundaries of disciplinary sub-specialization, demarcating discursive spaces in which Chinese ethnologists (and later foreign anthropologists) could house their careers and self-identify as spe-cialists in the history, language, and culture of this or that ethnicity or minzu. At the same time, the fifth order constituted a space in which a boundless number of "branches" and "dialects" could be stored without disrupting the discipline's core ontology. For those whose subspecialization required a more fine-grained analy-sis, as in dialectology or regional specializations, the taxonomy could be expanded to reveal the fifth order of dialects and ethnic branches. In those instances when a coarse granularity was more desirable, however, the fifth order could be collapsed into the fourth. Owing to this scalability, Davies' taxonomy could *absorb* complex-ity without requiring expansion, something that imperial catalogs could not.

Additionally, in contrast to late imperial texts, which relied heavily on exoge-nous markers of identity such as clothing or customary habits considered peculiar to observers, linguistic categorization focused on a feature of individual and com-munal identity that could be considered fundamentally personal, at once the foun-dation of group identity formation and the result thereof. This notion of language-based ethnotaxonomy being more emic, natural, and meaningful fed into the early Chinese ethnologists' view of themselves as the advocates of these marginalized groups, opponents of ethnocentric ethnography, and inheritors of the May Fourth tradition of fieldwork and direct contact with nonelite members of Chinese soci-ety. Although a colonialist, Davies had nevertheless based his taxonomy on exten-sive, direct observation, a fact that distinguished him from the bibliocentrism of imperial elites and aligned him with the fieldwork-centered model of modern so-cial science. Exemplified by eminent figures such as Gu Jiegang, May Fourth era scholars had searched out communities minimally influenced by mainstream Chi-nese culture, a search motivated both by a desire for unmediated knowledge about these communities and also an exoticizing and paternalistic sentiment.[70] As Chang-tai Hung has shown, scholars of the era began to look for research subjects in China's peripheral areas, believing that people in these parts of the country were the "least contaminated by Confucian values" and most in touch with the fundaments of hu-manity. Since "the greater distance from the Confucian-dominated center, the bet-ter for folk literature," Hung summarizes, "folklorists believed that, in peripheral, rural, and remote areas, especially among the national minorities, folk literature thrived, so the intellectual revolt against the traditional Confucian order encour-aged young folklorists to seek inspiration and fresh ideas from the relatively uncharted territory of the minority cultures."[71] In this respect, the non-Han peoples were ideal research candidates: doubly marginalized figures, silenced within canonical texts on account of being both rural and non-Han.[72] Equipped with linguistic methodology, researchers now had the tools with which to access these marginalized communities to an unprecedented degree.

At the same time, however, comparative linguistics enabled taxonomists to avoid the pitfalls of other available modes of inside-out categorization—for example, the collection of oral histories or folktales in which communities voiced their own understandings of their origins, migrations, and relations to neighboring groups. Unlike the folktale movements of decades prior, comparative linguistics did not need to concern itself with the subjectivities or sensibilities of those being categorized. Ironically, the marginalized communities of the borderlands were given a voice in this new form of categorization, but only to the extent that they provided taxonomists with "core vocabulary" such as man, woman, hat, pig, goat, river, sun, moon, and star. Once such data was elicited, the taxonomist could (and indeed needed to) retire to various "centers of calculation" to construct their ethnotaxonomic models.[73]

Over the course of the 1930s, Davies' language-based taxonomy became a focus of widespread attention within Chinese ethnology, received and debated by scholars who were at once intrigued by the model yet hesitant to adopt it wholesale. Even when accounting for this hesitancy, Davies' model would go on to have an immense impact on the ways in which early Chinese ethnologists went about categorizing their objects of study, the minzu of China. Building upon Davies' work, Ling Chunsheng, Ding Wenjiang, and Ma Changshou each published articles during the 1935–36 period in which they responded to the British officer's categorization. While taking issue with his categorization of certain groups, such as the Minjia, the adjustments that these scholars made were slight, restricted to largely cosmetic modifications of Davies' nomenclature. For example, each of these scholars dropped Davies' title and its explicit language-centered posture ("The Sinitic *Languages* of Yün-nan . . . ") replacing it with one more ethnological (e.g., "The Geographic Distribution of Ethnic Groups in Yunnan"). Ling Chunsheng, whose three-part categorization mirrored that of Davies' (a point Ling and his colleagues openly acknowledged), adopted presentational measures to differentiate his work from that of his British counterpart, adopting Davies' categories of "Shan language family" and "Tibeto-Burman language family," but amending them to read "Shan category" and "Tibeto-Burman category." He claimed that "basing ethnic categories on language is sometimes not entirely reliable" but that his work, although based "mainly on language," also drew upon aspects of history, culture, geography, and physical anthropology.[74] Ding Wenjiang and Ma Changshou performed similar adjustments in their respective articles.[75]

Ling's colleague and research partner Tao Yunkui saw past these aesthetic ad-

TABLE 6 Comparison of the Davies Model against Those of Key Chinese Ethnologists

Davies (1909)	Ding Wenjiang (1935)	Ling Chunsheng (1936)	Ma Changshou (1936)
Taxonomically stable groups			
Miao	Miao	Miao	Miao
Yao	Yao	Yao	Yao
Minjia	Minjia	Minjia	Minjia
Puman	Puman (Puren)	Puman	Puman
Dai	Dai (Baiyi)	Dai (Baiyi)	Dai (Boyi)
Tibetan	Tibetan	Tibetan	Tibetan
—	—	Guzong	—
—	—	—	—
Xifan	Xifan	Xifan	Xifan
Naxi	—	Naxi (Moxie)	Naxi (Moxie)
Nu	Nu	Nu	Nu
Luoluo (Yi)	Luoluo (Yi)	Luoluo (Yi)	Luoluo (Yi)
Lisu	Lisu	Lisu	Lisu
—	—	Aka	—
Luohei	Luohei	Luohei	Luohei
Woni (Hani)	Woni (Hani)	Woni (Hani)	Woni (Hani)
Jingpo (Kachin)	Jingpo (Kachin)	Jingpo (Kachin)	Jingpo
—	—	Qiu	—
Taxonomically volatile groups			
Burmese Groups			
Achang	—	Achang	Achang
Laxi	—	Laxi	Laxi
Zi (A-si, Tsai-wa)	—	Axi	Axi
Malu	—	Malu	Mala
—	Burmese (Mian)	—	—
Wa-related groups			
Benglong (Palaung)	—	Benglong	—
Wa	—	Wa (Kawa)	Wa
La	—	La (Kala)	La
K'a-mu	—	—	—
—	—	—	Pula
Zhuang-related groups			
—	—	—	Zhuang
—	—	Zhongjia	Zhongjia
—	—	Nong	Nong
—	—	Sha	Sha
—	—	Lü	—

justments, however, and in 1938 rearticulated the key issue at hand. Referring to the works by Davies, Ding Wenjiang, and Ling, Tao Yunkui wrote that "using language as a standard of categorization is, in actuality, linguistic classification. Ethnologists have simply taken the results of linguistic research and quietly transposed them atop their question." He continued by pointing out that these three scholars, "although quite knowledgeable about language, nevertheless are not experts. Thus, as for the question of language-based categories, we will have to wait until experts have a chance to conduct analyses before we can get a clearer picture."[76] Despite this critique, and despite their clear anxiety about their nearly wholesale adoption of Davies' model, these three taxonomists ultimately preserved Davies' language-based organizational structure and the great majority of his conclusions.

As tables 6 and 7 demonstrate, there was a remarkable degree of consistency across each of these taxonomies, and a vast gulf which separated all of them from earlier imperial modes of categorization. In each taxonomy, the Miao, Yao, Minjia, Puman, Dai, Tibetan, Xifan, Naxi, Nu, Luoluo (Yi), Lisu, Luohei, Woni (Hani), and Jingpo (Kachin) were uniformly recognized, and still others were recognized with nearly complete consistency (such as the Achang and the Wa). For those ethnic categories that were less taxonomically stable, they fell into one of three main categories: Burmese groups, groups related to the Wa, and groups related in some way to the Zhuang. The taxonomic uncertainty of Burmese and Wa groups such as the Laxi, Zi, Kamu, and others seems to have had a great deal to do with the contested and uncertain status of the region where they lived (due to the longstanding conflict between China and colonial Burma over border demarcation). Moreover, for the Burmese and, to a lesser extent, groups like the Kamu, their status as transnational groups in possession of (or at least associated with) a sovereign nation contributed to their taxonomic volatility. Their status as "stated" groups appears to have led to confusion over whether they were best framed in ethnic terms as Chinese minorities or in political terms as foreign nationals. The same debate pertained to the "Annam" people of modern-day Vietnam, who Ding Wenjiang included in his taxonomy. Ling Chunsheng and others criticized Ding's inclusion of the category Annam, arguing that such individuals should be understood not as Chinese minzu, but simply as Vietnamese expatriates. Even with these debates and adjustments, however, one fact was clear: these taxonomies were both completely unlike any ethnic taxonomy that had come before and remarkably similar to that of the Davies Model from which they drew their inspiration.

Beyond this immediate, surface-level continuity, an even clearer consistency obtained between the structures of Davies' model and the taxonomies of early Chinese ethnologists. In a word, the taxonomies of early Chinese ethnologists obeyed exactly the same taxonomic structure as the Davies Model, organizing them into the five orders of classification. Moreover, like Davies, they consistently identified the fourth order of classification as the domain of minzu and languages—that is,

TABLE 7 Taxonomic Structure (detail of Tibeto-Burman category only; ethnic groups are in italics)

H. R. Davies (1909)	Ling Chunsheng (1936)	Ma Changshou (1936)
1. Sinitic	1. Yunnan minzu	1. Minzu in Southwest China
1.1 Tibeto-Burman	1.1 Tibeto-Burman	1.1 Tibeto-Burman
1.1.1 Tibetan group	1.1.1 Tibetan group	1.1.1 Tibetan group
1.1.1.1 *Tibetan*	1.1.1.1 *Tibetan*	1.1.1.1 *Tibetan*
	1.1.1.2 *Guzong*[1]	
1.1.2 Hsi-fan group	1.1.2 Xifan group	1.1.2 Xifan group
1.1.2.1 *Hsi-fan*	1.1.2.1 *Xifan*	1.1.2.1 *Xifan*
1.1.2.2 *Naxi (Mo-so)*	1.1.2.2 *Moxie*	1.1.2.2 *Moxie*
1.1.2.3 *Nu (A-Nung)*	1.1.2.3 *Nuzi*	1.1.2.3 *Nuzi*
1.1.3 Lo-lo group	1.1.3 Luoluo group	1.1.3 Luoluo group
1.1.3.1 *Lo-lo*	1.1.3.1 *Luoluo*	1.1.3.1 *Luoluo*
1.1.3.2 *Lisu*	1.1.3.2 *Lisu*	1.1.3.2 *Lisu*
1.1.3.3 *Lahu*	1.1.3.3 *Luohei*	1.1.3.3 *Luohei*
1.1.3.4 *Wo-ni*	1.1.3.4 *Woni*[2]	1.1.3.4 *Woni*
1.1.3.4.1 Ma-hei		1.1.3.4.1 Mahe
1.1.3.4.2 K'a-to		1.1.3.4.2 Kaduo
1.1.3.4.3 Pu-tu		1.1.3.4.3 Pute
1.1.3.4.4 Pi-o		1.1.3.4.4 Piaoren
1.1.3.4.5 A-k'a		1.1.3.4.5 Aka
1.1.3.4.6 San-su		1.1.3.4.6 Shansu
1.1.3.4.7 K'u-ts'ung		1.1.3.4.7 Kucong
1.1.3.4.8 P'u-la		1.1.3.4.8 Nuobi
1.1.3.4.9 Lo-pi		
	1.1.3.5 *Aka*	
1.1.4 Burmese group	1.1.4 Burmese group	1.1.4 Burmese group
1.1.4.1 *Achang*	1.1.4.1 *Achang*	1.1.4.1 *Achang*
1.1.4.2 *Maru*	1.1.4.2 *Malu*	1.1.4.2 *Mala*
1.1.4.3 *Laxi*	1.1.4.3 *Laxi*	1.1.4.3 *Laxi*
1.1.4.4 *Zi (A-si, Tsai-wa)*	1.1.4.4 *Axi*	1.1.4.4 *Axi*
	1.1.4.5 *Qiuzi*	
1.1.5 Kachin group	1.1.5 Kachin group	1.1.5 Kaiqin group
1.1.5.1 *Kachin (Jingpo)*	1.1.5.1 *Yeren (Kachin)*	1.1.5.1 *Kaiqin*

[1]Whereas Davies regards the Guzong as a subset of the Tibetans, Ling treats them here as a standalone group.

[2]Ling does not indicate the groups he sees as composing the Woni (Hani). When compared to Davies and Ma, however, it appears that he maintains the same structure, with the exception of the Aka. Whereas Davies and Ma consider the Aka to be a branch of the Woni, Ling sees them as a standalone group. Otherwise, the three taxonomic structures are virtually identical.

the domain where category intersected present reality to form an ontology, much in the way that "species" constitutes the key ontological domain for naturalists. At least within the discipline of ethnology, language had become de facto the proxy for ethnic identity in China's hyperdiverse southwestern provinces, an approach that was first fully articulated by H. R. Davies.

"A CULTURAL LABORATORY PAR EXCELLENCE": ETHNIC TAXONOMY IN YUNNAN DURING THE WAR

Equipped with this new, highly economical system of categorization, Chinese ethnologists began to flesh out this taxonomic framework in the late 1930s. In 1937, the outbreak of war with Japan further accelerated this process, prompting unprecedented growth in the new field of study. In the wake of the Japanese invasion, approximately half of the one hundred and eight institutes of higher learning—concentrated in coastal cities such as Beijing, Nanjing, Shanghai, and Guangzhou[77]— were forced to retreat to the country's southwestern interior, bringing with them a wave of Chinese academics and a group of the nation's most renowned social scientists.[78] The interior regions were suddenly imbued with momentous geopolitical significance. Collectively, they became known as "Free China," the "Great Rear" *(da houfang)*, and, in general, as a place of national preservation in the face of war. With interior China as their new home, minzu scholars no longer divided their time between the office and the field. The two were now one and the same.[79]

Practically every Chinese social scientist went west. After a two-year visit to Europe and the United States in 1936 and 1937, Wu Wenzao returned to China in 1938, where he took a post at Yunnan University and established a research cooperative funded in large part by the Rockefeller Foundation.[80] Wu's prize student Lin Yaohua followed three years later in 1941 after completing his doctoral degree at Harvard University. Lin would later go on to Yanjing University in Chengdu and, in 1943, conduct intensive research on the Yi peoples of Liangshan. As he noted in the resultant study *The Lolo of Liangshan,* it was in the summer of 1943 that Lin first saw an Yi person with his own eyes.[81] Wu Zelin (1898–1990), whose postgraduate training was split between the University of Wisconsin, University of Missouri, and Ohio State University, made his way westward during the war, giving him the opportunity to live in Guizhou for three years and in Yunnan for five.[82] Originally trained in sociology, his wartime refuge was an experience that gave Wu "the opportunity to see with my own eyes and to come in contact first hand with more than ten minorities I had never even heard of before."[83] In a matter of a few years, Kunming became one of the most important bases of academic research, making it significantly easier for scholars to study the nation's interior and the non-Han peoples who populated it.

Fei Xiaotong captured it best when, in his celebrated study *Earthbound China,* he praised Yunnan as a "cultural laboratory par excellence"—a place wherein "the whole process of cultural development—from the primitive headhunters to the sophisticated and individualized city-dwellers—can be seen in concrete form."[84] "In a single day," Fei Xiaotong rejoiced, describing the experience of walking from the outskirts of Kunming into the city proper, "we will have traveled from Polynesia to New York."[85]

Fei's description of Yunnan as a "cultural laboratory" is revealing. During this period, the nascent discipline of ethnology, and the enterprise of ethnic categorization which structured it, developed traits normally associated with laboratory science. A laboratory, as Karin Knorr Cetina explains, constitutes an "enhanced" environment in which scientists free themselves from the limitations of the natural world. Operating within laboratories, scientists are no longer bound to studying natural objects or phenomena as they occur in nature—that is, from the ontological, spatial, and temporal limitations of understanding a given object or phenomenon "as it is," "where it is," or "when it happens."[86] Rather than dealing with objects "as they appear in nature," laboratory science "works with object images or with their visual, auditory, or electrical traces, and with their components, their extractions, and their purified versions."[87] Instead of examining the natural world contextually, laboratory science collects and mobilizes samples thereof, bringing them back to the lab to "manipulate them on their own terms."[88] Temporally, laboratories can "dispense with natural cycles of occurrence and make events happen frequently enough for continuous observation."[89]

In wartime-era ethnology, Yunnan province became just such a laboratory. Spatially, the concentration of non-Han peoples in local schools and universities provided researchers with unprecedented access to a wide range of non-Chinese languages and non-Han peoples. In 1942 and 1943, for example, Luo Changpei teamed up with a young student from Tengchong studying at National Dali Normal University. Over the course of two consecutive spring terms, the fourteen-year-old speaker of the Baiyi language of Lianshan provided Luo and his colleague Xing Qinglan the data necessary for their study *A Preliminary Investigation of the Baiyi Language of Lianshan*.[90] Despite the peculiar and circuitous geography of this arrangement, with interviews being conducted in Dali with a teenager from Tengchong representing the Baiyi language of Lianshan, comparative linguistic methodology placed little premium upon the examination of subjects in their representative social contexts. This combination of linguistic methodology and Fei's "cultural laboratory" enabled Chinese scholars to take full advantage of the region's many synthetic congregations of non-Han peoples, and thereby to split the difference between their commitment to field research and their need for an efficient means of extracting large quantities of data. By means of comparative linguistics, Davies' work demonstrated a method by which one could rapidly tame the taxonomic chaos of southwestern China. As a criterion, it would seem language was nothing short of a categorical silver bullet.

Temporally, this new ethnological laboratory enabled researchers to elicit data from their subjects on a far more intensive schedule. In the course of a few hours, for example, linguists could extract enough data from an informant to establish the rudimentary grammar of a given language and sufficient lexical data to locate that language within an ever-expanding classificatory framework.[91] Repeated over the course of months and years, researchers could start to assemble taxonomic models that encompassed, not just specific communities, but the entire province.

As ethnologists and linguists capitalized on this new cultural laboratory, the Davies Model became all the more axiomatic to and embedded within their work. Indeed, if Yunnan had become the laboratory of Chinese ethnology, the Davies Model had become its periodic table of elements. Closely following the outbreak of the war, Davies' work was translated into Chinese for the first time by historian and political philosopher Zhang Junmai (Carson Chang, 1887–1969).[92] Zhang's translation, which focused solely on the appendix of Davies' original work, was graced with a preface by the famous scholar, statesman, and calligrapher Zhou Zhongyue (1876–1955), a native of Yunnan who at one point served as secretary general of the Yunnan Provincial Government and a member of the board of directors of Yunnan University.[93] One year later, the work was translated into Japanese by Suyama Taku, prepared with a foreword by Ōkawa Shūmei.

Among many others, linguist Luo Changpei praised Davies' work for its scientific rigor[94] and Ling Chunsheng lauded it as the first standardized method for categorizing ethnic groups in the area.[95] At this time, ethnic taxonomy became a cottage industry of sorts within wartime Chinese ethnology. In 1938, Ling Chunsheng published a revised version of his earlier taxonomy, as did Ma Changshou in 1941.[96] These were followed closely by those of Ding Su (1941), Wei Huilin (1942), Rui Yifu (1943, 1944, and 1946), Lin Yaohua (1944), and Cen Jiawu (1944).[97] With each subsequent article, the discourse surrounding ethnic taxonomy became increasingly mired in details. However, as the Columbia-trained sociologist Huang Wenshan (1901–88) noted, by the close of the 1940s, most Chinese social scientists who encountered Davies' taxonomy tended to uphold the British officer's approach.[98] In 1941, National Central University Geology Professor Ding Su captured the essence of this trend with unmistakable clarity: "Among those who research ethnic groups in the southwest, there is no one who does not take H. R. Davies' taxonomy as his starting point."[99]

THE DAVIES MODEL IN THE PEOPLE'S REPUBLIC

Following 1949, the Davies Model was carried into PRC ethnology by the very same scholars who had integrated it into the discipline in the 1930s and 1940s. In fact, the Davies Model achieved an even greater level of saturation in the Communist period, owing to the unprecedented centralization of the discipline during the educational reforms of the early 1950s. Unlike Chinese ethnology in the Republican period, which was a multicentered consortium of scholars, institutions, publishing houses, and funding agencies, the early Communist state brought ethnology within a unified academic network. In mid-1951, state authorities commenced development of a countrywide network of nationalities institutes designed to help train minority cadres. At the core of this new network was the Central Institute for Nationalities (CIN), founded in Beijing in the summer of 1951. In addition to cadre development, the CIN was also designed to bring together the nation's leading ethnologists. The CIN incorporated the Ethnology Department of Yanjing University, the Sociology Department of Tsinghua University, and other centers of ethnological research, bringing together under one roof scholars such as Lin Yaohua, Fei Xiaotong, Wu Zelin, Yang Chengzhi, and others who had been directly involved in wartime scholarship.[100] Regional divisions of the CIN were established in the south, southwest, and northwest, creating a nationwide network entrusted with training minority cadres and engaging in ethnic scholarship. With this centralized academic structure, and the ascendancy of Republican-era scholars such as Lin Yaohua, Luo Changpei, Fu Maoji, and others, the Davies Model had become axiomatic.

We find this continuity most clearly in the work of ethnologists and linguists Luo Changpei and Fu Maoji who, during the early Communist period, managed to extend the linguistic model outside of academic circles and into the taxonomic worldview of local officials in Yunnan—again, the same officials who would later oversee the Classification. Two years prior to the project, in 1952, the pair convened in Yunnan to continue and complete a survey of local languages which Luo Changpei had begun during the war. This team of seven scholars, all of who would later take part in the Ethnic Classification Project in 1954, was overseen by Zhang Chong, who directed Fu and his squad to concentrate on minority script development and cadre training.[101] The team operated out of the Yunnan Institute for Nationalities, where they had easy access to students of many different ethnic and linguistic backgrounds.[102]

This extended interaction between Fu and Zhang over the period from 1952 through 1954 had a demonstrable effect on the way in which the Yunnan administration understood the ethnic demography of its province. The influence was subtle, but is readily apparent when comparing locally produced ethnic taxonomies between the years of 1951, prior to the visit by Fu, and 1953, after Fu had been in the province for approximately one year. In the ethnic distribution maps published by the Yunnan Province Nationalities Affairs Commission in 1951 for internal circulation (those first outlined in chapter 1), provincial accounts listed groups according to population size, without any attention paid to taxonomic structure (that is, to parent and child categories).[103] In the map published in 1953, however, roughly the same set of ethnonyms was organized, not according to population, but according to the same orders of classification articulated first by Davies and later by Republican-era Chinese ethnologists.

This new attention to categorical structure, particularly language-based structure, shows up elsewhere in 1953 documents as well. In late 1953, the Yunnan Nationalities Affairs Commission produced a "Chart of Yunnan Minorities who are the same but have different names."[104] In this chart, roughly the same 120-plus names are listed as on the various distribution maps, but this time organized into a clear hierarchy, topped by thirteen "large *zuxi*," under which were classified twenty-six "branches" *(zhixi)*, and then finally, the inventory of ethnonyms. The Provincial Nationalities Affairs Commission, in other words, was clearly adopting the language-based paradigm, as communicated to them by Fu Maoji, and using it to reorganize the ethnonyms they had been investigating since the formation of the PRC. When Fu and his colleagues looked at the people of Yunnan, they saw roughly twenty-six groups. Now, after only one year of interaction with Fu, Zhang and the Yunnan Nationalities Affairs Commission were starting to as well.

Returning to April 1954 and the opening weeks of the Classification project, we find the enduring presence of the Davies Model evident in the lectures by Luo Jiguang and Ma Xueliang. Reproduced here in one final tabular juxtaposition, the genealogy becomes clear (see table 8).

When Lin Yaohua, Wang Xiaoyi, and their colleagues departed for Kunming on May 7, 1954, this was the conventional model and working hypothesis that they brought with them and that would end up guiding their taxonomic work. Quite unlike Communist authorities in Yunnan and Beijing who, prior to the inaugural census, regarded Yunnan as home to upward of one hundred minzu, the ethnotaxonomy set forth by Chinese ethnologists and linguists included less than thirty.

CONCLUSION

Whereas scholars have become accustomed to treating the Ethnic Classification project as a Communist affair, the pedigree of the project's underlying taxonomic logic requires us to adopt a broader historical outlook that spans the 1949 divide. As this chapter has shown, and subsequent chapters will bear out, the official demography of Yunnan as it currently exists is but a partially modified version of the leading taxonomic theories of the Republican period, all of which regarded Yunnan as a province inhabited by roughly two dozen minzu. This paradigm was already quite robust by the end of the Republican period, developed by Chinese social scientists in a time before the country's academic community had been incorporated into the official state structure. It was their taxonomic worldview, not that of the Communist party, which argued on behalf of a radically synthetic mode of ethnic categorization. In order to understand how the ethnotaxonomy of the PRC was formed, therefore, we are behooved to abandon what might be termed the "Communist imposition hypothesis," and to pay much closer attention to PRC state's social scientific advisors.

This leads us to a second, related conclusion. Whereas conventional accounts of China's Ethnic Classification are quick to point out its political and methodological affinities with that of the Soviet Union, here we find much stronger ties to British colonial practice—particularly in its reliance on a mode of ethnic categorization

TABLE 8 Continuation of the Davies Model into the Classification

Davies (1909)	Ding Wenjiang (1935)	Ling Chunsheng (1936)	Ma Changshou (1936)	Luo Changpei & Fu Maoji (March 1954)[1]	Luo Jiguang & Ma Changshou (Classification Team)[2]
		Taxonomically stable groups			
Miao	Miao	Miao	Miao	Miao	Miao
Yao	Yao	Yao	Yao	Yao	Yao
Minjia	Minjia	Minjia	Minjia	Minjia	Minjia
Puman	Puman (Puren)	Puman	Puman	Puman	Puman
Dai	Dai (Baiyi)	Dai (Baiyi)	Dai (Boyi)	Dai	Dai
Tibetan	Tibetan	Tibetan	Tibetan	Tibetan	Tibetan
—	—	Guzong	—	—	—
—	—	—	—	Qiang	—
Xifan	Xifan	Xifan	Xifan	Xifan	Xifan
Naxi	—	Naxi (Moxie)	Naxi (Moxie)	Naxi	Naxi
Nu	Nu	Nu	Nu	Nu	Nu
Luoluo (Yi)	Luoluo (Yi)	Luoluo (Yi)	Luoluo (Yi)	Yi	Yi
Lisu	Lisu	Lisu	Lisu	Lisu	Lisu
—	—	Aka	—	—	—
Luohei	Luohei	Luohei	Luohei	Lahu	Lahu
Woni (Hani)	Woni (Hani)	Woni (Hani)	Woni (Hani)	Hani	Hani
Jingpo (Kachin)	Jingpo (Kachin)	Jingpo (Kachin)	Jingpo	Jingpo	Jingpo
—	—	Qiu	—	Qiu	Qiu
—	—	—	—	Jiarong	—

Taxonomically volatile groups

Burmese groups				
Achang	Achang	Achang	Achang	Achang
Laxi	Laxi	Laxi	—	—
Zi (A-si, Tsai-wa)	Axi	Axi	Zaiwa	Zaiwa
Malu	Malu	Mala	—	—
—	—	—	Burmese	Burmese
Burmese (Mian)	—	—	Chashan	Chashan
—	—	—	Langsu	Langsu
Wa-related groups				
Benglong (Palaung)	Benglong	—	Benglong	Benglong
Wa	Wa (Kawa)	Wa	Wa	Kawa
La	La (Kala)	La	—	—
K'a-mu	—	—	—	—
—	—	Pula	—	—
Zhuang-related groups				
—	—	Zhuang	Zhuang	—
Zhongjia	Zhongjia	Zhongjia	Buyi	—
Nong	Nong	Nong	Nong	Nong
Sha	Sha	Sha	Sha	Sha
Lü	—	—	—	—

[1] Luo and Fu, "Guonei shaoshuminzu yuyan wenzi de qingkuang," 21–26.

[2] Wang Xiaoyi, Interview, Beijing, January 21, 2003, citing his journal from the 1954 lecture on "The Utility of Language in the Course of Investigations (*Yuyan zai diaocha li de zuoyong*)."

derived from historical linguistics and, most importantly, its direct, genealogical connection to the scholarship of H. R. Davies.

As for Davies himself, the retired officer passed away in 1950 at the age of eighty-four.[105] By all accounts, he lived out his days entirely unaware of the immense impact that his work had on the disposition of Chinese ethnology. Had he witnessed the development of the discipline over the course of the 1940s, he might have been surprised to see a clear thread—an unbroken methodological and discursive genealogy—winding from his research in the late 1890s straight through to the Communist period. Following his death, and the tremendous political changes that swept the mainland, all memories of Davies were quickly buried or transformed. On May 11, 1951, for example, Liu Geping delivered a speech to the Government Administration Council entitled "Summary Report on the Central Nationalities Visitation Team's Visits to the Nationalities of the Southwest." One foreigner in particular was mentioned by name—Henry Rodolph Davies. Unlike the late Republican period, however, where his 1909 work was celebrated as the starting point for all ethnotaxonomic work conducted in the southwest, Davies was now summarily dismissed as an "imperialist spy" whose life history and work illuminated little more than the European violation of Chinese sovereignty.[106] In late 1954, the irony became even more pronounced. In September of that year, Yang Yucai, a high-ranking political member of the Yunnan Province Ethnic Classification, published an article in *Geographic Knowledge* in which he dismissed Davies' research as the "antiscientific" nonsense of a "capitalist careerist."[107] Little did Yang realize, it seems, that it was Davies' "antiscientific" theories that Republican-era Chinese ethnologists had used to make a sharp break with earlier, imperial modes of ethnotaxonomy and that, in the early People's Republic, guided the ethnic categorization of China's most diverse province.

Plausible Communities

In reality, many minorities do not fulfill the four characteristics that Stalin pointed out. So why should we call them "nationalities" (minzu)?
—LIN YAOHUA, LECTURE TO THE ETHNIC CLASSIFICATION RESEARCH TEAM, KUNMING, MAY 22, 1954

Wang Xiaoyi arrived in Kunming on Sunday, May 16, 1954, following a ten-day journey from the capital. With three days to spare before the team's orientation session, he was able to launder his clothes, trim his hair, attend a performance of local Dian opera, and familiarize himself a bit with the city. Here in the provincial capital, he and his fellow Beijingers would meet the second half of the Ethnic Classification research team and finalize plans for their upcoming fieldwork.

The local moiety was essential to the success of the project, a fact repeatedly impressed upon Wang and his colleagues prior to their departure. In addition to their extensive, firsthand knowledge of the province and its minority populations, the Kunming team also had access to a Communist state infrastructure necessary for even the most basic of research activities: the organization of interviews, transportation, lodging, and translation, among others. Wang recorded in his journal the advice of senior ethnologist Chen Yongling, his former advisor. "You will have to unite with the local and minority cadres," Chen stressed to the team prior to their departure. "Meals are best eaten together with the local cadres. You must team up with them. You mustn't make them feel that you Beijingers are always together, that you're a clique, that you and they have no connections. . . . When conducting research, you must not make the local cadres think that you are always together, secretly discussing this matter or that."[1]

Chen's advice reflected a broader change in Chinese academia since 1949, and particularly since the Communists' reorganization of universities starting in the early 1950s. Multiple disciplines were abolished, deemed bourgeois and contrary to the aims of the revolution. Social psychology was disbanded, as were law, political science, and sociology.[2] Ethnology survived because of its perceived utility to

Beijing, particularly in its efforts to more fully incorporate the minority regions of China's western provinces. Its survival, however, came at the cost of unprecedented centralization and official control, in terms of funding, publication channels, and theoretical perspectives. As Chen and others knew, scholars in new China would have to tread carefully, making sure not to project an air of superiority vis-à-vis their party supervisors. The members of the Classification team, as we will see, took this advice to heart. At the same time, they managed to maintain a great deal of autonomy, even in the face of direct orders from party representatives.

The two halves of the Ethnic Classification research team met on the twentieth of May, during a late afternoon session in the provincial capital. Like Wang and his Beijing colleagues, this select group of cadres, scholars, and students had been recruited by the state to help determine the ethnic composition of the province.[3] Within the Yunnan contingent, there were three prominent scholars: Fang Guoyu (1903–83), Yang Kun (1901–?), and Jiang Yingliang (1909–88), established researchers who, like Lin Yaohua and Fu Maoji, had come of age in the Republican period.[4] Fang was a native of Lijiang, a Naxi, and a graduate of Peking University. He authored numerous acclaimed works of history, ethnology, linguistics, and geography, including *The Brief of Catalogs of Historic Material in Yunnan, Manual of Mosu Pictographic Characters, History of the Yi Nationality,* and *Textual Criticisms and Explanations of Historic Geography in Southwestern China,* among others.[5] In 1950, he was appointed to serve as a member of the Yunnan Province Nationalities Affairs Commission and subsequently as a member of the Central Nationalities Affairs Commission. Yang Kun, who received his doctorate from the University of Paris, was instrumental in the formation of the Chinese Ethnological Association in 1936.[6] Less involved in ethnographic investigation than many of his peers, Yang was best known for his extensive introduction of French sociological theory to China, particularly the work of Marcel Mauss, Lucien Lévy-Bruhl, Claude Lévi-Strauss, and Émile Durkheim.[7] Jiang Yingliang, a graduate of Zhongshan University, had established himself as an expert of the southwestern border region and its minority populations and was one of the earliest and most vociferous Chinese ethnologists to criticize the Guomindang's minority policies in the southwest.[8] He was also among those who, with the Communists' abolition of sociology in the early 1950s, was prompted to move to the field of history—which, alongside ethnology and linguistics, was among the only disciplines that remained where one could study China's minority peoples. All three were professors at Yunnan University and were accompanied by a select handful of their students.

The balance of the local team was composed of government officials and civil servants, delegates of the Yunnan Province Nationalities Affairs Commission, the CCP Yunnan Province United Front Department, and Kunhua Hospital. The central figures were Li Qunjie, deputy head of the Yunnan Province NAC, and Zhang Chong, deputy governor of the province. A native of Lijiang, Li Qunjie (1912–2008) received degrees from both Donglu University and Zhongshan University, follow-ing which he served as a writer and editor for publications based in Shanghai and Hong Kong. Li joined the Chinese Communist Party (CCP) in May 1937, return-ing to Kunming the following month to organize a party branch and serve as its secretary. Following the arrival of the People's Liberation Army in early 1950 and the formation of the provincial government, Li was named vice-director of the Office of Culture and Education and was later appointed to the provincial Nationalities Affairs Commission.[9] Zhang Chong (1900–80) was a native of Luxi, and during the Republican period served as an officer in the National Revolutionary Army. Fol-lowing the end of the Eight-Year War of Resistance against Japan, Zhang relocated to Yan'an in 1946 and joined the CCP in the year following. Instrumental in polit-ical organization which preceded the Communist arrival, Zhang was quickly ap-pointed vice-chairman of the Yunnan Provincial Government and a member of the provisional Southwest Military Government.[10]

Li Qunjie and Zhang Chong were appointed to supervise the Classification and to serve as intermediaries between the research team and the state. Most impor-tantly, their job was to keep the team's academic camp in line and to prevent the enterprise from unraveling into protracted intellectual debate and esoteric delib-eration. This concern is understandable when we consider that it was Li and Zhang, and not the Classification researchers per se, for whom the deadline of the forth-coming National People's Congress loomed largest. In Beijing, the central Nation-alities Affairs Commission was awaiting their final report so that the appropriate number of (appropriately named) minority representatives could attend the inau-gural congress.

With this in mind, Li took command of the orientation session early, outlining clear directives regarding who the Classification team would research during the upcoming fieldwork, and how the status of these candidates would be assessed. Re-visiting the 1953–54 census results, Li issued three straightforward prioritizations: out of the roughly two hundred registered names, those with the largest popula-tions would be handled first; inland communities would be investigated before those living along the border; and certain politically sensitive groups would have their cases handled before all others. This last instruction referred directly to five groups: the Dai, Nong, Sha, Tujia, and Yi.[11]

Among the larger applicant groups, moreover, not every one would be subject to categorization. There were fourteen groups in the province, Li and his colleagues agreed, whose status as full-fledged minzu was beyond question and did not re-quire further authentication. These included the Dai, Hani, Hui, Jingpo, Kawa (later renamed Wa), Lahu, Lisu, Miao, Minjia (later renamed Bai), Mongolians, Naxi, Ti-betans, Yao, and Yi.[12] For these fourteen groups, no time would be spent on de-bating whether or not they constituted independent minzu. Rather, the job of the team was simply to determine their *composition*—that is, to identify which other applicant groups in the region might feasibly be amalgamated into one of these four-teen.[13] For those whose claims to minzu status were in doubt, the situation was something quite different. Zhang Chong chimed in at this point, emphasizing to the team that it was to "respect the differences between groups, but to emphasize their commonalities."[14] The experience of categorization efforts in the Soviet Union, he noted, demonstrated that combining small groups into larger ones was benefi-cial to the socioeconomic development of both minorities and the country at large. The Classification was to take amalgamation as its mantra.

For the academic contingent of the Classification, there was hardly anything dis-agreeable in Li's and Zhang's points. As seen in the preceding chapters, the four-teen groups they outlined were universally recognized by Chinese ethnologists. With the one exception of the Kawa, who were not included in Ding Wenjiang's taxon-omy of 1935, each of these fourteen groups appeared in the ethnotaxonomic schema of Henry Rodolph Davies, Ling Chunsheng, Ma Changshou, Luo Chang-pei, and Fu Maoji, and the lectures by Luo Jiguang and Ma Changshou.[15] Zhang Chong's preference for amalgamation was also completely in line with Chinese eth-nologists' longstanding commitment to categorical rationalization. Taxonomic synthesis had been a driving force in Chinese ethnology since its inception, as wit-nessed in their fervent embrace of comparative linguistics and the Davies Model.

With regards to the criteria of ethnic categorization, however, the situation was quite different. Unlike his first set of pronouncements, here Li Qunjie articulated orders that, if followed, would have had dire implications for the team and its abil-ity to complete the project in the time allotted. Li deferred to the official political line of the early PRC, instructing Classification researchers that all claims to inde-pendent minzu status would be assessed in strict accordance with the Soviet defi-nition of natsia as articulated by Joseph Stalin. Founded upon the evolutionary the-ories of Lewis Henry Morgan and Friedrich Engels, and formalized by Stalin in his 1913 tract, *Marxism and the National and Colonial Question,* this model contained two key elements.[16] First, for a group to be considered a nationality, it had to fulfill each of four criteria: the group had to share a common language, a common terri-tory, a common mode of economic production, and a common psychology (taken to mean culture). The second component of Stalin's model was even more stringent and involved ranking groups along a five-stage evolutionary scale encompassing primitive communism, slavery, feudalism, capitalism, and socialism. Precapitalist communities (i.e., those at the stages of primitive communism, slavery, and feu-dalism) could not be considered full-fledged nationalities and were to be relegated instead to one of the three other stages of human organization: clans, tribes, or tribal federations.[17]

Unlike the first set of instructions by Li and Zhang, this second stipulation posed a serious problem for Lin Yaohua, Fu Maoji, and the entire research contingent. The requirements outlined by the party directors of the Classification team were simply too steep for the non-Han groups of Yunnan. Minority groups in the region, by and large, did not engage in capitalist modes of economic production. If applied faithfully, this model of minzu would have permitted few if any groups to qualify as minority nationalities, thereby paralyzing the project and turning one-time scholars of southwest minzu into scholars of southwest clans *(shizu)*, tribes *(buluo)*, and tribal federations *(buzu)*. Indeed, such steep requirements had not even been applied dogmatically in the Soviet Union, where the census recorded, not each individual *natsia*, but rather *narodnost* (also translated as "nationality," but meant to signify an ethnographic rather than political entity).[18]

Nevertheless, Li's and Zhang's instructions were explicit and, as Chen Yongling and others had advised the Beijing scholars, open defiance of such instructions was not an option. And so, with these instructions, Li Qunjie and Zhang Chong had made certain that the academic members of the Classification team knew their place. "This project is not research for the sake of research," Li emphasized to the team, a comment suggestive both of his own, unspoken sentiment toward metropolitan intellectuals, as well as the larger, complex relationship between the Communists and the predominantly non-Communist community of university scholars. "The Classification will be scientific but not academic."[19]

How did the Beijing contingent react to these directives? As scholars and social scientists, these researchers held membership in an elite circle whose professional identities were grounded in notions of methodological rigor and a fidelity to the social world. Here was Li, however, outlining a research program encumbered with a host of political and pragmatic constraints. First, an entire range of small groups was being excluded precisely because there was no political cost to doing so. Even more unsettling was Li's intervention into the theoretical foundations of the project, a reformulation of the very meaning of minzu.

Before we examine the reaction of researchers to these particular issues, it is useful to pose the question in broader terms. What exactly did it mean for ethnologists and linguists to collaborate with a political regime for which minzu was, at least according to orthodox Marxist theory, an epiphenomenal and insubstantial fiction which was destined to melt away? No matter how strong their commitment to recognizing minzu, and to making it one of the central dimensions of citizenship in New China, there was no escaping the fact that the Communists approached minzu in a radically different way from their social scientific advisors in the academy. Faced with this Communist worldview, it is important to understand why Chinese ethnologists embraced this new relationship, and were willing to collaborate so energetically with a regime that denied the enduring existence of the very thing that their discipline was committed to understanding.

To address this set of questions, we must return once more to the early years of Chinese ethnology and recognize that this was not the first time these researchers had been obliged to negotiate their theoretical frameworks to accommodate the ideological orientation of the presiding Chinese regime. Since its inception, Chinese ethnology had been navigating the minefield of early twentieth-century ethnopolitics and the debate that raged between competing political parties over the essence of the Chinese nation (read minzu). As we will see, these scholars were eager to take part in policy formation, long being engaged in what this chapter will term "ethnological activism." They wanted to serve the state, to have their particular form of expertise enrolled, enlisted, and acted upon. They wanted to develop southwest China, incorporate its diverse peoples into the nation-state, and to help promote in the minds of these peoples more coherent group identities. As we will see, their overtures to the Guomindang went unrequited. Only under the Communists were their talents and their political activism put to full use.

THE REPUBLIC OF NINE PEOPLES: ETHNOLOGICAL ACTIVISM IN THE REPUBLICAN PERIOD

The first division of ethnology in China was founded in 1928 as part of the Academia Sinica.[20] Cai Yuanpei, the renowned president of Peking University and director of the newly established Academia Sinica, baptized the new branch of learning *minzuxue*—literally "the study of minzu." By adopting *minzu* as the Chinese equivalent of "ethnos," Cai was attempting to establish a monopoly over the term, at least within the academy, wresting it from the related but separate discipline of race science with which it shared certain conceptual affinities.[21] In China, scholars interested in physical anthropology and biometrics had been using minzu (among other terms) as a translation for the English word *race*. By equating minzu and ethnos, Cai was attempting to claim the term on behalf of sociocultural anthropology, to denote minzu as a holistic concept that, while encompassing the body, was not bound by it. As part of the terminological bargain, Cai ceded the term *zhongzu* to his counterparts in physical anthropology, arguing that it was the proper (and only) Chinese word for their object of study.[22] Beyond Cai, other social scientists were also committed to separating the two concepts. As James Leibold relates, Qi Sihe, Lü Simian, and others associated with Gu Jiegang's Yugong Study Society argued on behalf of a minzu-zhongzu division wherein the first was to be understood in terms of linguistic and customary difference, and the latter in terms of physical form and skin color. At the same time, Cai's use of the term *xue*, used in Chinese to translate the suffix "-ology," was intended to distinguish the new discipline from the longstanding tradition of Chinese writings on border peoples. By casting the new discipline as a "xue," Cai was declaring its membership in the broader family of comparative social sciences such as anthropology and sociology, and at the same time distinguishing it from earlier, imperial studies of non-Chinese people. To the latter he ceded an alternate term: *minzuzhi* or "ethnography." Later in 1935, this argument was further elaborated upon by Yang Kun, who systematically outlined the differences between ethnology *(minzuxue)*, ethnography *(minzuzhi)*, anthropology *(renleixue)*, and studies of race (translated, following Cai's lead, as *zhongzu*). At the very most, Yang was willing to describe imperial gazetteers in terms of "descriptive ethnology," to be contrasted against the "comparative ethnology" of his discipline.[23]

Although Cai's terminological intervention was targeted at the academy, its repercussions quickly spread outside of social scientific circles. By claiming *minzu* as the centerpiece of the new discipline, a term that was also being used by political theorists and authorities as a translation for "nation" and "nationality," Cai placed the new discipline in the center of a discursive battle that would soon rage between the Guomindang and the Communists. As soon as it was born, therefore, Chinese ethnology found itself the third member in a debate over the essence of Chinese nationhood.

The ebb and flow of this precarious position is captured vividly in a little-known episode in the mid-Republican period, shortly after the outbreak of war with Japan. In 1939, China's southwestern neighbor Siam officially changed its name to Thailand, a name that formalized an ethnonationalist bond between the nation's majority Thai ethnic group and the territorial state. The Siam situation proved unsettling for Guomindang authorities in Chongqing, who grew concerned that Thai ethnonationalism might spill over the border and spark parallel activities among the Dai people of Yunnan Province—a group who shared ethnonymic, cultural, linguistic, and historical connections with their neighbors.

In response to these developments, Ge Sangren of the Mongolian and Tibetan Affairs Commission set forth a bold policy recommendation in November 1939. To prevent parallel outbreaks of ethnonationalism among the diverse peoples of Yunnan Province, Ge recommended that "it should be forbidden to use names such as Miao, Yi, Man, Long, Luo, and Zhuang."[24] Language, he argued, should be purged of ethnic names and replaced with toponyms reflective of one's place of birth.[25] By late 1940, Yunnan Provincial Chairman Long Yun had become so concerned with the perceived threat that, on September 18, he adopted Ge's proposal, outlawed the use of ethnic names in the province, and ordered that the "borderland compatriots" be referred to as "persons from such-and-such a place." The policy made only one exemption: ethnonyms would continue to be permitted within the academy, but only in the context of scholarly publications.[26]

This episode sheds light on a deep contradiction latent within the Guomindang approach to the "nationality question." On the one hand, through its vehement refusal to countenance any taxonomy that categorized the Chinese populace into multiple minzu, the GMD implicitly recognized the symbolic power of identification, and thus the power, existence, and reality of ethnic identity itself. If the eradication of the ethnic name *Dai* could help prevent the emergence of a Thai ethnonationalistic movement, then there had to be a certain psychosocial power that flowed through these designations. At the same time, by assuming that a simple edict delivered from the metropole could bring local systems of identification to a halt, the Guomindang's policy vastly underestimated the power of names and local modes of categorization. Likewise, this policy sent a clear message to Chinese ethnologists: provided that the discipline confine its discussion of minzu to the rarefied space of academic journals, and maintain no illusions about its political clout, then it could function as normal. To the extent that they advocated a multi-minzu worldview in the public sphere, however, there would be negative repercussions.

Ethnologists adopted three main strategies in their attempt to navigate the precarious terrain of Republican-era ethnopolitics: appealing for the need to develop the social and economic infrastructure of the country's southwestern provinces, particularly in the war against Japan; calling attention to the ethnotaxonomic work of foreign scholars who were producing theories that consistently drove conceptual wedges between the peoples of the southwest and Chinese civilization more broadly; and drawing upon the more traditional, northern-centric concept of the "Republic of Five Peoples," and expanding it to include four major ethnic constituencies in the southwest.

In their first strategy, ethnologists attempted to advance their ethnotaxonomic worldview by calling attention to the region where most of their subjects resided, China's southwest. The southwestern hinterland, they argued, was among the poorest and most administratively disconnected in all of China, factors that rendered it susceptible to the divide-and-conquer tactics of foreign powers. Imperial forces were highly aware of this, moreover, as evidenced by the longstanding attempts of the French and British (and now Japanese) to expand their spheres of influence into Yunnan. To protect the integrity of the nation, scholars argued, it behooved Guomindang authorities to undertake research into the social and economic conditions of southwest China in order to lay the groundwork for regional development. Ethnology, they contended, was well equipped to undertake such research and provide national authorities with the information they required.

One of the more outspoken Chinese ethnologists was Jiang Yingliang, who would later go on to join the Classification project in 1954. In his 1938 study *The Question of Southwest Ethnic Groups in Wartime,* Jiang attempted to delineate a clear relationship between the minzu of the southwest and what the author called the "road ahead in the war of resistance."[27] Jiang called for a social scientifically informed centralization of policies toward these communities, urging the Chinese state to make use of specialists, rather than bureaucrats unacquainted with the complexities of local cultures and languages. By appointing ethnological experts to official positions, Jiang argued, the Chinese state could inaugurate an age of enlightened administration and counteract the trend toward economic disparity and sociopolitical inequality rampant in the region.

Jiang drew heavily on wartime imagery in support of his argument. He pointed to Han persecution of the Kawa peoples in Yunnan, the exclusion of the southwest minorities from the "Republic of Five Peoples," and the overall lack of ethnic and national consciousness among the Yi along the Yunnan-Burma border.[28] This overall state of affairs afforded the Japanese with opportunities to use "treacherous methods" to seduce "our forsaken southwest ethnic groups."[29] In the wake of war, Jiang inquired rhetorically, "can we still allow ourselves not to come up with vigorous policies, not to use our nation's strength to revise relations between the minzu of the southwest and the Han?"[30] The ethnic groups of southwest China, in Jiang's reckoning, "truly possess all the fundamental components of the ideal soldier. It's just too bad that this talent has been misused in inter-tribal struggle."[31] "If we give [ethnic groups in the southwest] a suitable form of education," he proposed, "instill in them a concept of the nation-state, resolve [the difficulties] in their lives, add a form of military training, and guide them to the front line of resistance against the enemy, would they not become the backbone of national defense?"[32]

Jiang painted an exotic portrait of the ethnic groups in southwest China, highlighting their frank, honest, hardy, and affable dispositions. These factors, he argued, were resultant from the lack of civilizing influences in the region, whose absence has allowed the southwestern peoples to avoid "contracting the cheating and hypocrisy of civilized man," and instead having "preserved the instinctive nature of primitive guilelessness."[33] Furthermore, demanding physical labor and their "extremely low standard of living" made them physically fit and easy to satisfy (gastronomically and sartorially speaking).

Jiang's arguments, tinged with paternalism, exoticization, and a brand of "internal orientalism" observed elsewhere by Louisa Schein, were echoed by his wartime colleagues.[34] Wu Zelin made similar assertions regarding the Miao of Guizhou, on the one hand noting the group's lack of a unifying consciousness, and on the other positing the extreme usefulness such solidarity would have in the war against Japan.[35] In a 1942 essay, Wu argued that:

> Some scholars go so far as to deny the necessity of border policy research, believing that, once central politics is put on track and once victory is achieved in the War of Resistance, the so-called problem of border nationalities will be readily solved. Those studying anthropology do not believe the problem to be so simple, and thus their opinion is a bit different. They believe that only by getting border policy and rural policy on track will central policy follow suit. In a certain respect, one could even say that border policy and rural policy are at the heart of the question of China's central politics at the present stage. Only when the prestige of the central government reaches the hearts and minds of the border people and the rural people will . . . it be possible to implement the central government's political orders.[36]

Ethnologists adopted a second strategy as well, this one calling attention to the threat of foreign-made ethnic taxonomies. Scholars pointed to the activities of Japanese agitators in the north who had laid the groundwork for the invasion of Manchuria by spreading the doctrine of Manchurian and Mongolian distinctiveness. Similar threats were starting to surface along the southwestern border as well. In his 1938 essay, "The War of Resistance and the Cultural Movement of the Border Ethnic Groups," Cen Jiawu drew attention to the work of Japanese scholars operating in southwest China, and likened it to the divide-and-conquer tactics Japan had deployed in years prior. Dispatched by the Japanese state, foreign scholars were developing classificatory schema designed to "destroy minzu solidarity," promote separatist sentiment among the Li and Miao, and thereby legitimate Japan's ultimate objective of invasion.[37]

In addressing this issue, ethnologists were attempting to strike a chord with local authorities who were also distressed by the activities of foreign taxonomists. On November 28, 1940, Yunnan Provincial Chairman Long Yun sent an urgent message to the Civil Affairs Bureau warning of a reported influx of clandestine, Japanese-supported Thai operatives filtering into the province to infiltrate the Baiyi areas of Fohai County, conduct "secret activities," plot "to provoke the Yi [barbarian] people," and lay the groundwork for a joint Japanese-Thai invasion.[38] Local authorities feared that these collaborators would "cheer on Dai chauvinism" and promote the formation of a "large republic with Thai peoples living in neighboring territories."[39] Long's concerns were not unfounded, moreover, as evidenced by Selçuk Esenbel's work on Japanese imperialist tactics elsewhere. Japan's invasion of the Dutch Indies, for example, was preceded by intensive efforts to build a coalition with local Muslim leaders disgruntled by Dutch rule. Indeed, as Esenbel has demonstrated, Japan had been actively cultivating a relationship with the Islamic world since the early 1900s. Through the foundation of such organizations as the Greater Japan Islamic League (Dai Nippon Kaikyō Kyōkai), the promotion of Islamic studies in Japan, the introduction of Japanese culture to Muslim communities abroad, and cultural projects such as the construction of the Tokyo Mosque, Japan was able to make inroads into the Islamic world and portray itself as an ally against Western (Christian) colonialism. Moreover, ever since Russia's October Revolution of 1917, Japan was able to strengthen and militarize this relationship with Islam, successfully portraying the Soviet Union as the common enemy of both Japan and the Muslim world. In this "citadel policy," Islamic communities of northeast and central Asia were conceived of (and often conceived of themselves) as buffers against antireligious Communist aggression. The year 1931 was a particularly momentous one in the relationship between Japan and Islam, witnessing both the Japanese invasion of Manchuria and the Turkic Uighur rebellion in present-day Xinjiang. These two events were part of a larger Japanese plot that, in addition to the planned Japanese annexation of Manchuria, sought to integrate the Islamic communities of present-day Xinjiang, Ningxia, and Gansu provinces under a pro-Japanese authority. Although the Turkish Islamic State of East Turkestan was eventually crushed, Japan's successful creation of Manchukuo in the northeast stood witness to the ways in which Japanese ethnoreligious policies, when combined with its military prowess, could result in the disintegration of the Chinese mainland. Likewise, the Japanese South Seas Association was busily dispatching representatives to the countries of Southeast Asia to engage in cultural activities and local language pedagogy.[40]

In addition to the taxonomies being produced by Japanese scholars, Jiang Yingliang pointed out classificatory theories that could likewise serve the purpose of division and conquest. The works of Thomas Blakiston, Verneau Keane, Jean Louis Armand de Quatrefages de Beau, Joseph Edkins, and Albert Etienne Terrien de Lacouperie, for example, all identified the Miao not as part of the "Yellow Race," but rather as members of the "caucasique" branch of the Aryan race.[41] Still other foreign scholars, Jiang pointed out, were advancing a theory of Miao identity that categorized them as part of the Thai, denying outright their affiliation with China.[42] By pointing out the dangers posed by foreign-produced taxonomies, ethnologists in Yunnan were attempting to develop a demand among state authorities for the very product they were eminently qualified to provide: an ethnic taxonomy of southwest China that was at once rigorously scientific and thoroughly nationalist. Ethnologists attempted to convince state authorities that the proper response to the divisive, foreign-born taxonomies was not to deny the existence of diversity, but rather to create their own taxonomy which, in recognizing the existence of diverse groups in China, would thereby incorporate them into the statebuilding process and prevent them from being enticed by the Japanese, French, and British.[43] This commitment on behalf of Chinese ethnologists paralleled that of the Communists and would become one of the most important foundations for state-social scientific collaboration following 1949.

A third strategy was to articulate a more moderate discourse on minzu that could act as an interface between the multi-minzu worldview of Chinese ethnology and the mono-minzu ideology of the GMD. We see this most clearly in the writings of Cen Jiawu, who attempted to find a place for the minzu of the southwest (xinan minzu) within the official Republican concept of the "Chinese nation" (Zhonghua minzu). Interestingly, Cen invoked the earlier Republican concept of the "Republic of Five Peoples" (wuzu gonghe) and argued for its expansion. In addition to being composed of the five main minzu outlined in the theory of the Five Peoples' Republic, Cen argued, the "Chinese nation" also encompassed "the Miao, Yao, Li, and Luoluo."[44] The southwest minzu, Cen contended, have "mixed blood on many occasions" with the Han and were a "principal component" of the larger Chinese people.[45] Although he never announced it as such, Cen was articulating something like a "Republic of Nine Peoples." Noteworthy is the fact that Cen's concept excluded a wide range of groups that he and all Chinese ethnologists agreed constituted minzu within and of themselves (such as the Bai, Dai, Hani, Jingpo, Lisu, Naxi, Puman, and Xifan, to name only a few). This was an exclusion that Cen was willing to make, however. By encompassing at least some of the minorities of southwest China, the objective was to secure for the scholars of the southwest a more formal place at the table of national politics. In this way, the push for the official recognition of ethnic diversity was motivated by their own desire for recognition—for official recognition of their discipline, their worldview, and their expertise.[46]

Despite these manifold attempts, ethnologists were never able to integrate their worldview fully into the official demographic ideology of the Guomindang state. The war with Japan, coupled with its oppositional relationship with the CCP, prompted the Guomindang to redouble its commitment to a homogenous China. The GMD enjoined ethnologists to abandon all talk of "ethnic groups" and to support the official position: namely, that the borderland communities being referred to so divisively and irresponsibly as "ethnic minorities" in truth constituted inseparable parts of a singular *"Zhonghua minzu."* To speak of "southwestern ethnic groups," "Yunnan ethnic groups," and the like was as bad, one critic put it, "as doing Japan's propaganda for them."[47]

The revolution of 1949 brought with it a markedly different relationship between Chinese authorities and ethnologists. In this new political environment, one in which the new regime was a forceful advocate of the idea of a multi-minzu China, the strategies analyzed here became largely unnecessary. The state no longer needed to be convinced that China was composed of a wide array of minzu—this, indeed, had been part of the Communist's platform for two decades. To the contrary, the state initiated relations with ethnologists, as witnessed in the formation of state-sponsored Nationalities Visitation Teams *(minzu fangwentuan)* dispatched to border regions throughout the country only nine months after the formation of the PRC—and led in part by Chinese social scientists. Ironically, the factor which had placed the discipline of ethnology at the heart of political tensions in the Republican period—its title *minzuxue*—was the very same one that left it unscathed during the Communist reorganization of higher education. Even as the CCP dismantled the discipline of cultural anthropology (indistinguishable from ethnology in many parts of the world), the need for an effective minzu policy allowed the discipline of "minzuxue" to remain intact.[48] State authorities regarded it as a "potentially socialist discipline," as Gregory Guldin has phrased it, whose principle of a multiethnic China coincided nicely with their own concept of a multinational China.[49] The ethnological conceptualization of minzu-as-*ethnos* and the Communist conceptualization of minzu-as-*natsia* together would form the twin pillars of the new "unified, multinational country" *(tongyi de duo minzu guojia).*

BURYING STALIN: LIN YAOHUA
AND THE CONCEPT OF ETHNIC POTENTIAL

Returning to May 20, 1954, and the meeting in Kunming prior to the fieldwork portion of the Classification project, we find that the post-1949 transition was not with-

out its challenges for Chinese ethnologists, even when accounting for the important conceptual affinities outlined earlier. The Beijing contingent, having adopted
the linguistic model as it taxonomic starting point, had arrived in Kunming confi-
dent in its ability to carry out the project in the time allotted. Following the advice
of their linguistic advisors, and maintaining a taxonomic worldview that had been
longstanding within their discipline, these scholars believed themselves to have a
firm grasp on the rough number and names of Yunnan's non-Han peoples. Fieldwork would take time, no doubt, but the project was altogether feasible, thanks to
the trove of Republican era ethnological experience upon which they could base
their recommendations to the state. By the close of the first full meeting of the Classification team, however, the research contingent found itself saddled with a host
of new burdens and requirements, the most onerous of which was Stalin's model,
as dogmatically interpreted by the political leadership of the project. If their project
were to be saved—if they were to avoid coupling the already complex work of categorization with the further subdivision of groups into different *types* of human
communities—the Classification researchers would need to find a way to circumvent the Stalinist formulation. This would need to be done tactfully, however, as the
memory and pronouncements of Stalin were still treated as politically sacred.

Retiring for the evening, Lin Yaohua and his colleagues had a chance to reflect
on the proceedings, and to develop a response. Two days later, on the morning of
May 22, Lin gathered his research colleagues together for an in-depth discussion
of the Stalin problem. In a lecture entitled "Opinions Regarding the Problem of Ethnic Classification," Lin directly addressed the issue of the Stalinist model and the
distinctions that Stalin had made between various stages of human organization.[50]
Careful not to overstep his bounds within the team, and even more careful to con-
vey unwavering deference to Stalin, Lin was nevertheless able to hammer out an
effective response to Li Qunjie and Zhang Chong.

Lin began the early morning lecture with a recapitulation of the Stalinist model
in its simplest and starkest form, one in which full-fledged minzu status could only
be conferred upon groups that had achieved a level of linguistic, territorial, economic, and cultural integration unique to the capitalist mode of production. Conceived of in tabular format, table 9 shows Stalin's understanding of the relationship
between different forms of human organization.

As demonstrated here, Stalin's parameters denied the status of full-fledged nationality to any precapitalist group. Rather, one finds a direct correspondence between particular forms of human society and specific stages of historical development: clans (*shizu*) and tribes (*buluo*) emerge during the period of primordial or
primitive communism; tribal federations (*buzu*) during the stages of slavery and
feudalism; and nationalities during the stages of capitalism and socialism.

Lin set out to articulate and justify the concept of a *precapitalist minzu,* a concept that, as noted earlier, was important within the Soviet Nationalities Identifi-

TABLE 9 Lin's Recapitulation of the Stalinist Model

Stages of Social and Economic Development	
Russian/Pinyin (English)	
klan/shizu (clan)	Primordial Communism
plemia/buluo (tribe)	
narodnost'/buzu (tribal federation)	Slave Society
	Feudalism
natsiia/minzu (nationality, ethnic group, natsia)	Capitalism
	Socialism

SOURCE: Lin Yaohua, "*Guanyu minzu shibie wenti de yijian* [Opinions Regarding the Problem of Ethnic Classification]," YNPA, Quanzong 2152, Index 1, File 46: 39–56 (May 15, May 22, 1954).

cation project and yet notably absent from the directions outlined by Li Qunjie and Zhang Chong. Lin posed the question to the group directly:

> In reality, many minorities do not fulfill the four characteristics which Stalin pointed out. So why should we call them "nationalities" *(minzu)?* Primarily, this is because, in China, it is customary to refer to all developing national blocs *(minzu jituan)* as "nationalities." And since this is the custom, there's really no need to make distinctions. Politically speaking, it's especially unnecessary to make such distinctions. The historical relations between different nationalities are complex, and if we go around distinguishing between which groups are nationalities and which are not, it could very easily have negative political repercussions.[51]

While vague references to the potential downsides of a Soviet-style categorization laid the groundwork for his response, Lin knew that he would need to develop his point more concretely, lest it be taken simply as an abandonment of the Stalinist model. Demonstrating his political acumen, Lin began by citing a carefully chosen passage from another of Stalin's writings, *Marxism and the Problem of Linguistics.* Here, Stalin had conceded that "of course, the necessary components of the nation—language, territory, common culture, etc.—do not simply descend from the heavens. Rather, they are gradually created during the pre-capitalist period. These components, however, are at this time in a stage of infancy, and at most form nothing more than a potential that, in the future, under advantageous conditions, will help form into a nationality."[52] Here was the loophole Lin needed. Stalin himself had conceded that even clans and tribes contained the germ of full-blown nationality, a quotient of latent potential. Stalin outlined this idea more fully in his evolutionary theory of linguistic development. "As for the continuous development of language," Lin quoted Stalin once more, "tribal languages *(buluo yuyan)* develop out of clan languages *(shizu yuyan),* the languages of tribal federations *(buzu yuyan)*

TABLE 10 The Introduction of *minzu jituan*

minzu jituan	shizu (clan) *klan*	Primitive Communism
ethnos (Greek)	buluo (tribe) *plemia*	Primitive Communism
narod (Russian)	buzu (tribal federation) *narodnost'*	Slave Society
	buzu (tribal federation) *narodnost'*	Feudalism
	minzu (nationality, ethnic group) *natsiia*	Capitalism
	minzu (nationality, ethnic group) *natsiia*	Socialism

SOURCE: Lin Yaohua, "*Guanyu minzu shibie wenti de yijian*": 44–45.

develop from tribal languages, and national languages develop out those of tribal federations."[53]

By seizing upon this idea of potentiality—the notion that there could be precapitalist, prenational groups who were already in possession of the potential to form nationalities in the future—Lin was able to move away from the factors that *distinguished* different forms and stages of human organization and emphasize instead the one factor which *united* them: the *potential* for full-fledged nationality or ethnicity. It was this potential that, for Lin, served as the common denominator among each of Stalin's stages, and raised at least the possibility of defining groups in terms of what they *could become rather than what they were at present*. To give shape to this idea of potential, Lin Yaohua artfully introduced a new concept into the debate. "We need to ask," Lin continued, "what are they like, these precapitalist groups that are bound to become minzu?"[54] "Let's call them '*minzu jituan*,'" he proposed, a term which we might translate as "ethnonational blocs."[55] To clarify his neologism, Lin prepared a table (see table 10).

In this second step, Lin appended the first table with an additional column. Lacking any internal subdivisions, this column encompassed all of Stalin's different types of human communities and each of the five historical stages. That is to say, *minzu jituan* was an ahistorical umbrella term that contained not only full-fledged nationalities of the capitalist stage, but also Stalin's clans, tribes, and tribal federations.[56] It stood above them all, turning the step-wise ladder of human organizational development found in the strictest interpretation of Stalin's model into a spectrum: an unbroken continuum of more-or-less potential, more-or-less realized group identity whose most fully actuated state was the minzu, its most primitive the *shizu*. Thus, whereas a "precapitalist minzu" was logically invalid according to Li Qunjie's presentation of the Stalinist model, a precapitalist *minzu jituan* was not. To call something a precapitalist *minzu jituan* was the equivalent of saying that a particular cluster of prenational groups demonstrated the potential to develop into a nationality in the future. To call something a *minzu jituan* was to identify what might termed

TABLE 11 The Connotative Expansion of minzu

minzu ethnos narod	Primordial Communism Slave Society Feudalism Capitalism Socialism

its "ethnic potential": the potential for a cluster of smaller groups to come into a state of unity despite differences in the present.

Having introduced and clarified the concept of *minzu jituan*, Lin was prepared for the final step in his reinterpretation: the simple yet daring act of removing the qualifier *jituan*. In this final act of transitivity, the term *minzu* was made to stand in for that of *minzu jituan*, stretched out to encircle a greater conceptual area than ever before (see table 11).

With this, minzu inherited all of the properties previously attributed to *minzu jituan* and was delinked from that of *natsia*. This is evident in his final table where minzu no longer corresponds to *natsia* or to any particular stage of historical development. Rather, in Lin's reconceptualization, minzu correlated to the Russian term *narod* ("people") and the Latin term *ethnos*, and encompassed each of Stalin's five stages (see table 11).

In his closing remarks, Lin assured the local cadres present that he had not lost sight of the highly circumscribed role he and his researchers were meant to play. "Don't forget that academic research is to serve political practice. The work of minority research before us is certainly not purely for the sake of academic research. It must unite with politics, particularly with the problem of national security."[57]

Li Qunjie and Zhang Chong ultimately accepted Lin's interpretation of minzu and the notion of ethnic potential upon which it was predicated. Indeed, from the perspective of state authorities, the notion of ethnic potential could hardly have struck a more perfect balance between empirical rigor and political practice—precisely the sort of scientific yet nonacademic approach that the political leaders of the Classification had demanded. Although it required the expertise of social scientists, whose technologies of analyzing the historical and anthropological contours of the Chinese ethnosphere far outstripped those of the Communist state, Lin's minzu was fundamentally a futurological entity, something that could only be realized through the application of a separate set of technologies monopolized by the state: the mass media, systems of representative government, language planning, mass education, and so on. A minzu was no longer simply something that "was" in the ethnographic present, a definition that would have privileged the social scientific worldview and turned ethnologists into something like a council of elders whose insight could only be heeded and never questioned. Instead, it transformed the question of minzu from one of existing communities to *plausible* communities—potential communities whose activation depended upon the state's ability to hasten the so-called advantageous conditions cited in Stalin's writings on language. It ran parallel to Zhang Chong's emphasis on ethnic synthesis, moreover, being committed as it were to the identification of ethnic clusters for whom synthesis was feasible. As Lin went on to argue: "As for those ethnonational blocs *(minzu jituan)* who constitute one minzu, but who due to pressure of reactionary rule have come to live under many different names (of which there are many examples in Yunnan) . . . merging them together is to be encouraged."[58] This version of minzu was not only amenable to state intervention but in fact depended upon the state for its realization and animation.

POTENTIAL MINZU AND THEIR PROBLEMS

Researchers and their political patrons reached a middle ground. The Stalinist model would be upheld *in theory*, but would be applied more loosely (an act that, somewhat ironically, was also the case in the Soviet Union). In addition, political authorities agreed that linguistic categorization was the most effective and economical way to identify plausible communities, and officially selected language as the "primary criterion of classification."[59] Team members agreed that they would organize their research itinerary and methodology in accordance with the ethnic contours of leading language-based taxonomic theories, theories that, as we saw, trace back to the late Qing work of Henry Rodolph Davies and the Republican era adjustments of early Chinese ethnologists. These preexisting models would form the "preliminary theoretical evidence regarding which groups are standalone nationalities and which are branches." Fieldwork would then be conducted only to the extent necessary to "amend these preliminary theories" and submit viable taxonomic recommendations.[60]

With respect to these "preliminary theories," Lin Yaohua outlined a series of groups who constituted what I have termed here as "plausible communities." These included the fourteen presupposed minzu outlined earlier, along with three additional groups: the Zhuang, Dulong, and Achang. More specifically, we see in the team's preliminary theories the first evidence of where researchers planned to put all of the many other smaller ethnonymic groups that appeared in the census register, the distribution maps of the central and provincial NACs, and other ethnotaxonomic texts. When viewed alongside the more coarse-grained taxonomic template outlined in chapter 2, these preliminary theories demonstrate on a more fine-grained level a key factor in the project: namely, that even prior to the fieldwork stage of the project, the team already had a thoroughly detailed plan about which groups it planned to recognize as full-fledged minzu, and under which specific minzu categories it was prepared to subordinate the rest. Again, these theories derived from the work of Chinese ethnologists dating back to the late Republican period. With that in mind, we can look more closely at Lin's "plausible communities," as well as the particular problems that each would pose the team.

The Yi, as we have seen, were identified at the outset as a group that should be officially recognized as a standalone minzu. The main issue confronting the team pertained to the profusion of communities in the province who might feasibly be categorized as subsets of the Yi, rather than independent minzu in their own right. For candidates such as the Pula, Huayao, Lalu, Luomian, Luowu, Menghua and others, the team debated between two alternatives: "Can they be standalone minzu?" *(shifou keyi lie wei danyi minzu)* and "Are they branches of the Yi?" *(shifou Yizu de zhixi)*.[61] Lin proposed that upward of thirty groups could be folded into the Yi, including the Alu, Aluopu, Axiepu, Axipu, Azhe, Gepu, Gu, Laji, Lawu, Limi, Luobapu, Luoliang, Luoluopu, Luomi, Milainiu, Mili, Miqi, Misanba, Mosu, Muji, Naisu, Nasu, Nazha, Niusu, Nuole, Nuonuo, Nuosu, Pula, Qi, Sannipu, Tanglang, Zijun, and Zongpu.

Lin's objective, as seen here, was to funnel as many of the small pieces of the provincial ethnoscape into the Yi. Once again the logic was decidedly linguistic, although now coupled with other factors that shaped the potential of the proposed minzu configurations: "If we decide according to language and territory," Lin explained, "they are all Yi." At the same time, Lin anticipated potential resistance to this plan. "There are many who do not agree," he continued, "because of (1) large differences in dialect, (2) scattered territory *(diqu fensan)*, and (3) differences in economic life. Consequently, if we force them to merge into Yizu, it will result in real difficulties, and the people of each will not agree. However, if we do not merge them, and turn each autonym into a separate minzu, this is not in accordance with the requirements of national development. Thus, we should not do this either. For these reasons, we think that the primary problem would be inciting an Yi Problem *(yizu wenti)*."[62] As demonstrated here, Lin was committed to taxonomic synthesis, but wary of pushing too far, lest it inflame those groups in the region who would not suffer categorical subordination.

We also see this tension in Lin's treatment of the Hani, Lahu, Lisu, and Naxi, four of the presupposed minzu. Linguistically speaking, Lin explained, all four were branches of the Yi. However, due to territorial drift and separate development, "there is no need to place them within the Yi on account of language." What was more, Lin noted, the Hani and Lahu had already formed autonomous territories, with the Naxi and Lisu about to do so as well.[63] In addition to avoiding potential resistance, there was a further benefit to dissociating these groups from the Yi in that, once established as standalone minzu in their own right, they could function as additional centers of synthesis. The Naxi, Lin proposed, could absorb the Baxi, Malimasha, and Moxie. The Hani could absorb even more, including the Aka, Asu, Asuo, Axilama,

Baihong, Biyue, Budu, Bujiao, Bukong, Duoni, Haini, Kabie, Kaduo, Nuobi, Qidi, Suoni, Yani, and the Yeni.

Five other presupposed minzu could function as centers of synthesis as well, Lin suggested. The Bai could absorb the Lemo and Nama. The Dai could absorb the Dailü, Daina, Daiya, Bunong, Buyi, Budai, and Buzhuang. The Jingpo could absorb the Lang'e, Laqi, and Zaiwa. The Zang could absorb the Baiba, Xifan, and Yuanba. The Kawa could absorb the Benglong, Bulang, La, and Puman. These proposed mergers, it should be noted, were not without their ambiguities. With regards to the proposed expansion of the Dai, Lin explained that the "Buyi, Bunong, Budai, Buzhuang, Dedai, and so forth certainly have no difference of language with the Dai. The difference is only one of dialect. Their territorial distribution, however, is spread out and their economic lives are different. Their religions are different as well. Merging them into one group is inappropriate, but so too is turning them all into standalone minzu."[64]

As for the four remaining presupposed minzu—the Miao, Yao, Meng, and Hui—they would not function as centers of synthesis. They should be recognized, Lin confirmed, but no other groups in the province could feasibly be merged into them.

Borderline Groups

Alongside the presupposed groups was a smaller set of borderline groups whose status was in question. These included the Zhuang, Nong, Sha, Tujia, Achang, and Zaiwa. The cases of the Zhuang, Nong, and Sha, which need to be addressed together, bring to light how Yunnan's Ethnic Classification project interacted with and was complicated by the ethnopolitics of neighboring provinces. As Li Qunjie explained in his address to the team, research had shown that the Sha and Nong were branches of the Zhuang. However, he explained, researchers would still need to conduct fieldwork, largely for political reasons.[65] The reason for this requirement was a political one. Prior to the 1954 project, the first province to legislate on the identities of the Nong and Sha was Guangxi, in whose provincial censuses these two ethnonyms had also appeared. In the course of provincial nationality work, Guangxi authorities had grouped the Nong and Sha, along with a third, the Buyi, under the single rubric "Zhuang." In the Guangxi classification, the Nong were recategorized as the southern branch of Zhuang (nan Zhuang) while the Sha were recategorized as the northern branch (bei Zhuang).

At the same time, these ethnonymic groups had also appeared in the census registers of Yunnan's neighbor to the east, the diverse province of Guizhou. In contrast to Guangxi, however, the Buyi in Guizhou were not categorized as a subset of Zhuang, but rather as a full-fledged minority.[66] Thereafter, Guizhou authorities re-

TABLE 12 Categorization of the Buyi, Nong, and Sha in Adjacent Provinces

Appeared in the respective provincial censuses as	In Guizhou, categorized as	In Guangxi, categorized as
Buyi	Buyi	Zhuang
Sha	Buyi	Zhuang
Nong	Zhuang	Zhuang

categorized the ethnonymic group Sha as a branch of the Buyi. To complicate matters further, Guizhou authorities categorized the Nong neither as independent nor as Buyi, but as a subset of the Zhuang. In tabular format, each province's categorization were as shown in table 12.

Come 1954, these discrepancies left the Yunnan Province Ethnic Classification Team in a precarious position: its taxonomic decisions regarding the Nong and Sha would have to be based not only upon their own survey, but also on political considerations emerging from the preexisting decisions of classification work conducted in other parts of the country. Moreover, no matter which route they chose—to recognize the Nong and Sha, to categorize them as Zhuang, or to categorize them as Buyi—they could not avoid contradicting the classificatory conclusions of their provincial neighbors.[67] In early June, prior to the fieldwork phase of the Classification in Yunnan, Yunnanese officials received a letter from the Guizhou Nationalities Affairs Commission encouraging them to follow Guizhou's lead, urging Yunnan to categorize the Sha of Yunnan as Buyi. Guizhou authorities even went on to muse about how much more rational it would be were Guangxi Province to follow suit as well, and recategorize the Zhuang as Buyi so that there might be a standardized understanding of ethnicity throughout the southwest. However, because the Classification took place in strict accordance with provincial jurisdictions, and because the enterprise of ethnic categorization was inseparably connected to other political issues, this daydream never came true.[68]

The Tujia posed a very different type of problem, being one of the only cases in which the primary taxonomic questions were matters of taxonomic *analysis* rather than synthesis, that is, decomposing the category into its constituent parts rather than determining how it might absorb other candidates. The reason for this difference is to be found in the name *Tujia* itself. The Chinese character *tu* means "domain," "land" or "territory," and when applied to people, denotes that a person is a "local" or a "native."[69] Because many groups had referred to themselves as "locals" in the provincial census (*tujia, tujiaren,* and a number of other similar terms), the result was a proliferation of peoples scattered throughout the region with similar names, but who shared no cultural or linguistic characteristics in common. Prior to the Classification, the Yunnan Province NAC had attempted to sort this problem as best it could, proposing the following resolution of the Tujia:

1. The "Tujia" of Dali and Lijiang were to be recategorized as Yi, based on their language and their autonym (La-lu or La-lo-pa).
2. The "Tulao" of Wenshan were to be recategorized as Dai.
3. The "Liaozu" were also recategorized as Dai.
4. The "Tuliao" of Mengzi were to be recategorized either as Yi or a branch of the Yi.
5. The "Tuzu" of Wenshan were to be recategorized as Zhuang.[70]

The problem was far from resolved however, making it one of the most pressing for the 1954 team.

The Achang was one of the few groups Lin recommended for official recognition who were not among the a priori minzu. At this point, however, the recommendation was only preliminary, as it remained to be seen more clearly what their relationship was to the Yi. The Achang language, Lin explained, belonged to the Yi family. In addition, the territory they occupied was adjacent to the Yi, making even stronger the case for amalgamation. Nevertheless, Lin concluded provisionally that it was not appropriate to put them together with the Yi, for reasons he did not elaborate upon. "We will temporarily treat them as a standalone minzu."[71] The Zaiwa posed a separate problem. Lin was uncertain whether linguistic differences with the Jingpo counted as differences of language or simply of dialect. Lin was unsure whether the two were "a mixture of two different minzu" or "two branches of one tribe."[72] He categorized them temporarily as one, but knew that this was unsatisfactory. The Jingpo language, as Lin pointed out, was part of the Yi language family, while that of Zaiwa "fundamentally could be Burmese."[73]

Points of Confusion

Finally, Lin listed four categories of groups who could not be granted the status of minzu, or whose status needed to be considered further. These included the Miandian, Man, Gaomian, and Dan. Some groups were so confusing to Lin that they defied all efforts at hypothesis. Addressing roughly sixteen ethnonyms, Lin described them quite simply as "names we completely do not understand." These included names such as Abu, Ake, Buxia, Chaman, Jingdong, Kongge, Luogelüe, Mengbu, Nanni, Punan, Xiandao, and Yuzhang, among others.[74]

CONCLUSION

Come the first week of June, the team prepared to head out of Kunming and into the province to conduct fieldwork. As they did, they brought with them an elaborate, working model of the province, an ethnotaxonomy based on the twin pillars of language-based categorization and the concept of ethnic potential.

Through a detailed examination of the Stalin question, and the manner in which it was dealt with during the Classification, this chapter advances two conclusions. First, whereas existing scholarship on Chinese ethnicity provides an accurate portrayal of the content of Stalin's criteria, it has yet to clarify what role this paradigm played in the Ethnic Classification project. Stalin's model was not, as many scholars assume, an active ingredient in the decision-making process of Classification researchers—not, at least, if one is referring to the highly inflexible, four-part definition of *natsia* that is so frequently cited in the literature. Instead, Lin Yaohua reconceptualized minzu in such a way that it opened up the possibility for groups not yet in possession of Stalin's four required attributes to be categorized as full-fledged minzu in advance, giving rise to the possibility of "precapitalist nationalities."

The second conclusion pertains to the implications of Lin's notion of minzu—in particular, the fact that Classification researchers were planning from the outset to base their taxonomic recommendations not strictly on the inherent qualities or characteristics of the communities under examination, but also an assessment of the state's capacity to interpose itself and bring about the actualization of the proposed minzu categories.

Once we recognize that the Ethnic Classification was based upon a dynamic and futurological definition of minzu—that is, that it was primarily concerned with assessing the plausibility of certain categorical groupings rather than their fidelity to ethnic realities circa 1954—it behooves us to reconsider the ways in which we have traditionally gone about understanding and critiquing the project. Anthropological critiques of China's official ethnotaxonomy (i.e., the fifty-six-minzu model) are often based on a notion of correlative accuracy, a fidelity between micro- and macrocosm that analysts have assumed to be the core requirement of any taxonomy. The taxonomic approach of the Classification did not operate according to this same assumption, however, adopting instead one that split the difference between traditional modes of correlative categorization and, even more importantly, a much more futurological and experimental mode. Simply put, critiques that focus on the fidelity of 1954 Classification categories entirely the miss the point, insofar as fidelity was never the overarching goal of the project.

As we will see in the next chapter, the Classification team produced these new categories with the full understanding that the state would intervene at a later stage to close the gap between their forecasted categories and on-the-ground realities. To borrow a concept from Prasenjit Duara, Ethnic Classification researchers were fully cognizant that their work would require subsequent "strategies of closure"[75] undertaken through the state's expenditure of vast administrative, propagandist, and socioeconomic energies in the postproject era.[76] Without these, this sprawling, internally heterogeneous and phenomenally complex project could never have achieved the status of a cohesive, self-evident "common sense" that it now enjoys in the PRC.[77] To understand the logic and practice of the Classification, then, we must study it for what it was and for what its practitioners and patrons openly understood it to be: an unabashedly *ethnogenetic* taxonomic enterprise.

With these considerations in mind, we now rejoin the team during the first phase of fieldwork, where we will be able to witness firsthand the ways in which its classificatory praxis was guided by this concept of ethnic potential.

The Consent of the Categorized

The Achang of Yingjiang and the Achang of Lianghe have the same name, but they are different. Our languages are different. . . . Our customs and clothing are different. Doesn't that mean that we are not the same as the Achang of Lianghe?

—XIANG LAOZUO, ETHNIC CLASSIFICATION INTERVIEWEE, SELF-IDENTIFIED ACHANG OF YINGJIANG COUNTY, 1954

By means of political persuasion work, this division can be eliminated. Thus, we believe that the Achang of Yingjiang and the Achang of Lianghe are two branches of the same minzu, and that treating them as one minzu unit would be more appropriate.

—YUNNAN PROVINCE ETHNIC CLASSIFICATION RESEARCH TEAM, ACHANG REPORT

By the time Wang Xiaoyi arrived in the field, the sky had been dark for some time. It was the fourth of June, the rainy season, and the southern town of Mojiang was caught in the heavy embrace of a torrential downpour. Wang and his teammate Chang Hongen, a young linguist from the Academy of Social Sciences in Beijing, took shelter for the evening with plans to begin work the following morning. Their two-person squad was one of five that, in order to make the most efficient use of limited time and personnel, divided the province into more manageable regional units during the first phase of fieldwork. The other four squads were based in Wenshan-Mengzi, Ailaoshan, Xishuangbanna, and Kunming, and each was assigned a specific set of minzu candidates to classify. The Wenshan-Mengzi squad was charged with investigating the Tulao, Pula, and Nong candidates, among others. The Ailaoshan squad, based in Midu and Menghua counties, was assigned to research candidates hypothesized to form branches of the Yi. The Xishuangbanna squad, based in Jinghong (Cheli) and its environs, was given the Bailang to research. The Kunming squad, staffed by the team's more senior members, was committed primarily to intensive linguistic analysis. As for Wang and Chang, the two of them constituted the entirety of the Mojiang squad, charged with examining nominee groups in and

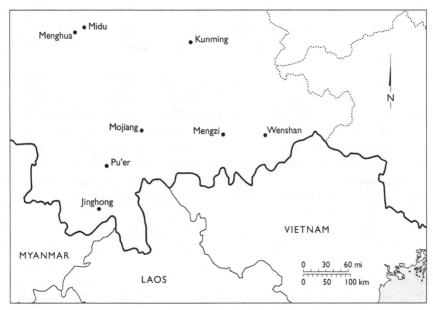

MAP 2. Bases of Operation during Phase One of the Classification

around Mojiang and Pu'er counties who the Classification team hypothesized to be subsets of the Hani.[1]

Having examined the central importance of Chinese ethnologists and linguists in the preceding two chapters, it is vital not to overemphasize their autonomy within the larger Classification project or to dismiss the role of political authorities. In this chapter we will examine two core dimensions of the project in which Chinese Communist influence was paramount: the administrative logistics of the expedition and the methods the team would use in order to secure the consent of those being categorized—a question with which Chinese ethnologists had never concerned themselves before. In both of these arenas, the social scientific contingent of the Classification team was dependent upon state and party infrastructure. Indeed, Wang Xiaoyi and Chang Hongen relied heavily upon logistical support from local political offices every step of the way. Prior to their arrival, lodging in the county seat had been arranged by local officials, as had their transportation from Kunming.[2] This was true of the other squads as well. Upon reaching their various destinations, researchers resided in a variety of government buildings, including local government seats, military installations, and primary schools.[3] Once in the county seat, their reliance on the local government grew only more pronounced. Before traveling deeper into the province, local offices had to secure arrangements in advance, which explains why the path of the Classification team mirrored the administrative hierarchy of the country: first, Wang and Chang traveled from Beijing to Kunming, then from Kunming to the Mojiang county seat, and finally from the county seat to various villages and subcounty destinations, where the pair rarely ever spent the night.

The squad's research itinerary relied upon Yunnan's political infrastructure as well. In order to reach representatives of the various minzu candidates, whom Wang and Chang had no time to find on their own, they depended upon cadres at the Yunnan Province Nationalities Affairs Commission and other subprovincial offices to arrange their fieldwork interviews.[4] Local cadres put Classification researchers in touch with members of their staffs who, for example, self-identified as Amu, Budu, Bukong, Kaduo, Lalai, and Qidi.[5] When appropriate interview candidates were not readily accessible, local offices went to even greater lengths, transporting relevant non-Han individuals from their home villages to the county seat where Classification researchers could interview them, typically for a few hours. In such instances, authorities provided interviewees with small stipends to offset lost wages.[6]

For Wang and Chang, this collaboration between the political and research halves of the Classification could scarcely have operated more smoothly. Their political patrons did their jobs so well that the two researchers were free to carry out their field research as usual, albeit at a highly accelerated pace. During their twenty-nine days in the field, the pair traveled constantly, cycling back and forth between approximately ten villages and the county seats of Mojiang and Pu'er, conducting brief interviews with respondents hailing from approximately twelve ethnonymic groups.[7] With so little time to spare, Classification research did not involve anything approaching the sort of detailed ethnographic research that Nicholas Tapp has assumed.[8] Rather, it involved a rapid succession of brief interviews with very few representatives from each of the applicant groups: anywhere from a few hours to at most a few days, and involving small groups of interviewees never exceeding ten people, and most often with far fewer. During each session, Chang Hongen recorded core vocabularies and Wang Xiaoyi inquired cursorily as to the disposition of the local economy and customary practices such as those surrounding marriages and funerals.

To compensate for these stringent conditions, the team attempted whenever possible to interview local minority elites, minority cadres, religious leaders, tribal chieftains, and village elders.[9] On August 18, 1954, for example, Wang and his squad members interviewed four self-identified Nisu individuals in the county seat of Xinping, three of whom were either local officials or cadres: Zhang Wenbin, the deputy head of Xinping County; Yang Huiyuan, a young cadre at the Xinping post office; Pu Xunchang, a cadre at the Xinping Trading Company; and finally a "middle level farmer" (zhongnong) also with the surname Pu. Elsewhere, interviewees included secretaries from local Chinese Communist Party (CCP) branches, local commune officers, and heads of local militia divisions.

The first and most basic reason for this preference was linguistic: minority elites were more likely than laypeople to speak Chinese. Conversing with "commoners" *(laobaixing)* required the use of as many as two translators, one assistant translating between the local minority language and the local dialect of Chinese, and another translating between that dialect and standard Mandarin *(putonghua)*.[10] Second, Classification researchers assumed that relatively upper-strata individuals would have developed, either through their tenure in office or advanced age, a more comprehensive understanding of the local ethnic terrain, and thus be in a better position to provide researchers with synoptic accounts of ethnic relations and thereby facilitate the relatively rapid completion of their work.

Even with the help of upper-strata minority informants, however, fieldwork did not always proceed smoothly. As phase one unfolded, one crucial dimension of the project began to expose the limits of the researchers' traditional fieldwork methodology. Unlike ethnological investigation undertaken in the recent past, in which the objective was to develop explanatory models that withstood collegial criticism only, researchers in the Classification were now obliged to assess the opinions and self-perceptions of the research subjects themselves. One of the most important factors in the assessment of the ethnic potential of a proposed minzu category was to estimate whether it would elicit support or resistance, particularly from elites *(shangceng renshi)* who would play an integral role in all subsequent phases of Chinese Communist minority work. For the first time, Chinese social scientists' clean-cut, synoptic, objectivist models of identity would need to come into direct contact with the subjectivities of their informants, a profoundly complicated interaction that necessitated an adjustment in their classificatory praxis.

Wang and Chang did their best to navigate this question of self-consciousness, but the process was often convoluted and frustratingly slow. For one thing, the social scientific-cum-statist concept of minzu had little to no significance for many of their interviewees, a fact that census officials first discovered in 1954. Consequently, the two researchers often had to employ circuitous, colloquial phrasings, attempting to approximate as best they could the type of collective human identity with which they and the state were concerned. Some of these phrasings included:

"Are you all part of the same family?"
"Did you all used to be part of the same family?"
"Are you all descendant from the same ancestor?"
"What do you call yourself?"
"What do such-and-such people call you?"
"Do you all speak the same language?"[11]

Moreover, even if the term *minzu* had carried weight at the local level, the team had made it a policy to avoid broaching the topic of "ethnic classification" to their interviewees, for fear that such disclosure might put their informants on guard.[12] Historically, the arrival of centrally dispatched investigation squads were rarely associated with desirable outcomes, typically involving one of two things with which surveys were intimately related: taxation and military service. To keep the purposes of the team's arrival more or less confidential, the team employed two different titles: the "Yunnan Province Ethnic Classification Research Team" and the "Yunnan Province Nationalities Affairs Research Team." The first of these was for internal use only. The second was used publicly.[13]

Ultimately, just as the 1953–54 census results revealed to the CCP the limits of its own ethnotaxonomic expertise, the fieldwork stage of the Classification produced a similar revelation for the team's social scientific contingent with respect to consensus building. They were model builders, and never before in the history of their disciplines had their ethnic or linguistic taxonomies been subject to the review or scrutiny of those being categorized. Indeed, their criteria and methods of categorization were effective precisely because they bypassed the subjectivities of the groups in question, creating models largely through the comparison of lexicons and grammars rather than through a consideration of mutual intelligibility or shared group consciousness (it was, after all, the lack of such group consciousness they often lamented, particularly during the war). As such, the very practices that had proven so effective for researchers in the past now left them at a loss. Thus, just as the CCP had turned to ethnologists for their assistance, a process that opened the door to social scientific approaches to Communist ethnopolitics, in the fieldwork phase of the project we find Chinese ethnologists coming to rely heavily upon Communist methods of assessing and molding the political consciousnesses of communities at the local level. If researchers helped the state see the peoples of Yunnan categorically, the state would now help researchers (and itself) secure the consent of the categorized.

Before we examine these methods as they were employed during the Classification, it is important to understand a bit about their origins and development. For this, we must return once again to the Republican period, to the early social research projects of the Communist Party.

"INVESTIGATION MEETINGS" IN THE HISTORY
OF CHINESE COMMUNIST FIELDWORK

As examined in chapter 2, a core component of the self-identities of Republican era scholars was the commitment to "direct observation"—that is, the commitment to scholarship built upon a foundation of lengthy, unmediated, and sometimes grueling forays into the lived realities of everyday people rather than through the mediated, comfortable world of bibliocentric research. The concept of direct observation was translated into Chinese using the term *shidi, shi* denoting "true," "real," or "factual," and *di* denoting "place" or "locality." The term, which was cited throughout social scientific literature in the period, was typically used to qualify words such as "investigation" *(diaocha),* to signal that one's study had been conducted "on the spot" or "in the field," rather than in the relaxed atmosphere of one's atelier or library.

Being Republicans first, and Chinese Communists second, members of the CCP were no exception to this general trend. Before he was the leader of the Communist Party, and before he was the Great Helmsman of the People's Republic, for example, Mao Zedong was an amateur sociologist. On January 4, 1927, for example, Mao set out on a thirty-two-day tour of five counties in Hunan, forming the empirical base for his well-known treatise *A Report on an Investigation of the Peasant Movement in Hunan.* In May 1930, he went on to conduct investigations in the town of Xunwu, the site of recent peasant rebellions. Lying at the intersection of the provinces of Jiangxi, Fujian, and Guangdong in southern China, Xunwu provided Mao with the opportunity to carry out research into the economic, political, and social structures of those cities and towns that he felt offered insight into the potential for socialist revolution in China.[14] In the case of Xunwu, Mao conducted his work in violation of party directives, defying orders to attend a party conference in Shanghai.

During these forays, Mao improvised a style of interviewing that later came to be formally known as "investigation meetings" *(diaocha hui).*[15] Mao introduced his *diaocha hui* in greater detail in his essay "Oppose Book Worship," published in the same month as his research trip in Xunwu. In that essay, he celebrated these fact-finding sessions as "the only way to get near the truth."[16] The investigation meetings, he explained, should always be conducted with a minimum of three people. Any fewer than this, and the information procured would be too narrow to use.[17] With regards to informants, Mao preferred those with the most comprehensive and synthetic understanding of local conditions. They should be aware of the composition of the peasantry, knowing how many owner peasants, semi-owner peasants, and tenants lived in the town. They should be able to provide information on the number of rich, middle, and poor peasants, as well as the number of small, middle, and large merchants. To this end, Mao preferred to speak with older people "rich in experience," young people who have worked in "struggle," and an appropriate selection of workers, peasants, and intellectuals. Soldiers and vagrants were useful on occasion, Mao continued, but it was vital to the effectiveness of the session to exclude anyone who was irrelevant to the questions under discussion. Mao was also patently uninterested in producing a proportionately representative sample, and thus discouraged the use of any more than twenty interviewees at a time.[18] He was equally unconcerned with comprehensiveness. Universal investigation, he contended, was impossible and unnecessary, the preferable method being that of conducting a limited number of investigations in a set of carefully chosen, exemplary villages and cities.[19]

As Yung-Chen Chiang has explained, these group sessions "provided a mechanism of checks and balances to insure that reality would be accurately represented." "So sanguine was he about the effectiveness of the group interview format," Chiang continues, "that he was completely oblivious to a host of methodological issues involved."[20] Here, Chiang underestimates Mao, taking him for a naïve ideologue. In fact, Mao was aware of the effects of the group format and the way in which it shaped the information thus procured. This method of research enabled Mao to elicit two forms of data simultaneously: the answers to the questions he was posing as well as the group dynamics of those being researched. By observing which of his interviewees were most outspoken, most deferential, most contrarian, and so on, he was able to identify who the key figures were, both in terms of potential allies to socialist revolution and potential opponents. As Roger Thompson explains, "Mao's informants were more than sources of information. . . . They could also be participants in the factional and revolutionary struggles that had been rending Xunwu for over a decade."[21] As Thompson goes on to note, Mao's method "not only served his revolutionary purpose but directly challenged the methodology and perspectives of Western social scientists and their Chinese associates."[22] Mao opposed what he perceived as the superficial objectivity of Western social science and did not shrink before tying his work explicitly to particular political projects. To that end, it was at best unnecessary and at worst duplicitous to couch social scientific research in any notion of unbiased approach: better to interview those individuals whose opinions held sway in the local area rather than attempting to create an evenly representative sample; better to focus one's attention on local power holders than to dilute one's time in search of a statistically significant number of discussants. Mao would later explain his views using an idiomatic expression "To shoot an arrow, have a target *(youdi fangshi)*." "Some comrades are shooting arrows without a target," Mao explained, targeting his criticism at those who engage in research for its own sake. Other comrades, he continued, "stroke the arrow fondly, exclaiming, 'What a fine arrow! What a fine arrow!' but never want to shoot it."[23] With the vivid sense of humor for which he was well known, Mao disparaged this breed of intellectual—the book learners—as "half intellectuals." "You can open and close a book at will; this is the easiest thing in the world to do, a great deal easier than it is for the cook to prepare a meal, and much easier than it is for him to slaughter a pig. He has to catch the pig . . . the pig can run . . . he slaughters him . . . the pig squeals. A book placed on a desk cannot run, nor can it squeal."[24]

Mao's group interviews also created conditions of possibility for the formation of certain consensuses during the interview process. Unlike one-on-one interviews, in which people are more able to voice dissenting or divergent opinions, group interviews tend to result in the articulation of ad hoc orthodoxies. Whereas there is no doubt that such group-think would have resulted in far more coarse-grained data for Mao than one-on-one interviewing, for Mao the point was served. His goal was never to determine the opinions of individuals, but rather to determine and assess the plasticity of the opinions of groups. He saw research as a necessarily participatory process wherein the understanding of something required participating in its transformation. As Mao argued in the course of his essay "On Practice" (1937), "If you want knowledge, you must take part in the practice of changing reality. If you want to know the taste of a pear you must change the pear by eating it yourself."[25]

After relocating to the new base of operations in Yan'an, Mao further advocated the implementation of investigation meetings. The investigation meeting method "is the simplest, most practicable and most reliable method, from which I have derived much benefit. It is a better school than any university."[26] During the Yan'an period, Mao's investigation would become a cornerstone of the "mass line" technique of policy formation, in essence forming the first half of the well-known couplet "from the masses to the masses."[27] "The basic method of leadership," Mao explained, "is to sum up the views of the masses, take the results back to the masses so that the masses can give them their firm support and so work out sound ideas for leading the work on hand."[28]

Following 1949, this mode of field research—one in which the boundary between information and transformation was porous by design—continued to be employed. For party organizers in Yunnan, we find examples from the early years of the People's Republic, during the establishment of autonomous minority areas. As local officials attempted to build the centrally mandated minority districts, administrative factors behooved them to amalgamate various ethnonymic communities into a smaller number of larger groups, much in the same way that Classification researchers were being instructed to in 1954. In a session dating back to before the Classification, for example, representatives of the Asong, Baijiao Luoluo, Datou Luoluo, Huayao Luoluo, Huoshao Luoluo, Laowu, and Xiangtan were convened to discuss the possibility of being reclassified under the single moniker "Yi," a decision that would have important implications for the balance of power within the newly formed administrative unit. The representatives present decided that, except for one group (the Laowu, for whom further consideration was deemed necessary), the proposal was acceptable.[29] In another instance, local representatives of the Baihong, Kaduo, and others gathered to vote on a similar measure, this time relating to their potential reclassification as "Hani." Once again, representatives arrived at a consensus supporting the merger of thirteen ethnonymic groups as Hani.[30] In each case, the process was similar: invite a small number of minority powerholders to serve as "representatives" of their particular ethnonymic groups, set in motion a discussion (or debate) over a particular issue, come to a working conclusion, and then enroll those same elites to carry out the mass implementation of the consensus thereby reached. Most importantly, while these meetings were couched in terms of open inquiry—in certain cases, asking the group leaders what *they believed* their categorical designations should be—nevertheless, the scenarios were far from symmetrical. It was the local party members, after all, who were engineering the sessions and deliberately congregating the specific ethnonymic groups they intended to synthesize.

As evidenced by firsthand reports from the Classification, the fieldwork portion of the project drew heavily upon the investigatory methods developed by local political offices in their early, pre-Classification nationality work. The mechanisms at work can be observed through a series of intriguing group interviews in which Ethnic Classification researchers set the stage for consciousness-transformation.

PARTICIPANT TRANSFORMATION:
STAGING REALIZATION AMONG THE TULAO

The Tulao was an applicant group centered in Wenshan and Mengzi counties with a total estimated population of seventy thousand people.[31] Along with six other applicant groups—the Heiyi, Long'an, Nong, Sha, Tianbao, and Tu of Funing County—the Tulao was hypothesized by researchers to form a subset of the Zhuang, one of the a priori minzu.[32] Researchers had linguistic evidence to support such a hypothesis and yet, once again, such data were insufficient for the purposes of determining the ethnic potential of such a categorization. To assess the viability of this taxonomic merger, the team needed to determine whether their informants would support the amalgamation. Only this would turn this imaginable community into a plausible one.

The team undertook this examination in two steps. First, researchers assessed whether the applicant groups in question would be willing to merge with *each other.* Second, if this merger was deemed feasible, they then set about determining whether this newly formed composite could be folded into the Zhuang. In the first of these steps, researchers congregated representatives of the specific non-Han groups who they postulated to be part of the Zhuang and who they knew, by means of prior lexical and grammatical analysis, to share linguistic traits in common with one another.[33] Knowing in advance that their interviewees should, at least in theory, be able to communicate with one another, researchers encouraged interaction during the session in the hope that their informants would come to self-identify with the hitherto "other" groups in the room. If and when the such an opportune moment arrived—that moment of realization—researchers would then broach the idea of categorical amalgamation and gauge their informants' reactions. In this respect, these interviews constituted precisely the same kind of "asymmetric dialogues" that Stevan Harrell describes in his analysis of the Chinese Communist "civilizing process."[34] Like Harrell's dialogues, many of the Classification interviews were encounters that, while far from one-sided, were designed to privilege the central representatives in charge of arranging and orchestrating them. This asymmetry was embedded in the organization of the sessions, as demonstrated in the case of the Tulao.

In the process of assessing the ethnic potential of an expanded Zhuang category, these staged epiphanies were highly effective. Tulao representatives openly attested to the transformative power of the group discussion. Not until the interview session, one group of interviewees explained, did they realize the bonds they shared with other groups in the region.[35] As one representative was recorded as stating, "If it weren't for Chairman Mao, we would have never come together—only now do we know that we all come from the same roots."[36] Likewise, during their interview with representatives of the Heiyi from Funing County, Classification researchers invited a Nong cadre to attend as well. The two informants "conversed and were able to communicate with one another," thereby supporting the team's hypothesis.[37] The Funing County representative of the Tu was handled similarly, as evidenced by the specificity of his conclusion. "The Tu is the same as the Nong, Tianbao, Heiyi, and Long'an," he decided with an assurance that, which to him felt spontaneous, was in fact carefully choreographed. "In the future," he continued, "we can join to form the same *zu*."[38] Testimonials like these found their way into Classification reports, providing subjective support for taxonomic merger that could be aligned with objective data pertaining to language, historical origins, and so on.

Having established the viability of a taxonomic equivalence between the applicant groups, the second step involved setting this newly conceptualized ethnic admixture equal to the Zhuang. In the team's final report on the Tulao, the methodology in mind is particularly evident: "The 'Tulao' was originally a branch of the Zhuang, but their language has since become an independent dialect of the Zhuang language. It's best if we combine them with the Zhuang, but . . . it will require some deliberation and persuasion work."[39] The groundwork for an enlarged Zhuang category began to take shape through asymmetric, orchestrated group sessions such as these—what I term "participant transformation."

"PERSUASION WORK" IN ACTION

In certain cases, staged epiphanies such as these failed to convince the interviewees, either because the non-Han representatives were simply unable to understand each other to the degree hypothesized by linguists, or because they did not equate shared speech with shared identity. Both situations bring to mind observations made by Eric Hobsbawm and others, who point out that the equation of language and identity is by no means a universally shared assumption, and that the treatment of language as a surrogate for identity can be objected to on at least two grounds. First and most basically, linguistically inflected identification purges identity of the many components that make it a complex and flexible phenomenon. Identity operates along multiple axes, wherein the relative importance or salience of any one axis is not fixed, but rather changes over time and in relation to contextual factors. By collapsing collective identity and making it coterminous with the boundaries of speech communities, language-centered categorization makes the untenable claim that language is the preeminent marker of identity at all times. As Hobsbawn notes, this is at best a construction of the nationalist age and, at worst, an unfounded assumption by researchers as to the minds of nonliterate peoples.[40]

Secondly, the very idea of "language" is a far more elusive concept than linguistic classification would lead us to believe. Left to its own device, as Hobsbawm explains, "non-literate vernacular languages are always a complex of local variants and dialects intercommunicating with varying degrees of ease or difficulty, depending on geographical closeness or accessibility."[41] Linguistic analysis, however, much like the nationalist mythology to which it is eminently serviceable, "attempts to devise a standardized idiom out of a multiplicity of actually spoken idioms, which are thereafter downgraded to dialects."[42] That is to say, the linguistic notion of a standalone "language" is a theory-laden rather than neutral concept. As taxonomic categories, they bear the imprints of classificatory decisions made by linguists regarding methods of comparison and standards of measurement. Scholars trained in diachronic linguistics typically conducted their comparisons using a highly mediated process involving the transcription and compilation of multiple vocabulary lists, which were then used as the basis of evaluating the potential genetic relationships between different speech communities. Whereas such methods undoubtedly raise the prospect of uncovering historical relationships between different forms of speech, such linguistic comparisons do not test mutual intelligibility *per se*. In this way, they attempted to engineer a measure of parity or commensurability between local concepts of ethnic identity and those promulgated by the social scientific state.

When confronted with such opposition, Classification researchers stepped up their interposition by attempting to persuade their interviewees as to the similarities in their speech and the correlation between language and ethnicity.[43] In essence, they were delivering a synthesis of the very ethnological worldview developed in China during the 1930s and 1940s. A telling example of this phenomenon is with the Mili, researched during the first phase of the Classification by the squad in Ailaoshan. The Mili was a candidate group with a registered population of approximately five thousand people who, along with the Lalu, Micha, and Menghua, were hypothesized to form a branch of the Yi.[44] Once again, researchers had prior knowledge to support this idea, but did not yet have the consent of the categorized.

As with the formation of the Zhuang, the team adopted a two-part process, first assessing the viability of a merger between the various applicant groups, and then contemplating the merger of this composite with the Yi. "At first," the Classification report explained, the Mili interviewee "believed himself to be different from the 'Lalu,' the 'Micha,' and the 'Menghua.'" However, "by means of comparing their languages, clothing, housing, customs, and so forth," the researchers were able to convince the Mili representative that his group was one and the same as the aforementioned three. Yang Zhengyun, the representative of the Mili in attendance, was then recorded as conceding that, "I suppose we're one part of a single group."[45]

From the perspective of conventional social scientific theory, an intervention such as this would likely be dismissed as a form of data contamination. Rather than fitting their taxonomy to the subjectivities of their respondents, researchers were trying to mold the consciousness of their respondents to fit the taxonomy. Owing to the definitional flexibility of ethnic potential, however, as well as the Classification project's status as a bureaucratic-cum-academic enterprise, this was perfectly permissible and, from the perspective of researchers, necessary. Classification research was an openly constitutive element of non-Han ethnic identity, in essence part of a first wave of state intervention charged with refashioning local society. By staging these group interview sessions and "educating" incredulous informants, the mission of researchers was never one of dispassionately recording the ethnic sphere as their informants believed it to be. Rather, they were attempting to engineer a measure of commensurability between local concepts of ethnic identity and those promulgated by the emerging social scientific state. Supported by such a plastic definition of ethnicity, Classification researchers were thus able to make their taxonomic recommendations not so much based on an assessment of ethnic relations in the ethnographic present, but by estimating which potential group identities were more achievable and feasible than others. Linguistic and cultural differences were significant only when they were seen as constituting insurmountable obstacles to the formulation of those ethnic taxa posited in the team's guiding taxonomic hypotheses.

OBJECTIONS OVERRULED:
THE PROBLEM OF THE THREE ACHANG

In the cases of the Tulao and the Mili, Classification researchers were able to re-shape (if not create) the consciousness of their non-Han interlocutors during the interview process. In other cases, however, respondents were far more vociferous in their opposition to the team's taxonomic theories. During the first phase of research, for example, the research squad based in Kunming came in contact with three applicant groups who identified themselves in the census as Achang. The three communities resided in separate counties—Yingjiang, Lianghe, and Lianshan—and interacted with one another infrequently. According to the representatives of each self-identified Achang community, moreover, these three applicants were not part of the same group.

Xiang Laozuo, a self-identified Achang from Yingjiang, seized upon the team's language-based methodology and used it to refute the researchers' claims. He pointed out that "the language of the [Yingjiang] Achang is more mutually intelligible with that of the Zaiwa and the Jingpo than it is with the Achang of Lianghe."[46] Another self-identified Achang, Zhao Geguo from Lianghe County, echoed this sen-

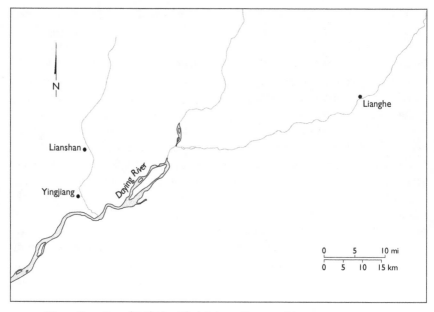

MAP 3. Home Counties of Self-Identified Achang Communities

timent in his testimony, also recorded in the team's final report. In a separate interview with Classification researchers, Zhao made reference to Xiang Laozuo above,
arguing that:

> The Achang commoners from Lianghe County have issues. Namely, the Baoshan Spe-
> cial District has one Achang Committee Member—one Xiang Laozuo. He is an Achang
> from Yingjiang. But the Achang of Yingjiang and the Achang of Lianghe speak different
> languages, our customs are different, we don't interact, we don't intermarry. The com-
> moners [in Lianghe] feel that this delegate can only really represent the Achang of
> Yingjiang, not the Achang of Lianghe.[47]

Zhao went on to address the third Achang community, the Achang of Lianshan.
"The Achang of Lianshan are Jingpo Achang. Their language, customs, and their
clothing are all completely identical to the Jingpo. They have absolutely no connection to the Achang, and in Baoshan Special Administrative Area, they have a
Jingpo Delegate who represents them."[48] Zhao concluded with a simple observation, "The Achang of these three locales are not the same. We don't interact, we don't
intermarry, we're totally unrelated."[49]

Notice in particular the foci of Zhao's comments: sociality, mutuality, interaction. Whatever the three self-identified Achang communities looked like on paper,
he argued, they did not intermarry. However similar their languages may have

looked or sounded in the eyes and ears of metropolitan scholars, they could not understand one another. In what world could a group of people so divided be considered identical? Notice as well that, for Zhou, the existence of three different yet isonymic communities did not pose an inherent problem. As Zhao noted, the Achang of Lianshan were represented in the local government by a Jingpo delegate, which seemed to suit their preferences just fine.[50] In this way, Zhao's protest illustrates vividly the tensions that surfaced during the Classification between local, non-state forms of categorization and metropolitan, official modes committed to encompassing the entire country and all its inhabitants. From the perspective of Classification researchers and their political patrons, however, such categorical laxity was intolerable. Once again, therefore, their primary concern was shifted away from mapping out *existing divisions in the ethnographic present* and towards assessing *plausible unities in the ethnographic future.*

Having conducted linguistic comparisons of two of the three self-identified Achang groups—those from Yingjiang and Lianghe counties—Classification researchers remained committed to their hypothesis that these group spoke dialects of a single language, even if they were mutually unintelligible in the meantime. The data supporting this belief was questionable, however: having compared a word list of seven hundred words, only 333 words were found to be similar or identical. This 46 percent rate of similarity fell below the 50 percent threshold that Classification researchers tended to observe elsewhere, but researchers compensated for this discrepancy by emphasizing grammatical similarities between the two tongues. According to ethnographic data, moreover, the three communities shared certain cultural practices in common.[51] Their empirical data was shaky, but Classification researchers were unwavering in their commitment to the creation of a singular Achang group.

Standing atop this unstable empirical footing, researchers argued in their summary report that, from the perspective of objective factors, the Achang of Yingjiang, Lianghe, and Lianshan were best categorized as members of a single minzu rather than three. The resistance of this interviewee, the team felt, was the result of a false consciousness: the Achang in each locale had lost track of their common origin due to the divergent cultural influences (one having been influenced mainly by the Han, and the others by the Dai and Jingpo). To resolve this tension, Classification researchers advised the implementation of "political persuasion work" (*zhengzhi shuofu gongzuo*), their final report reading as follows: "By means of political persuasion work, this division can be eliminated. Thus, we believe that the Achang of Yingjiang and the Achang of Lianghe are two branches of the same minzu, and that treating them as one minzu unit would be more appropriate."[52]

This example provides a clear illustration of the blunt means by which Classification researchers sometimes went about reconciling the reactions of their interviewees with the taxonomic models that they brought into the project. In the case of the Achang, they simply overruled the objections of their informants, and submit-

ted taxonomic recommendations they knew would require future state intervention. In terms of support, the best that the team was the able to elicit from Xiang
Laozuo was a reluctant concession: "When I attended a meeting in Mangshi, I ran
into five representatives of the Lianghe Achang. When they spoke, I was unable to
reply, and when I spoke, they were unable to understand. However . . . if today that
group of people has already been called 'Achang' then there's nothing left to do but
to agree."[53]

As evidenced by the tone of Xiang's remark, it is clear that the 1954 team was
unsuccessful in its attempt to persuade him of a shared identity between the
Achang of Lianghe and those of Yingjiang and Lianshan. He clearly still had reser-
vations. Why, then, did Xiang give in? Most likely, Xiang's compromise stemmed
from one of two sources. On the one hand, it is very possible that "minzu," as a relatively new concept, was not something that had the power or currency to invoke
an urgent or recalcitrant response from Xiang. Although the Communist state was
planning to build a nationwide political economy of ethnic identity, circa 1954 it
remained little more than an embryonic plan. It is important, therefore, that we recognize the historicity of the project, and that researchers were asking minority interviewees to pass judgment on a concept whose future significance could not have
been fully appreciated at the time. On the other hand, even if Xiang had grasped
the importance of this one interview in 1954, it is also highly likely that his compromise was prompted by a realization and recognition of the vast inequality in
power that separated him from that of the centralized Chinese state.

THE NAMES THAT CAN BE NAMED:
THE SELECTION OF OFFICIAL ETHNONYMS

Having returned to Kunming and submitted their phase one reports to Lin Yaohua, the fieldwork teams were able to enjoy a few days of rest. As July wound to a
close, Classification researchers traveled to West Mountain, a few miles outside of
Kunming near the banks of Dian Lake. The pace of research had weighed heavily
upon the team and soon a number of researchers fell ill. On the thirtieth of July,
Lin Yaohua developed a serious cold and spent the following week in the infirmary.
Wang Xiaoyi fell ill shortly thereafter, bedridden while his colleagues prepared for
the second and final stage of field research.

The first phase had concluded successfully and in complete accordance with the
itinerary first laid out by Li Qunjie. The Yi, Nong, Sha, Dai, and Tujia received the
team's foremost attention, and researchers had handled the majority of candidates
whose populations exceeded ten thousand. More importantly, as demonstrated by
their work in phase one, the social scientific contingent had clearly begun to embrace its connection with the state, pursuing amalgamation wherever possible and
deploying a host of strategies to shape and mold the consciousnesses of their in-

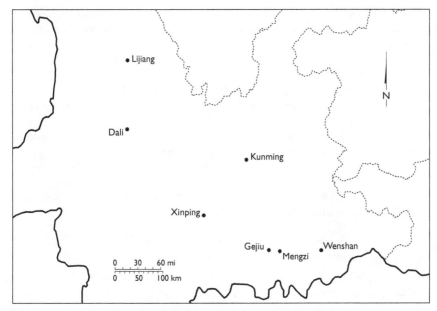

MAP 4. Bases of Operation during Phase Two of the Classification

terviewees. When confronted with the recalcitrant Achang representative Xiang Laozuo, for example, the Classification researchers did not yield. Rather, they drew heavily upon the notion of ethnic potential as innovated by Lin Yaohua, outlining categories that, although not fully existent in the ethnographic present of 1954, they believed could be made real through the future intervention of the Chinese state.

On August 9, researchers began preparation for the second and final phase of fieldwork, with one squad based in Dali and Lijiang; a second in Xinping; a third in Wenshan, Mengzi, and Gejiu; and a fourth in Kunming.[54] During this phase, the team would begin to consider another crucial component of their work, the question of what each of their proposed minzu composites might be called. Again, unlike ethnotaxonomic work undertaken in the Republican period, which was not subject to the sentiments of those being categorized, here in the Classification project, the symbolic power of naming would need to be considered in depth.

In preparation for the beginning of phase two, Deputy Research Director Fang Guoyu, who in addition to his academic post also served as a Lijiang County congressional representative, began to ponder these post-Classification issues. While in Kunming during phase one, he submitted a formal request to the Yunnan People's Congress to "confirm the names of nationalities in Yunnan and submit them to the center for formal publication."[55] More specifically, he proposed the following three-step process for rationalizing the ethnonyms of Yunnan once and for all:

First, for groups who have already expressed their support for the ethnonyms developed by the central government, we request that the central government issue a formal notification calling for the common usage of the confirmed name, and outlawing the use of any others. Moreover, [we request that the central government] provide an explanation of the prior spellings and pronunciations of these ethnonyms.

Second, for groups whose names have yet to be confirmed, we need to contemplate proper names for them. Especially for those groups from which representatives have been elected to attend the National People's Congress, their names must be confirmed and then submitted to the Central Electoral Commission. Also, we request that the central government issue a formal notification.

Third, with regards to the autonyms and heteronyms of the different branches of each nationality, we need to contemplate and, through necessary procedures, unify these names. Each nationality, or each branch, should only use one name, one spelling, and one pronunciation. These names should not be changed at will.[56]

The essence of Fang's proposal is captured in these closing sentences: one name, one spelling, one pronunciation, not to be changed at will. In this we find a radical departure from the policy of self-categorization that guided the CCP's initial approach to ethnic categorization and that began our story in chapter 1. What Fang envisaged was something that Chinese ethnologists had been pursuing since the 1930s: a standardized ethnonymic index capable of unifying ethnological research and, through its integration with the centralized state, serving as the organizing logic of the regime's ethnopolitical infrastructure. In other words, Fang and his colleagues envisioned the sanctification of an ethnotaxonomy that could help stabilize Chinese ethnology as a "normal science," in the Kuhnian sense, and China itself as a "normal state."[57]

On August 12, 1954—three days before fieldworkers began to fan out into the province one final time—Fang's proposal was approved by the Yunnan People's Congress. It was a moment that, despite its relative obscurity within the history of the Chinese social sciences, represented something of a victory for Chinese ethnology. After more than two decades of unsuccessfully petitioning the Republican state, Chinese ethnologists were now being called into service by a regime amenable to their social scientific worldview. Not only that, but now their specific ethnotaxonomic framework—once limited to the rarefied world of academic journals populated by perhaps dozens of fellow scholars—was to become the official demographic taxonomy of the People's Republic of China.

THE PROBLEM OF AUTONYMS IN THE
SELECTION OF OFFICIAL ETHNONYMS

The selection of official ethnonyms posed a unique challenge in China's southwest, and in Yunnan in particular. Many communities in Yunnan were nonliterate circa 1954, and thus their autonyms existed exclusively in the realm of orality. For the new demographic paradigm of the PRC to work, these names would have to be transcribed and standardized using Chinese characters. As with any language, however, Chinese is ill-equipped to capture faithfully the sounds produced in other tongues, and thus what resulted was often a complex process of negotiation wherein various "branches" of a newly proposed ethnic group debated over which of their autonyms should be used and how each should be sinicized.

The smoothest way to elicit the support of minority respondents was to use the names by which they referred to their own ethnic identity. In certain cases, this process worked smoothly. In the case of the Minjia, for example, Classification researchers recommended that "Bai" serve as the official name of the group, a recommendation supported by the team's interviewees. "The majority of people in this ethnic group," researchers observed, "only know their autonym 'Baizi.' Save for a small number of people, most do not know about the name 'Minjia.' Thus, in order to respect this group's autonym, it's best to use the name Baizu."[58] The same was true for the two character compound "Lisu," which the team felt approximated well the autonym of the community in question. The only question, researchers felt, was whether the characters should be appended with the radical *ren*, signifying "human," in order to make it more palatable to the group. Ultimately, the team decided that such a change was not necessary. "It has a long history of usage, and does not carry any pejorative connotations. Thus there is no need to change it."[59]

In other cases, the use of autonyms posed challenges, particularly in those cases when minzu were to be formed out of an assemblage of candidates whose autonyms differed. In the case of the Kawa, for example, researchers and political authorities were considering three different official names—Laka, Wa, and Burao. According to researchers, the name "Wa" was "acceptable among the Sheng Kawa [one of the applicant groups], but the Kawa of Banhong are totally unwilling to be called 'Wa' since they consider it have a derogatory meaning." "Burao" was an attractive alternative, since it was the autonym of the Shengka applicant group. The problem with this name, however, was that it could not satisfy the other applicant groups, whose autonyms were different. "Laka" was another possibility that the team considered. Laka was a neologism designed by the research team to synthesize the autonyms of two different Aka subsets. However, as the team pointed out, "for reasons of custom, we fear it won't be readily accepted."[60] Ultimately, the neologism proposal was dismissed, and the team recommended the use of the amended heteronym Wa—as it remains today.

Another case of proposed neologism involved the Nu and Qiu, two candidates whose categorization involved a particularly curious line of argumentation. As researchers discovered early in the project, the languages of different "Nu" communities were, in certain cases, mutually unintelligible. The Nu of Fugong were unable to communicate with the Nu of Gongshan, for example. Their grammars were largely the same, researchers noted, "but differences in vocabulary are extremely large."[61] Committed to Zhang Chong's call for synthesis, however, the team developed a remarkable rationalization for treating the Nu as a single, coherent minzu: although different Nu communities were unable to understand each other's languages, they tended to rely on a *lingua franca*—the Lisu language—to communicate with one another. "If we use Lisu as the common language of the Nu," the team recommended, "this will certainly not get in the way of their development."[62]

Having rationalized the Nu as a plausible group, the team went on to propose the further expansion of the category—this time extending the boundaries to include another applicant group, the Qiu. Once again, however, linguistic differences stood in their way. Upon comparing 459 words taken from the Qiu language of Gongshan, and the Nu language of Fugong County, only 10 percent were found to be identical, and 25 percent to be similar. The team concluded that these two communities "cannot speak to one another" even though their grammars were "basically the same."[63] In one final comparison—between the Qiu of Gongshan and the Nu of Bijiang—the team speculated: "perhaps these are not the same languages, but two different, yet intimately related, languages."[64] Based on the team's field notes, it would appear that only one comparison yielded supporting evidence, a lexical comparison of 459 words from the Gongshan Nu and the Gongshan Qiu that resulted in a similarity rating of 73.3 percent (40 percent identical, 33.3 percent similar in meaning and pronunciation).[65]

Despite these differences, the team recommended that the Nu and Qiu of different counties in Yunnan be merged into a single minzu. This raised the problem of official designation, however: to choose either "Nu" or "Qiu" as the official designation would symbolize the subordination of one to the other, a politically unskillful move, as would the selection of either group's autonym. To resolve this issue, researchers proposed the possibility of developing a new ethnonym, that of "Luzu." This name was preferable to other available options, researchers suggested, since it "conveys that it is not the Qiu that is being merged into the Nu, but rather the Nu and Qiu who are merging to form the newly named Luzu."[66] Years later, the Qiu would be recognized as a standalone minzu, rendering this particular decision moot. Nevertheless the case of the Nu and Qiu in 1954 illustrates once again the team's commitment to synthesis and the strategies they adopted in order to ensure that their categorical decisions would, to the greatest extent possible, elicit the consent of the categorized. This was an essential dimension in determining the ethnic potential of each proposed taxonomic configuration.

HETERONYMS IN THE NAMING OF COMPOSITE MINZU: THE ZHUANG AND THE YI

In the last two of these cases above, tensions emerged precisely because the Classification team was attempting to use the autonym of particular applicant groups as the official ethnonym of the resulting minzu category. In other cases, however, there were simply too many groups involved to consider using any one applicant group's autonym as the official name of the entire composite. In such cases, the use of a heteronym was preferable, since it helped avoid the complex problems that often accompanied self-designations. This is particularly true of the "Zhuang," a heteronym that was used as the official ethnonym of a wide array of disparate groups in Yunnan. By using this name, provincial authorities in Yunnan avoided some of the complicated issues that confronted their counterparts in Guizhou.

As explained earlier, Guizhou provincial authorities dealt with the categorization of a number of applicant groups who shared linguistic traits in common with certain communities in Yunnan. However, instead of categorizing them all as "Zhuang," as the Yunnan Classification team did, Guizhou opted to recognize them as "Buyi." The name Buyi was selected because it reflected the autonym of the applicant groups in question. Seemingly, then, the case of the Buyi in Guizhou should have proceeded more smoothly than the categorization of the Zhuang in Yunnan—after all, one would expect there to be less resistance and complication when the state opted to use an autonym as the official name of the group rather than an exonym. In reality, however, the case of the Buyi in Guizhou was far more contested and complex than the Zhuang in Yunnan.

In the early years of the PRC, the Guizhou Province Nationalities Affairs Commission dealt with the categorization of the Buyi at a convention named the "Representative Meeting of Zhongjia (Buyi) to Research the Rectification of Ethnic Names." Representatives from five special administrative areas convened in Guizhou in late August 1953 and, with the assistance of Yu Shizhang of the Chinese Academy of Social Science Linguistic Research Institute, tried to sort out the confusion of names. After five days of deliberation, the forty representatives came to an agreement that they should be categorized as a single group, and that their official name should be a Chinese transliteration of the group's autonym.[67]

The problem of classification did not end there, however. "The delegates all knew," a report from the proceedings explained, "that the Buyi and Chinese languages are different, and that the Buyi language contains many sounds that written Chinese cannot reproduce. If one wants to transcribe the autonyms of the Buyi with the utmost accuracy as to how they sound in the Buyi language, one encounters difficulties. Thus, everybody agreed that, as long as we can use Chinese characters that have relatively close pronunciations . . . that will work."[68]

The problem still remained, however: which autonym to use? Delegates in the room maintained different opinions, not only about which Chinese characters were best to use, but also what the "official" autonym should be. They proposed a host of variants: "Buyi," "Buyueyi," and "Buyue," among over twenty others. One source of contention was pronunciation. Certain delegates argued that the name "Buyueyi" best approximated the group's autonym, while others were uncomfortable with the

TABLE 13 Comparison of Various Groups to the Shuitian

Group Compared With	Lange	Luo	Shuiyi	Talu	Zhili	Ziyi
Number of words	270	878	525	281	908	740
Identical and/or similar words	207	795	371	219	708	668
Percentage of similarity	>76	>90	70	>77	>77	>90
Number of different words	63	83	154	62	200	72
Percentage of difference	>23	>9	>29	>22	>22	>9

SOURCE: *Yunnan sheng minzu shibie yanjiuzu* [Yunnan Province Ethnic Classification Research Team], "*Yongsheng 'Luo' 'Shuitian' 'Zhili' 'Ziyi' 'Liming' shibie xiaojie* [Summary report on the classification of the 'Luo,' 'Shuitian,' 'Zhili,' 'Ziyi,' and 'Liming' of Yongsheng]," YNPA, Quanzong 2152, Index 3, File 78 (1954): 100.

idea of using three characters—the majority of ethnic groups in the region, after all, employed either one- or two-character ethnonyms. In addition to the basic problem of pronunciation, the symbolic meaning of the Chinese characters played a role too. The character "yue" in "Buyue" carried considerable historical importance, one delegate argued, presumably because it connected the group to the "Nanyue" of Chinese antiquity. By the end of the five-day session, the delegates eventually returned to their starting point of Buyi, but adjusted the first character "bu," with the respectful addition of the "ren" (human) character component.[69] This lengthy process was entirely avoided in Yunnan, by opting to use an exonym as the group's official name, rather than an autonym.

By far the largest exogenously named minzu in Yunnan is the Yi, an a priori group that, by the close of the 1954 project, would end up inheriting over thirty new "branches" *(zhixi)* to become the fourth-largest minority group in China.[70] The process of subsuming these groups under the super-sign Yi was much more complicated than simply filing them under a new ethnic header. For one thing, the Nuosu of Liangshan—the archetypal Yi group that Classification team leader Lin Yaohua had first researched in the early 1940s—was traditionally feared and hated by many of their neighbors due to a longstanding history of aggression and slave-taking.[71] Reports from 1954 clearly illustrate this fact, remarking how, for example, the Langsu, Tagu, and Liude (three candidate groups hypothesized to be branches of the Yi) "have terrible relations with the Liangshan Yi to the north, because the Yi had often kidnapped their sons and daughters and turned them into slaves."[72] In their efforts to categorize certain groups under the umbrella term *Yi*, therefore, Classification researchers had to avoid referring to the Nuosu at all costs. Any direct comparisons would have met with the vehement and insurmountable opposition of many of the aforementioned thirty candidate groups. Confronted with these issues, the research team developed a complex practice of building the Yi. This methodology drew upon three key techniques, which I term gateway groups, transitivity, and aster-linear organization.

TABLE 14 Comparison of the Shuitian with the Yi and the Lisu

Group Compared With	Yi of Liangshan	Lisu of Bijiang
Number of words	875	772
Identical and/or similar words	455	376
Percentage of similarity	52	48
Number of different words	420	396
Percentage of difference	48	>51

SOURCE: *Yunnan sheng minzu shibie yanjiuzu* [Yunnan Province Ethnic Classification Research Team], "*Yongsheng 'Luo' 'Shuitian' 'Zhili' 'Ziyi' 'Liming' shibie xiaojie*": 100–101.

First, rather than systematically comparing each of the applicant groups to the archetypal Yi, which would have met with the ire of the interviewees, the Classification researchers began by choosing a few specific groups in the region for whom they felt, for a variety of reasons, a direct comparison to the Yi could be made. The three main "gateway groups" included the Shuitian of Yongsheng County, the Yi from the eighth district of Xinping County, and the Tujia of Yangbi.[73] Beginning with the Shuitian, Classification researchers conducted comparisons between them and a host of other candidate groups whom the team hypothesized to be subsets of the Yi. These included the Lang'e, Luoluo, Shuiyi, Talu, Zhili, and Ziyi. And once again, this process relied upon the comparison of word lists and grammars (see table 13). In each case, each of the compared groups was determined to speak the same language as the Shuitian, and thus to share common genealogical origins (see table 13).

The same process took place with the Yi of Xinping and the Tujia of Yangbi. The Yi of Xinping served as the gateway group between the Yi of Liangshan and nine other applicant groups: Ache, Chesu, Lalu, Luowu, Menghua, Micha, Mili, Shansu, and Zijun. The Tujia of Yangbi acted as the gateway group between the Yi of Liangshan and the self-identified Tujia of Yongsheng, Xiangyun, and Dengchuan Counties.[74] Having established classes of equivalence between the three gateway groups and the eighteen other applicant groups, the team then proceeded to set these gateway groups equal to the Yi of Liangshan. In the case of the Shuitian, the Classification team compared them against both the Liangshan Yi and the Lisu of Bijing County, which suggests that the team was considering the possibility of recategorizing the Shuitian as either Yi or Lisu (see table 14).

The levels of similarity and difference here were remarkably close, with only slightly more commonalities found between the Shuitian and the Liangshan Yi. For the Classification team, however, this was enough. "From the chart above," the team members concluded, "one can see that the language of the 'Shuitian' . . . is identical and/or similar to Yi, whereas it is comparatively further away from the Lisu lan-

TABLE 15 Comparison of the Yangbi Tujia with the Yi and the Lisu

Group Compared With	Yi of Liangshan	Lisu of Bijiang
Number of words	692	701
Identical and/or similar words	392	388
Perentage of similarity	56	55
Number of different words	392	313
Percentage of difference	44	45

SOURCE: *Yunnan sheng minzu shibie yanjiuzu* [Yunnan Province Ethnic Classification Research Team], "*Yongsheng Shuitian, Luoluo, Zhili, Ziyi, Lang'e, Talu deng minzu de yuyan* [The Languages of the Shuitian, Luoluo, Zhili, Ziyi, Lang'e, and Talu Nationalities of Yongsheng County]," YNPA, Quanzong 2152, Index 3, File 78 (October 1954): 76.

guage."[75] Even more interesting was the team's subsequent conclusion. "In accordance with these situations," they reasoned, "one can also conclude that the 'Shuitian,' 'Zhili,' 'Luo,' 'Ziyi,' 'Liming,' 'Lang'e,' 'Talu,' and 'Shuiyi' languages are all dialects of Yi."[76]

This last conclusion was made possible by an epistemological and methodological approach we might call transitivity. Once the Shuitian and, for example, the Zhili, were found to be sufficiently similar (linguistically), they were then treated as categorically identical in all subsequent taxonomic operations. Once two groups were set equal to one another, any pursuant categorizations of the one necessarily and "naturally" applied to the other. Hence, once the Shuitian were equated with the Liangshan Yi, then so too was the Zhili, Ziyi, Talu, and so on. In other words: if *a* equaled *b*, and *b* equaled *c*, then Zhili equaled Yi.

The same underlying assumption was applied to the Yi of Xinping and the Tujia of Yangbi. The Classification team compared both of these groups against the Liangshan Yi (and also against the Lisu, in the case of the Yangbi Tujia) and found a rate of linguistic similarity that, in their judgment, warranted categorical amalgamation. As with the Shuitian, the case was also highly suspect. In their comparisons of the Yangbi Tujia against the Liangshan Yi and the Lisu of Bijiang County, the rates of linguistic similarity and difference were practically identical (see table 15).

Faced with this evidence, the Classification team acknowledged in their report that "it is very difficult to conclude whether the Tujia language belongs to the language of the Lisu or of the Yi." Nevertheless, on the basis of certain morphological traits, the team decided that the Tujia language (and, with it, the Tujia themselves) was a subset of Yi.[77]

Classification researchers then set about linking up the Yangbi Tujia with further groups in the region. In a separate set of lexical comparisons, the Yangbi Tujia were compared with the Tujia of the Fourth District of Yongsheng. This yielded

a 70 percent rate of similarity, more than enough for the team to set the two taxonomically equivalent to one another. In turn, the Tujia of the Fourth District of Yongsheng was compared to the Tujia of the Third District of Xiangyun County, yield-
ing a rate of similarity of 60 percent. Having established this chain of comparisons,
the team once again relied on the concept of transitivity to set the Tujia of Xiangyun
County equal to the Tujia of Yangbi—and, thereby, to the Yi.[78]

Through the selective usage of gateway groups and this principle of categorical
transitivity, the 1954 team was thus able to build the Yi indirectly, using what I term
aster-linear organization. In diagram form, the Yi super-group appears as shown
in figure 1.[79] Here one finds a very small number of direct linear connections between the Liangshan Yi and the gatekeeper groups, who in turn are orbited by a
dense aster-shaped constellation of still more groups. Whereas the Yi was conceptualized linguistically, as in the language-based ethnotaxonomic models of the 1930s
and 1940s, this is how the Yi was *built*.

In addition to helping circumvent critical questions of subjectivity and consent,
the team's indirect method of categorization helped avoid a second methodological pitfall. If researchers had based their taxonomic conclusions on a series of one-
to-one comparisons between applicant groups and the paradigmatic Yi, it is quite
probable that many of the comparisons would have returned negative results. Looking at the percentages given in figure 1 (which indicate the degree to which two
groups were linguistically similar, as based on lexical comparisons), one can postulate that there were a number of groups that, had they been compared directly to
the Liangshan Yi, would have proven to be linguistically quite dissimilar. Had researchers conducted a direct linguistic comparison of, let us say, the Lalu and the
Yongsheng Yi (instead of the indirect one they performed by means of the Xinping
Yi), the linguistic statistics would have likely yielded negative results that even the
synthesis-minded Classification team could not have ignored. Likewise, this skep-
ticism applies to hypothetical Mili-Yongsheng Yi, Shuiyi-Liangshan Yi, and Zijun-
Yongsheng Yi comparisons, among others. Admittedly, because researchers did not
conduct such comparisons, there is no way to conclude definitively that direct linguistic juxtapositions would have resulted in similarity rates of under 50 percent—
after all, the vocabulary that separated Shuiyi and Shuitian might have constituted
commonalities between the Shuitian and Liangshan Yi. Likewise, even if they had
resulted in low rates of linguistic similarity, there is nothing to suggest that the 1954
team might not have gone forth and grouped them together regardless, as in the
case of the Achang. However, the evidence strongly suggests that Classification researchers employed indirect method of categorization for two reasons: first, to avoid
sensitive, deal-breaking issues of identity (particularly with respect to the Yi of
Liangshan) and, second, to bolster their arguments by presenting only the most affirmative quantitative data. Classification researchers were not in the business of pos-

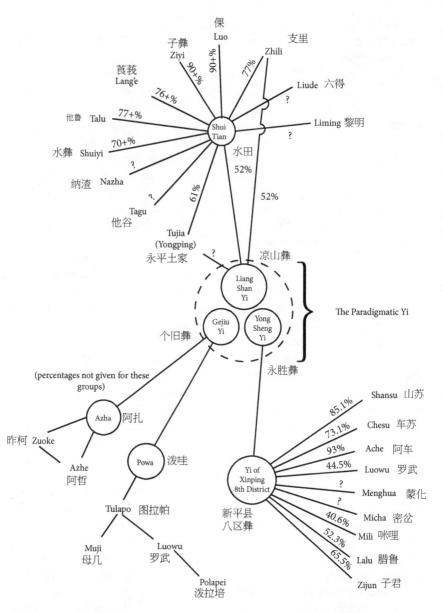

FIGURE 1. The Yi Complex. Percentages here were derived from lexical comparisons between the connected groups. Researchers typically compared vocabularies of anywhere from 200 to 500 words. In certain cases, specific percentages were not given—only general notes about the linguistic "similarity" of two groups.

ing further questions to their superiors. Their mandate was to advance conclusive, substantiated taxonomic recommendations.

CONCLUSION

The team returned to Kunming in the final days of September. All told, the Classification team had recommended for official recognition only five groups that were not a priori. These included the Achang, Bailang (Bulang), Nu, Xifan, and Zhuang (a category already recognized by the neighboring provinces of Guangxi and Guizhou). As for the rest, the team recommended that they be taxonomically merged with one or another of the a priori ethnic groups, or recategorized as the Zhuang (see table 16).

Phrased differently, and with attention paid to the central concept of "ethnic potential" examined in the preceding chapters, these taxonomic recommendations listed the names of those groups that the team considered the most viable, the ones into which the state should invest its energies of social engineering.

Through a close examination of the team's taxonomic work in action, four important aspects of the team's taxonomic practice become evident. First, we now see how "ethnic potential," the conceptualization of minzu outlined in the preceding chapter, shaped and guided the team's fieldwork methods. Drawing upon decades of ethnotaxonomic work, embodied in the models whose genealogy we traced in chapter 2, the team already possessed all the "objective" data it needed to make a strong case to the state. What it needed now was confirmation that the groups being categorized would comply with their theories or, at the very least, not resist them too strongly. Through the deployment of a number of different strategies, the team's fieldwork was geared toward procuring such confirmation or, in the complex case of the Yi, avoiding conflict to the greatest extent possible.

Second, we have seen how Ethnic Classification methodology drew upon research methods that derived from Chinese Communist praxis, most notably the investigation meeting pioneered by Mao and systematized by the CCP. Being concerned with assessing the plausibility of potential ethnic configurations in the future—rather than simply with a strict empirical evaluation of ethnic identities existing in the present—this research method was well-suited. By gathering together small groups, whose composition was designed according to information known only to the interviewers, and then carrying out "asymmetric" dialogues with their interviewees, Classification researchers were able to assess, on a small scale, the potentiality of those ethnic categories that objective data indicated to them should be reasonable. In this way, they were able to assess the subjective dispositions of key ethnic elites without empowering them fully—lest these interviewees become too cognizant of the process in which they were involved and thus attempt to steer it in their own favor.

TABLE 16   Taxonomic Conclusions of the 1954 Ethnic Classification Research Team

Applicant	Categorized As	Applicant	Categorized As	Applicant	Categorized As
Achang	Achang	Boluo	Yi	Shuitian	Yi
Bailang	Bulang	Bowa	Yi	Shuiyi	Yi
Heipu	Dai	Chesu	Yi	Tagu	Yi
Zhemin	Han	Lalu	Yi	Talu	Yi
Hani, Haoni, Biyue,	Hani	Lang'e	Yi	Tu	Yi
Kadu, Ganniu,		Liming	Yi	Tujia (1)	Yi
Amu		Liude	Yi	Tujia (2)	Yi
Kadu	Hani	Luo	Yi	Tujia (3)	Yi
Lawu	Hani	Luowu (1)	Yi	Tujia (4)	Yi
Nuobi	Hani	Luowu (2)	Yi	Tulapa	Yi
Suobi	Hani	Menghua (1)	Yi	Zhili	Yi
Kucong	Hani	Menghua (2)	Yi	Zijun	Yi
Benren	Kawa	Micha	Yi	Ziyi	Yi
Lemo (Nama)	Minjia	Mili	Yi	Zuoke	Yi
Nu, Qiu	Nu	Muji	Yi	Heiyi	Zhuang
Xifan (1)	Xifan	Nazha	Yi	Longan	Zhuang
Xifan (2)	Xifan	Polapei	Yi	Nong	Zhuang
Ache	Yi	Pu (Aza, Pula)	Yi	Sha	Zhuang
Axi	Yi	Sani	Yi	Tianbao	Zhuang
Azha	Yi	Sanmin	Yi	Tulao	Zhuang
		Shansu	Yi		

Third, in that process of assessing the ethnic potential of hypothetical ethnic categories, we see the continued centrality of language and linguistic categorization. To assess the plausibility of certain conglomerations, the consistent method was to test whether the representatives of different applicant groups could understand each other's speech. Furthermore, as in the case of the Tulao, such linguistic assessments had two effects: in addition to providing empirical evidence of mutual intelligibility (thereby adding support to the plausibility of such a minzu configuration), it also induced a sense of surprise or realization in the minds of those being interviewed. In the course of the interview itself, certain respondents were surprised to find they could communicate with the other attendees of the diaocha hui, moments of "induced realization" that aided the team in securing what it ultimately needed were its taxonomic recommendations going to be effective: the consent of the categorized.

Finally, we see very clearly how the promise of state intervention greatly influenced the Classification researchers' taxonomic recommendations. Whereas Li Qunjie and Zhang Chong had once feared the bourgeois, "ivory tower" pedigrees of the team's social scientific contingent, it was now clear that the academic members had not just accepted this marriage between social scientific and state socialist practice, but had embraced it fully. In this respect, whereas the Classification team's ethnotaxonomic models trace their origins to Republican-era social scientific traditions, the Classification team's methodology is best understood as a hybrid of two traditions of social research: the ethnological tradition developed by Chinese academics in the Republican period and Communist methods developed before and just following the founding of the People's Republic.

5

Counting to Fifty-Six

"Fifty-six minzu, fifty-six flowers?" That's how the song is sung. And yet in the great garden of the Zhonghua minzu there blossoms many a secret flower. Do you know who all of these minzu are?

—"EXPOSING 'THE YET-TO-BE-CLASSIFIED MINZU OF CHINA'"

The question of whether the categories correspond to the previous reality of ethnic consciousness is unimportant, because for at least forty years the Yi have been the Yi.

—STEVAN HARRELL

On September 15, 1954, the first National People's Congress (NPC) convened in Beijing as scheduled. At the opening ceremony, Mao Zedong proudly welcomed the arrival of just over twelve hundred representatives from all corners of the country.[1] The roles and responsibilities of the NPC, Mao and his fellow party leaders explained, were to be far-reaching and comprehensive, dealing with the most sensitive of national issues: the formulation and passage of laws, the revision of the constitution, the election of the chairman and vice-chairman, the formulation of the administrative geography of the country, the national budget, the deliberation and settlement of international treaties, and all matters of war and peace, among others.[2] In reality, congressional power would prove to be far more circumscribed than this, and yet the symbolic message retained its power: if the six hundred million people of China had "stood up" on October 1, 1949, here their representatives would sit back down and get to work on consolidating the new state.

As Mao delivered his speech, Classification workers were still in the field, in cities and towns throughout Yunnan. As such, only the recommendations from phase one of the project would have a direct impact on the proceedings. The results of phase two would have to be implemented later. Even so, the Chinese Communist Party (CCP) had made good on its promise of extensive minority representation, more than any Chinese regime in history. Within the congressional committee on Nationalities Affairs, thirty different minzu were represented, with eight others included among the other delegates. In contrast to the China of Chiang Kai-shek, the China of the CCP had become a veritable mosaic. In contrast to the China of Sun Yat-sen, with his conservative and northern-centric conceptualization of the republic of "Five Peoples," the China of 1954 had expanded to encompass the myriad non-Han peoples of the southwest, an expansion that ethnologists and linguists had long advocated. Over the subsequent three decades, moreover, the Chinese family would welcome eighteen more siblings, and these fifty-six would be incorporated into an elaborate web of discourses and practices.

Before this new system could be stabilized, however, quite a few problems would need to be resolved. The first such glitch appeared on that fall afternoon in the form of one Long Mingchuan. As one of the forty-five delegates from Yunnan and one of the members of the first congressional committee on Nationalities Affairs, Long's peculiar trait was his minzu designation: Long was listed in the congressional registers as a member of the Nong minzu. The Nong, however, was not a minzu, at least not according to the conclusions of the Yunnan Province Ethnic Classification Research Team. It was a branch of the Zhuang, as evidenced by their language, their history, and so forth.[3]

This glitch did not take long to fix. The year 1954 would be the last time a Nong-as-such would ever report to the National People's Congress. Henceforth, if Long Mingchuan were selected to represent Yunnan again, it would be as a Zhuang or, if in the 1980s, perhaps as a Buyi. And never again would the state commit the error it had made in the census of 1953–54. The policy of self-categorization was a thing of the past, with all subsequent registration campaigns following the template used by other modern states: henceforth people would select their ethnonational identity from among a menu of preset options, options that would obey the spirit of Fang Guoyu's earlier policy proposal: one name, one spelling, one pronunciation, not to be changed at will.

Long's attendance as a representative of the nonexistent "Nong Nationality" attests to the fact that even though the Classification had developed the ethnotaxonomic blueprints for China's unified multinationalism, it would take much longer to develop a functioning ethnotaxonomic orthodoxy. Classification researchers were the architects of this system, but they still required engineers—in this case, state authorities—to turn their designs into reality. The first issue we will explore, then, is the constellation of policies and practices in the post-Classification period designed to make the new official discourse of Chinese diversity into both a ubiquitous standard and a taken-for-granted, natural fact. This enterprise has taken place in a wide variety of venues, including print media, film, museums, academia, political administration, tourism, consumer culture and, most recently, cyberspace.

The subsequent disappearance of the short-lived Nong nationality casts light on a second important dimension of the Classification, one that draws our attention back to the census of 1953–54 and the advent of the Classification: Where have all the unrecognized minzu categories gone? Where are the hundreds of other ethnonyms that, officially speaking, can no longer properly be called ethnonyms? What happens to those categories that the state decides not to see? As we will see, many remain accessible, although they are dispersed in some unlikely places. Others, however, are lost for good. By simultaneously surfacing and canonizing the officially recognized minzu and sublimating and subordinating the rest, the Chinese state has been remarkably successful in turning the fifty-six-minzu model into common sense.

THE UBIQUITOUS FIFTY-SIX

The Post-Classification Decade

Beginning in the latter half of the 1950s, and continuing through to the launch of the Cultural Revolution in 1966, state authorities began naturalizing the new ethnotaxonomic orthodoxy through processes of inscription and elaboration. The newly recognized minzu designations were inscribed into an increasingly large network of discourses, practices, and artifacts, and at the same time elaborated or "filled out" via the prolific production of ethnological imagery, sound, and knowledge. These processes of inscription and elaboration have, with each passing year, become more carefully calibrated with the state's ethnotaxonomic orthodoxy.

One of the earliest and most important periods of ethnonymic inscription was in the creation and official naming of autonomous minority counties, prefectures, and regions. The logic of naming these administrative regions had been outlined before the Classification in the August 9, 1952, document, the *General Program of the People's Republic of China for the Implementation of Regional Autonomy for Nationalities.*[4] Two basic types of autonomous areas were outlined: areas dominated by a single minority; and areas "inhabited by one large minority including certain areas inhabited by other smaller minorities" or "jointly established by two or more areas, each inhabited by a different minority."[5] In the case of the first, the autonomous administrative area would contain the official name of the dominant non-Han minzu, as with the Xishuangbanna Dai Autonomous Prefecture, the Chuxiong Yi Autonomous Prefecture, and the Dali Bai Autonomous Prefecture. For mixed-minzu areas, the official names of the largest minzu would be included, in order of size. Examples include the Wenshan Zhuang-Miao Autonomous Prefecture and the Honghe Hani-Yi Autonomous Prefecture, among others. One of the first and most important sites of ethnonymic inscription, then, was the administrative divisions of China itself, with the new ethnotaxonomic orthodoxy being embedded in all official communications, maps, and so on.[6]

Official ethnonyms were also inscribed in the country's new system of national identification cards. Like the census schedule in 1953–54, these cards included one's name, gender, date of birth, place of residence, and minzu classification. Importantly, children of two-minzu couples were permitted to adopt the ethnonymic status of only one parent, a policy that continues to the present day. As such, there is no legally recognized "bi-minzu" designation in China—no space for legally recognized "hyphenated identity." Rather, a child of less than eighteen years has his or her minzu status selected by the parents and, upon his or her eighteenth birthday, is granted a two-year window of time in which reclassification is possible (but again, only from between the ethnonational status of one's mother or father). After the age of twenty, no further reclassification is permitted.[7] What this law quietly shores up is the stability and persistence of the fifty-six-minzu model through time, acting as a check against the potentially destabilizing effects of intermarriage and cultural hybridization. No matter how much the "contents" of each category changes—for example, in which children of two-minzu households perhaps come to share the linguistic, religious, and cultural traits of one parent, while sharing the minzu designation with the other—this law ensures that the fifty-six minzu model can encompass everyone in China without undergoing any changes.

Accompanying these efforts towards ethnonymic inscription was an even broader and more prolific enterprise geared toward the creation of new ethnological knowledge patterned after the official ethnotaxonomic orthodoxy. In 1955, state authorities called upon the Central Institute for Nationalities in Beijing to organize a nationwide linguistics research expedition geared in part toward determining which of each newly recognized group's myriad "dialects" would be considered the official standard (the way that *putonghua* is recognized as the standard dialect of Chinese). To that end, senior linguists at the institute—who included Classification researchers and consultants Fu Maoji, Ma Xueliang, and Luo Jiguang—helped organize and oversee the training of more than four hundred research personnel in phonetic transcription and basic linguistic fieldwork. The group then divided into seven teams and fanned out to all corners of the country starting in 1956. The first team was charged with researching the Zhuang, Buyi, Dong, Shui, and Li—and, interestingly for our purposes, for determining whether or not the Nong and Sha "dialects" could use the newly revised Zhuang script. The second team focused on the Miao and Yao, and was headed by Ma Xueliang. The third team was responsible for investigating the Achang, Bulang, Benglong (De'ang), Dai, Dulong, Hani, Jingpo, Kawa (Wa), Lahu, Lisu, Minjia (Bai), and Naxi. As with team two, this team was staffed with Classification researchers, including Luo Jiguang and Chang Hongen. The fourth team was dedicated entirely to the research of the Yi and its dialects. The fifth, sixth, and seventh teams fanned out into China's northern and northwestern regions, focusing on such linguistic groups as the Dongxiang, Kazakh, and Tajik. As one can surmise from the cases of the Yi and Hani examined earlier—categories that inherited dozens of dialect "branches" over the course of the Classification—

this process was no simple matter. In many cases, these putative dialects were mutually unintelligible, making the selection of standards a highly politicized process.[8]

At the same time that researchers were determining the standard dialects of each newly recognized minzu, the Chinese state also sponsored one of the largest ethnological research expeditions in human history: the Social History Research Investigations, or *shehui lishi diaocha*. These expeditions involved hundreds if not thousands of newly recruited and trained researchers operating in practically every corner of the country. In addition to a voluminous set of research documents, the Social History Research Investigations culminated in a collection of novella-sized treatments of each recognized group, written, edited, and published after the Classification.[9] In this collection of primers, known as the *jianshi* or "Concise History" series, the official narrative of each newly recognized minzu was laid out with brevity and clarity, while omitting the complicated and messy processes by which they achieved their recognized forms. In the *jianshi* series, we witness a pair of parallel processes: first, an extensive production of new knowledge that conformed to the categories blueprinted in the Classification and, second, a systematic process of "silencing the past" and forgetting that the Classification ever took place.[10] Each of the Concise Histories projected its respective minzu as far back into time as possible, conveying the sense that it had always existed, either in embryonic, semimature, repressed, or fully mature form. As Siu-woo Cheung has observed, the state went out of its way to involve minority elites in the writing of these histories, in an effort to enlist and enfold them into this new orthodoxy, and to avoid at all costs the sense that minzu identities had been imposed from above. As Cheung has observed with regard to Guizhou Province, "it is through the process of self-representation (such as writing the official minzu history) according to the master narrative of the minority institute in which they are groomed that the native elite transform their local identity into an institutionalized minority identity."[11] This genre of historical writing has persisted into the present day, as evidenced in 2004 when the Ethnic Publishing House (Minzu chubanshe) issued a reprint of the series originally released in the early 1980s.[12]

This state-sponsored production of ethnological knowledge was not limited to the printed page, moreover. Within a year of the advent of the Social History Research Investigations, yet another team was dispatched to undertake a nationwide anthropological film project. Referred to collectively as the "Chinese Minority Nationality Social History Scientific Documentary Film" series *(Zhongguo shaoshu minzu shehui lishi kexue jilu yingpian)*, the project culminated in such films as "The Yi Nationality of Liangshan," "The Wa Nationality," "The Dulong Nationality," "The Jingpo Nationality," and so forth.[13] Based on carefully edited and scripted plans, many with upward of three hundred separate shots, these films helped animate the newly recognized minzu in the minds of the viewing audience by supplying vivid audiovisual content.[14]

The Post-Mao Ethnic Revival

The first phase of the Cultural Revolution, lasting from 1966 to 1969, marked a brief and violent hiatus from this otherwise largely consistent process of inscription and elaboration. Called upon to root out and destroy connections to China's traditional past, Maoist extremists targeted many facets of non-Han minority communities and cultures, from language and architecture to religion and social practices. As many scholars have noted, minority language education was halted in many parts of the country, a significant number of religious sites were destroyed, the discipline of ethnology was disbanded, and in general non-Han groups became the target of harassment and, in many cases, outright violence. Far from celebrating China's ethnic diversity, the objective in many areas became one of assimilation.[15]

In the wake of the Cultural Revolution, Communist authorities returned to many of the ethnonational policies and practices of the 1950s and early 1960s. Retreating from the ultra-leftist notions that viewed minority culture as one of the many facets of "traditional" and "feudal" China in need of destruction and erasure, China of the late 1970s and 1980s began "reconstituting the ethnic," as Ralph Litzinger has shown.[16] In southwest China, one of the most important dimensions of this revival—and one that again witnessed the ascendance and increased ubiquity of the country's officially recognized minzu groups—was the emergence of cultural tourism.[17] Once the purview of foreign adventure travelers and backpackers, the provinces of Yunnan and Guizhou increasingly became the destinations of choice for a rising Chinese middle class. Supported by a rapidly developing tourism infrastructure, encompassing travel agents, domestic air carriers, and local hotels, travelers from coastal cities and inland metropolises like Chongqing could enjoy a "taste" of Miao, Naxi, and Dai culture, among others, and return home with a host of affordable ethnic souvenirs: Miao batik, ancient Naxi/Dongba script, and so forth. As with other examples of "invented traditions," it mattered little from which of the "branches" of each minzu that the particular colors, shapes, and recipes of such souvenirs derived—they represented one of China's fifty-six minzu, and from this they derived their touristic value.[18] The minzu of the southwest became commodities, with the fifty-six-minzu model serving as the organizing logic of the goods and services within the emerging economy. Kiosks in the Kunming airport began to tempt sojourners with collections of "nationalities dolls" (minzu wawa), conveniently available in a complete, fifty-six-minzu box set. For the sports card enthusiast, a preferable option might be one of the many different versions of "nationalities cards" (minzu kapian).[19] Whatever one's hobby or medium, an "ethnic" option often existed—and, if it did, the organizing principle would certainly be the state's official minzu taxonomy.

The post-Mao period also witnessed the influx of yet another group intrigued by the minorities of China: foreign anthropologists and historians. Scholars of Chinese minorities adopted a very different approach to the question of ethnic diversity, and in many ways sought to interrogate the fifty-six-minzu model by demonstrating its internal incoherence and inconsistencies. At the same time, scholars working in the 1980s—as well as those they mentored in subsequent decades—in large part continued to observe the fifty-six-minzu model tacitly, using it as the logic of professional identification. In a survey of anthropological work on China, for example, Susan Blum provides an excellent overview of the Chinese ethnic studies subfield, outlining a group of scholars who, quite tellingly, subspecialize in accordance with the familiar boundaries.[20] Whereas not every one of the fifty-six minzu has received the attention of international scholarship, as Blum notes, "the ethnic map is being filled in."[21] The historical trajectory of the Chinese ethnic studies subfield has, in this way, produced a somewhat ironic state of affairs in which scholars, many of whom seek to problematize the fifty-six-minzu model, have developed the field increasingly along a path that reproduces this model. While there are studies that call into question the naturalness of Miao identity, Yi identity, Zhuang identity, and so forth, nevertheless they tend to rely upon the fifty-six-minzu paradigm to provide their knowledge infrastructure. By simultaneously critiquing and employing the fifty-six-minzu model, such studies arguably contribute to the overall fortification of the paradigm, demonstrating as it were that the fifty-six officially recognized minzu categories are capable of containing contradictions and inconsistencies. And even if ethnological subspecialization itself does not directly contribute to the reinforcement of the system, a global organizational framework has emerged within Chinese ethnology that does. For example, the category of Achang discussed earlier can no longer be considered strictly a Chinese or ethnological category, insofar as "Achang" has since become a standardized, operative category within the Library of Congress (LOC) subject heading system as well. Beyond its ethnonymic function, by which it designates and demarcates people, "Achang" is now also a globally recognized infrastructural taxon—specifically, DS731.A25—that assists in the coordination and organization of knowledge produced about the Achang and by Achang specialists. While not all of the fifty-six minzu have their own LOC designations, and while a number of LOC designations exist beyond the fifty-six minzu model, nevertheless, a host of minzu categories have by now become part of not only the PRC system of ethnological infrastructure, but the global knowledge infrastructure as well. Other examples include DS731.P34 (Bai), DS731.H34 (Hani), DS731.M87 (Hui), DS731.C49 (Jingpo), DS731.L33 (Lahu), DS731.N82 (Nu), DS731.T74 (Tujia), and DS731.Y5 (Yi). Most importantly for our purposes is the way in which these categories have extended to the point where each is capable of containing the full spectrum of approaches—from the radically deconstructionist to the patriotically primordialist—without the risk of being subverted. In many ways, the system of categorization in China has, through its globalization and neutralization, outflanked and by now encompasses its detractors as well as its supporters.[22]

The 1990s and Beyond

Over the past two decades, the fifty-six-minzu model has become an even more important and common organizing principle within the realm of Chinese public spectacle and political ritual, supported by an extensive promotional industry. In preparation for National Day in the year 2005, for example, the Chinese Academy of Social Sciences oversaw a nationwide search for minority twins, one from each of the officially recognized groups. Why 2005? Again, we find our answer in the central, load-bearing concept of unified multinationalism and the fifty-six-minzu model. Whereas all nation-states are prone to celebrating their decennial, semi-centennial, and centennial anniversaries, the fifty-sixth anniversary of the People's Republic provided an opportunity that just could not be squandered.[23] The 2008 Olympics only accentuated this trend. On June 16, 2008, the Central University for Nationalities seized the historic moment to celebrate the upcoming Olympics. What was this historic opportunity? June 16, 2008, marked "fifty-six days until the fifty-six minzu welcome the Olympics."[24] The Olympics also brought the fifty-six-minzu model squarely into Hong Kong television. In the propaganda film *Fifty-Six minzu, One Dream,* pop sensation Zhou Bichang crooned "harmonious" lyrics atop a stage of immense proportions. Although challenging for the young and altogether life-less performer, the dimensions of the stage were necessary in order to accommo-date the familiar backdrop: the laconically swaying, fifty-six-person wide chorus line, each person bedecked in his or her representative ethnic garb.[25] And at the opening ceremonies of the games, in a moment haunted by the memory of the Ti-betan uprisings only months earlier, a procession of fifty-six children dressed as the fifty-six minzu presented People's Liberation Army troops with the flag of the People's Republic. Although it was later discovered that most of these children were, in fact, Han, the symbolism remained clear.[26]

This ethnotaxonomic orthodoxy has extended outside of official channels as well, becoming common fare in the more decentralized online realm. On YouTube, the fifty-six-minzu model can be found in the diatribes of young Chinese nationalists, who draw upon the magic number to argue for the inalienability of Tibet. Another video, titled "China is a united multi-ethnic nation of fifty-six ethnic groups," lay-ers one image of multiethnicity atop another. Posted by the user onechinaprc, the collage contains one particularly striking image: an aerial shot of fifty-six elabo-rately dressed minzu subjects, themselves arranged to form the number "56."[27]

In addition to such "sacred" displays of patriotism, the fifty-six-minzu model has since been incorporated in the "profane" as well, as insinuated in the opening pas-sage of this book. Pinup style vignettes have begun to surface, entitled "Girls of the fifty-six ethnic groups" and the like. A series of websites poll readers on which of the minzu boasts the most beautiful women, providing photos of each and then open-ing up space for comments. In response to one such poll, one reviewer expressed his admiration for "those foreign-looking girls," by which he was indicating minority women of Central Asian descent. Another reader, number 73, felt the same, casting his vote for the Kazakh *(Hasake)* girl. Two posts later, reader number 75 burst his bubble: "That's a Han girl wearing Kazakh dress. Number 73 is an idiot."

LOST IN CATEGORIZATION

To the extent that the fifty-six officially recognized peoples of China have achieved ubiquity, the unrecognized groups have undergone a diametrically opposite process of disappearance. Whereas a search on the Yi yields an incalculable collection of results, a search for nonofficial categories such as Ache, Chesu, and so on, does not. And the results one does encounter are inevitably linked to or nested within a broader discussion of the Yi. This raises the question: Where have all the unrecognized minzu categories gone? Where are the Aka, Ache, Chesu, Sha and the hundreds of other ethnonyms that, officially speaking, can no longer properly be called minzu? Just as the canonized ethnonyms are found in certain domains, so, too, do the unrecognized names cluster in certain sites. In the balance of this chapter we will explore three such domains: the discursive realm of taxonomic synonymy, the "yet-to-be-classified minzu," and the emergent discourse of "newly discovered" groups.

As borne out in the foregoing discussion, the destination for many of the now-unrecognized groups in China was *inside* one of the fifty-six minzu. This was true, for example, for the Classification in 1954, and also for the mop-up projects that ensued. In 1960, for example, a small team of researchers returned to Yunnan to revisit the cases of those nominees whose categorization had been sidelined by the 1954 team. Named the "Yunnan Province Ethnic Classification Comprehensive Investigation Team," the 1960 expedition combined researchers from the Yunnan Province Nationalities Affairs Commission, the provincial Nationalities History Institute, and the provincial Language and Script Steering Committee.[28] Dispatched to four areas in all—Jinping, Lijiang, Wenshan, and Xishuangbanna—their job was to take care of the numerous taxonomic cases left unfinished by their predecessors, which the team estimated at roughly eighty ethnonymic groups encompassing some thirty thousand people.[29]

As in 1954, the clear majority of groups encountered were funneled into one or another of the then recognized minzu categories. Indeed, many of the large composite categories we encountered in chapter 4—such as the Hani, the Yi, and the Zhuang—swelled to become even larger than before. Into the Hani, the 1960 team inserted the Ake of Jinghong county, the Bubeng of Yiwu, the Buxia of Jinghong, and the Pin. The Yi further absorbed the Benren of Jinghong and Yiwu, the Guola of Yiwu, the Mengwu of Maguan and Xishou, the Nanjing of Zhenxiong, the Sa of Qiubei, the Sanda of Jinggong, and the Zhuohe of Maguan. In addition to these ethnonyms, which were among those registered in the inaugural census, the 1960 team encountered a number of previously unregistered groups that it relegated to the category of Yi as well. These included the A'cixia of Lancang, the Bo of Qiubei, the Datou of Pu'er, the Luo of Funing, and the Lawu of Wenshan, Luxi, and Lemo counties. The Zhuang further absorbed the Ao of Funing, the Donglan, the Qing of Hongwu, the Shui of Luoping and Yilang, the Shuihu of Luoping and Fuyuan, the Tusi of Qiubei, the Yang of Guangnan, and the Zheyuan. In addition, the 1960 team uncovered a series of previously unregistered ethnonymic groups, which they also placed in the category of Zhuang. These included the Baiyi of Maguan and Wenshan, the Laji of Maguan, the Longjiang, the Pubiao of Xishou, and the Yang of Funing.[30]

Many of the other newly recognized minzu inherited additional branches as well. The Bulang absorbed the Ben of Baoshan and Lianghe, the Bujiao of Yiwu, the Kongge of Jinggong, and the Wa (Va) of Mojiang. The Dai absorbed the Bajia of Menghai, the Manzhang of Jinping, and the Pu'er of Jinping. The Jingpo absorbed the Laokang of Lancang and Menglian. The Lahu inherited the Kucong of Yiwu and Jinping. The Lisu absorbed the Yongbai of Changning. The Naxi inherited the Ruanke of Lijiang. The Xifan of Lanping, Ningliang, and Lijiang were once again recommended as a standalone minzu, to be named Pumi.[31] The Han absorbed the Douyun of Maguan and Hekou, and the Jingdong of Tengchong. Compared to this long list of mergers, the team submitted only six recommendations for recognition, two of which (the Benglong and Pumi) had already been made. The other included the Youle of Jinghong, the Gelao, the Gaomian, and the Mang.[32]

Consequently, when one goes looking for any of these groups in the realm of discourse, it is necessary to peer through the lens of one or another of China's fifty-six minzu. To arrive at Ake or Buxia, one must look through the lens of Hani; for the Bujiao or the Kongge, through the lens of Bulang; and for the Laji and the Pubiao, through the lens of Zhuang. Likewise, any data procured from the study of these groups must be attributed to, stored within, and brought into alignment with Hani, Bulang, and Zhuang, respectively. Any deviation from this—for example, to refer to the Bujiao as the "Bujiao zu" (Bujiao Nationality)—is not merely "unorthodox" or "nonstandard," but rather a violation of the embedded linguistic codes that govern the logic of ethnopolitics in post-Classification China. There exists no such thing as a "Bujiao zu," because *zu* is a suffix that can only be appended to the fifty-six official recognized minzu. The same logic applies to the nonofficial names of recognized minzu. For example, whereas "Mosuo" is recognized as another name for "Naxi," there is no such thing as a "Mosuozu."

Not all of the unrecognized groups of China are found within one or another of the fifty-six minzu, however. There is also a broad, miscellaneous category known as the "yet-to-be-classified minzu" *(wei shibie minzu),* which in the census of 1990 totaled some 749,341 people.[33] For Yunnan, this category predominantly encompasses those ethnonymic groups living along the border between China and Southeast Asia, particularly between China and Burma. In recent years, and particularly with the rise of the domestic tourism industry, this so-called fifty-seventh minzu has become the focus of increasing attention among China's new class of tech-savvy cultural connoisseurs. "Outside of the fifty-six minzu," one blogger asks, "how many minzu are there that have not been recognized?"[34] Sites detail the names, locations, and cultural practices of many such "hidden flowers," complete with photographs. On March 16, 2007, user Liu Zhenlin posted at length on the yet-to-be-classified minzu, declaring that their "intangible culture completely fulfills the country's standards for being protected. . . . We cannot forget the yet-to-be-classified minzu of the southwest."[35]

Plumbing the depths of absentia even further, one finds ethnonymic communities that stand outside of both the fifty-six-minzu model and the semiofficial category of "yet-to-be-classified." These communities (if, indeed, they constitute communities) might be termed the "orphans of infrastructure" within China's ethnotaxonomic system, to borrow a term from Susan Leigh Star.[36] Looking again at the 1960 follow-up investigation, we see that in multiple cases, researchers were simply unable to find many of the communities that had been left unexamined in 1954. "[We] undertook field research," the 1960 report explained, "and found that certain ethnonyms either no longer exist, or that we were unable to determine their location." In all, fifteen ethnonymic groups fell through the cracks in this way, including the Ahei, Buhei, Daixi, Deng, Gaomian, Ji, Kepan, Laxu, Li, Menghua, Mengtong, Mosu, Nanni, Punan, and one category whose ethnonym is illegible in the report. "As such," the report continued, "there was no way for us to create preliminary opinions regarding their ethnic categorization."[37]

During the same investigation, nearly thirty other ethnonymic groups were also dismissed outright, once again for reasons of population size. For unidentified groups with populations greater than one thousand, the team was to conduct onsite investigation and submit preliminary conclusions as to their categorical status. For those with populations between one hundred and one thousand people, the goal was a "general understanding" and the collection of relevant research material. In the case of ethnonymic groups whose populations fell beneath twenty person each, however, the report explained that they "cannot possibly form the special characteristics of a standalone minzu."[38] These included the Aban, Ahei, Ali, Aluo, Ani, Aying, Gui, Hei, Hongya, Jin, Kejia, La, Lanzhua, Longxi, Meng, Misi, Mofeng, Moluo, Nahua, Nini, Pingtou, Po'ke, Pu, Puni, Sanjiao, Shoutou, Talang, Tang, Wei, Wu, Yao, and the Zong.[39] No attempt was made to investigate these registrants, not even to merge them with other minzu.

To be unrecognized is not the same as being nonexistent, however. As demonstrated in recent anthropological work, many unrecognized groups can be found in exactly the same counties and townships where census officials encountered them in 1953 and 1954. Indeed, over the recent decades, a familiar cast of char-

acters has undertaken an investigation of these groups, including Western sojourners and Chinese ethnologists. In *Operation China*, a manual published in
2000, Paul Hattaway set out to outline "all the peoples of China" in order to assist
missionaries in their work of conversion. Targeted at a very particular audience,
the report presents data on the geographic location and population of different
communities, as well as the degree (in percentages) to which each had "never heard
the gospel," been "evangelized but did not become Christians," or were "adherents
to any form of Christianity."[40] For our purposes, what is fascinating about this text
is the list of groups it includes, many of which are identical to those one finds in
the unpublished census data of 1953–54. Moreover, many appear in precisely the
same locales, with population statistics that, while they certainly cannot be taken
at face value, nevertheless seem to correspond in some measure to the statistics
from five decades earlier.[41]

   In Xishuangbanna, for example, the Ake appeared in the 1953–54 census with
a population of 1,002, and the Sanda with 459.[42] Circa 1985 and 1996, the same
ethnonymic groups were found, with populations of roughly one thousand each.[43]
In Mile county, the Azhe was registered in the first census with a population of
12,925 people.[44] County reports in 1984 registered this group once again, estimating its population at 36,447.[45] Gengma and Zhenkang counties also remain home
to one of the larger unrecognized non-Han groups, the Benren, although a sharp
drop in population figures suggest dramatic changes in the region. Registered in
1953 and 1954 with a population of 12,412 in Gengma and 13,798 in Zhenkang, a
recent report from 1995 listed the same group with a collective population of only
one thousand.[46] In Xinping county, the self-identified Lalu group was registered in
1953–54 with a total population of 7,039 people.[47] According to a report from 1999,
they numbered 28,700 in the county, and 38,000 regionally.[48] In the county of Yongsheng, the self-registered Lude appeared in the inaugural census with a population
of 105; the Tagu with a total of 1,207 people; and the Naza with 430. In a 1999 report, the Lude (rendered using a slightly altered Chinese character transliteration,
Liude) were estimated at 1,400; the Tagu with a total of 3,500, and the Naza with a
population of 1,300.[49] The counties of Weixi and Lijiang, each home to only one
self-defined Malimasha registrant in the early PRC, are now home to an estimated
one hundred Malimasha families.[50] Gejiu and Mengzi counties remain a center of
the Muji, registered in 1953–54 with a combined population of 10,085, and in 1999
with over fifty thousand.[51] Likewise, Lijiang remains a center of the Tanglang ethnonymic group, registered in the first census with 586 people, and decades later
with 947.[52] As these figures remind us, a community need not be seen by the state
in order to maintain their coherence through time (see table 17).

   Christian missionaries have not been the only community to demonstrate interest toward the unrecognized non-Han communities of China. In recent years,
there has also emerged a latent "ethnological activism" among Chinese anthro-

TABLE 17 Geographic Distribution and Population of Selected Unrecognized Groups, Past and Present

Ethnonym	1953–1954		Contemporary	
	Population	*Distribution*	*Population*	*Distribution*
Azhe	12,925	Mile	36,447 (c.1984)	Same
Benren	26,210	Gengma, Zhenkang	1,000 (c. 1995)	n/a
Lalu	7,039	Xinping	28,700 (c. 1999)	Same
Lude	105	Yongsheng	1,400 (c. 1999)	Same
Muji	10,085	Gejiu, Mengzi	52,050 (c. 1999)	Same plus Jinping, Pingbian, and Hekou
Naza	430	Yongsheng	1,300	Same
Sanda	459	Xishuangbanna	1,000 (c. 1996)	Same
Tagu	1,207	Yongsheng	3,500 (c. 1999)	Same
Talu	723	Yongsheng, Huaping	7,000 (c. 1999)	Same, plus Ninglang
Tanglang	586	Lijiang	947 (c. 1996)	Same

pologists and linguists. In 1992, linguist Sun Hongkai of the Chinese Academy of Social Sciences commenced work on a multipart series dealing with the "newly discovered" languages of China, some of which are none other than those spoken by communities who failed to receive recognition during the Classification.[53] Whereas the authors of the series never go so far as to refer to these groups as "zu," their central thesis—that is, that there are multiple, distinct languages in China that cannot legitimately be categorized as belonging to one or another of the existing fifty-six minzu—borders precariously close to taxonomic revisionism. This is particularly true when we consider the centrality of linguistics within the original classification, as the foregoing discussion has shown.

Even more intriguing, there is strong evidence at this point that Chinese ethnologists are once again advancing theories that press and strain against the ethnotaxonomic orthodoxy preserved and demanded by state authorities. In the 1930s and 1940s, as we have seen, Chinese ethnologists were forced to deploy multiple strategies in the face of a Chinese regime committed to a particular definition of minzu. Circa 2008, it would appear that some ethnologists are once again up to their old iconoclastic tricks. Unable to apply the term *minzu* to anyone but the officially recognized peoples, some scholars on the mainland have begun to adopt the Taiwanese neologism *zuqun* as their new approximation of the English term "ethnic group."[54] Whereas the dynamics of this shift have yet to reveal themselves fully, I would suggest that one reason for this is once again political: it enables Chinese ethnologists to engage in the discussion of ethnicity without violating the dictates of the officially sacrosanct model, to move away from being "prisoners of the science imposed upon them by the Communist Party," as Stevan Harrell has phrased it.[55] So long as nonrecognized ethnicities are not referred to as *zu,* and so long as no suggestion is made that the Chinese garden is home to more than fifty-six flowers, then anthropologists and linguists are free to refer to any *zuqun* that they please. Nevertheless, the development of such a counterdiscourse once again raises the prospect for a theoretically grounded subversion, as it did in the first half of the twentieth century.

Conclusion

A History of the Future

The Ethnic Classification Project portrayed in these pages is Herculean and fragile all at once. The project was monumental, as one can sense most palpably in the way it has saturated all subsequent modes of Chinese ethnological knowledge and formed a prism through which our understanding of Chinese ethnicity and the Chinese nation-state is unavoidably refracted. Whether in the arena of administrative geography, language planning, family planning regulations, consumer culture, education, print and broadcast journalism, scholarship, or otherwise, these categories of minzu identity serve as the persistent identifiers. They are the anchors to which a wide array of knowledge, policies, sentiments, and actions are grounded.

At the same time, we have seen how the project was undertaken by researchers and political authorities who faced highly stringent time constraints, and produced results that, left to their own devices, were powerless to bring about a convergence between the state's discourse on minzu (or what Stevan Harrell refers to as the ethnological "metalanguage") and the "practical" languages of ethnic identity at the local level.[1] Rather, the success of the Classification has depended upon unceasing efforts by the Communist state to intervene through a wide array of social engineering projects—public education, museums, dance performances, standardization of minority languages, the training of minority cadres, and so forth.

To the extent that such post-Classification programs have proven effective, the fifty-six-minzu model has become more taken for granted, more commonsensical, and thus for all intents and purposes, more accurate. The more accurate the official demographic paradigm becomes, in turn, the more the ethnotaxonomic theories of Republican Chinese ethnologists and the Ethnic Classification researchers are naturalized as simply "a job well done"—a prophetic "history of the future." In other words, the accuracy of the taxonomic conclusions of the 1954 Classification project has changed over time.

When we survey the literature on ethnic minorities in contemporary China, evidence strongly suggests that the vector of such historical change has been in the direction of greater accuracy. According to the work of numerous anthropologists, it would appear that minority groups in contemporary China really do seem to identify themselves more or less in accordance with the minzu designations put forth by the 1954 team. As quoted in the epigraph of the preceding chapter, Stevan Harrell has noted that the ontological status of the category "Yi," while constituting a fascinating question for foreign scholars interested in problematizing China's current ethnotaxonomic orthodoxy, no longer seems to be a vexing problem for Yi people themselves (or not, at least, for Yi scholars who work on the Yi). Mackerras has noted a similar situation among the Bai and Zhuang, as has Louisa Schein for the Miao, and both Dru Gladney and Jonathan Lipman with respect to the Hui.[2] This trend makes a great deal of sense, especially when we consider that, with each passing year, more and more citizens are *born into* the fifty-six-minzu model. Unlike the Ache interviewees examined in chapter 4, who the state would have to transition into the new ethnotaxonomic model through processes of "persuasion work," their grandchildren will have been "born Yi." Thus, while there remains a certain degree of resistance—Colin Mackerras points to dissatisfaction among the Shuitian (classified as Yi) and Siu-woo Cheung to the Gejia of Guizhou (categorized as Miao)—overall such resistance has been eclipsed by compliance.[3] As Lipman notes, the Communist state has been "remarkably successful in imposing the language of the minzu paradigm on its entire population, including scholars and intellectuals of the 'minority nationalities' themselves."[4] The prophecy seems to be coming true, with the "potential" minzu categories outlined during the Classification becoming more "actual" every year.

To say that the Classification is becoming more accurate, however, is not to say that the fifty-six-minzu model is self-sustaining or invulnerable. One need only place the contemporary model within a broader historical framework—viewing it, for example, alongside the history of the late Qing—to know that no ethnotaxonomic discourse can ever become fully self-sustaining. Its continuity requires perpetual management by the state and continued participation by the people. As Kevin Caffrey notes, the Classification project "is part of a process, and it does not end," since the strength of its social effect remains largely reliant upon acts of reaffirmation and renewal in the postproject world.[5] Without these, the system can readily fall into decline or, more simply, return to a state of taxonomic polyphony. When this happens, however, the fifty-six-minzu model will not simply dissolve, nor will the ethnotaxonomy of the future return to anything like the pre-Classification period. By the present day, it occupies a far too central role in the common sense of modern China to simply disappear. Rather, it will become the building blocks of a new order, stripped and salvaged for parts in much the same way that late imperial texts were dismantled and repurposed by Chinese ethnologists in the 1930s and 1940s. Whatever world comes next, it will surely be built *out of* and not simply *atop* the world that presently exists. The Classification will forever constitute a vital part of Chinese history, whatever the future holds in store.

Ethnotaxonomy of Yunnan, 1951, According to the Yunnan Nationalities Affairs Commission

1	Zang	25	Huayao	49	Limi
2	Lisu	26	Sani	50	Mian
3	Moxie	27	Axi	51	Xifan
4	Minjia	28	Tulao	52	Zhongjia
5	Tujia	29	Miao	53	Heihua
6	Yi	30	Nong	54	Taiyi
7	Hui	31	Sha	55	Lang'e
8	Benglong	32	Pula	56	Tagu
9	Shantou	33	Yao	57	Mingji
10	Benren	34	Muji	58	Zhili
11	Kawa	35	Tu	59	Shu
12	Menghua	36	Qiu	60	Talu
13	Luohei	37	Nu	61	Qi
14	Puman	38	Langsu	62	Meng
15	Aka	39	Tu'e	63	Mili
16	Bo	40	Chashan	64	Baike
17	Kaduo	41	Achang	65	Man
18	Bukong	42	Malimasha	66	Sanda
19	Biyue	43	Tanglang	67	Liutou
20	Budu	44	Baijia	68	Abu
21	Woni	45	Bailang	69	Laopin
22	Dai	46	Luowu	70	Kamu
23	Micha	47	Xiangtang	71	Kakang
24	Sanmin	48	Li	72	Kadan

73	Huanyang	93	Suobi	113	Luomian
74	Ake	94	Amo	114	Liangshan
75	Kongge	95	Ximoluo	115	Minlang
76	Silang	96	Luomian	116	Zijun
77	Qima	97	Miyi	117	Baizi
78	Shuiyi	98	Kabie	118	Dongshu
79	Shuitian	99	Chabo	119	Menggu
80	Nazha	100	Asuo	120	Luowu
81	Adong	101	Bajia	121	Sansu
82	Chesu	102	Nalu	122	Santuohong
83	Naniao	103	Ami	123	Baiyi
84	Heipu	104	Asu	124	Shuihu
85	Laniao	105	Lami	125	Axian
86	Mili	106	Qidian	126	Azhe
87	Duota	107	Qidi	127	Pu'er
88	Nuobi	108	Youle	128	Kelao
89	Kucong	109	Bujiao	129	Mengwu
90	Alu	110	Bubang	130	Laji
91	Muhua	111	Buxia	131	Douyun
92	Lalu	112	Tuli	132	Dan

SOURCE: Yunnan Province Nationalities Affairs Commission, "*Yunnan xiongdi minzu zhuyao fenbu diqu jiantu* [Simplified Map of the Main Regional Distributions of Brother Nationalities in Yunnan]," YNPA, Quanzong 2152, Index 3, File 3 (1951): 5.

NOTE: All ethnonyms appear in the original with the suffix -*zu* removed for purposes of clarity.

Ethnotaxonomy of Yunnan, 1953, According to the Yunnan Nationalities Affairs Commission

	Name	Population		Name	Population
1	Yi	1,145,840	22	Axian	2,000
2	Menghua	27,707	23	Liangshan	1,963
3	Dali Tujia	36,743	24	Zijun	1,860
4	Axi	22,300	25	Ximoluo	1,700
5	Muji	18,211	26	Ache	1,555
6	Sani	16,980	27	Minlang	1,554
7	Sansu	14,564	28	Tagu	1,500
8	Micha	12,101	29	Santuohong	1,313
9	Lijiang Tujia	10,000	30	Xiangtang	1,302
10	Sanmin	10,000	31	Tanglang	1,180
11	Luowu	6,401	32	Chesu	1,027
12	Lalu	5,889	33	Heipu	864
13	Shuitian	5,800	34	Nuobi	833
14	Azhe	5,000	35	Lami	600
15	Pula	99,847	36	Lang'e	1,600
16	Youle	4,881	37	Shu	450
17	Shuiyi	4,000	38	Suobi	414
18	Talu	2,654	39	Nazha	350
19	Baiyi	2,600	40	Zhili	260
20	Qidi	2,536	41	Mingji	250
21	Heihua	2,300	42	Miyi	234

	Name	Population		Name	Population
43	Alu	37	81	Nong	247,158
44	Asu	9,633	82	Sha	143,143
45	Woni	202,888	83	Zhongjia	4,645
46	Luohei	142,962	84	Shuihu	4,645
47	Aka	34,335	85	Douyun	900
48	Kaduo	32,595	86	Hui	243,553
49	Budu	24,326	87	Tulao	98,095
50	Biyue	16,914	88	Menggu	3,532
51	Bukong	11,900	89	Man	9,633
52	Kucong	3,853	90	Tu	58,235
53	Duota	504	91	Mian	600
54	Lisu	163,013	92	Dan	450
55	Tu'e	200	93	Baike	1,400
56	Shantou	66,740	94	Mengwu	None given
57	Chashan	50	95	Ake	850
58	Achang	7,173	96	Kongge	None given
59	Langsu	50	97	Laji	825
60	Nu	9,384	98	Asuo	602
61	Qiu	721	99	Bubang	500
62	Minjia	452,922	100	Bujiao	500
63	Moxie	150,318	101	Li	414
64	Malimasha	570	102	Sanda	411
65	Zang	35,495	103	Kelao	383
66	Xifan	25,829	104	Dongshu	300
67	Dai (Tai)	436,186	105	Bailang	166
68	Huayao	17,019	106	Laopin	75
69	Tuli	1,428	107	Limi	50
70	Baiyi	637	108	Qi	49
71	Pu'er	637	109	Datou	9,633
72	Puman	None given	110	Buxia	9,633
73	Pu'er benren	4,104	111	Huanyang	9,633
74	Kawa	125,205	112	Kamu	9,633
75	Baoshan benren	13,700	113	Kakang	9,633
76	Benglong	1,150	114	Kadan	9,633
77	Miao	260,125	115	Kabie	9,633
78	Baijia	5,800	116	Kana	None given
79	Meng	543	117	Silang	9,633
80	Yao	41,113	118	Qima	9,633

	Name	Population		Name	Population
119	Abu	9,633	122	Ami	9,633
120	Qidian	9,633	123	Chabo	9,633
121	Amo	9,633	124	Bajia	9,633

SOURCE: Yunnan Province Nationalities Affairs Commission, "*Yunnan sheng xiongdi minzu fenbu lüetu* [Preliminary Distribution Map of Brother Nationalities in Yunnan Province]," YNPA, Quanzong 2152, Index 3, File 4 (1953): item 1.

Minzu Entries, 1953–1954 Census, by Population

Name	Population	Name	Population
Han	11,632,155	Xifan	16,091
Yi	1,493,347	Azhe	15,928
Bai	658,172	Nu	13,003
Dai	483,347	Xiangtang	11,888
Zhuang	477,160	Kucong	10,457
Hani	441,085	Muji	10,085
Miao	360,468	Xie	10,067
Lisu	249,467	Lalu	7,040
Hui	216,454	Ben	6,415
Kawa	158,842	Lao	5,595
Naxi	141,727	Mili	5,047
Lahu	134,854	Lemo	4,807
Benren	120,564	Meng	3,507
Jingpo	106,803	Benglong	3,126
Pula	103,620	Heisu	2,975
Yao	72,184	Lami	2,644
Zang	66,816	Du	2,413
Tu	42,729	Douyundou	2,327
"Other minzu"		Tamiao	2,178
(qita minzu)	38,148	Shuitian	2,172
Bulang	32,148	Shuihu	2,025
Achang	19,621	Dalao	1,970
Huayao	16,719	Shui	1,960

Name	Population	Name	Population
Bajia	1,782	Buxia	216
Zijun	1,637	Bujiao	176
Sa	1,443	Qing	161
Mahei	1,260	Tusi	134
Mengwu	1,243	Illegible	119
Shanhou	1,240	Heipu	118
Lang'e	1,223	Zi	113
Tagu	1,207	Lude	105
Tujia	1,188	Yongbai	104
Danren	1,054	Mosu	96
Ake	1,002	Qu	88
Ximoluo	993	Zhong	65
Man	954	Guola	63
Chaman	900	Paijiao	63
Huasu	845	Laxi	62
Lama	800	Gaomian	60
Talu	723	Ao	58
Canyi	720	Mata	56
Douyun	697	Gelao	50
Lulu	676	Pin	50
Baijia	602	Deng	47
Tanglang	586	Nanjing	46
Tulao	493	Yuenan	45
Jiazhou	475	Buwa	42
Sanda	459	Zong	39
Naza	430	Nanni	38
Zhili	428	Azhe (alternate character)	37
Ruanke	425	Jingdong	36
Kabie	421	Lazi	24
Dingge	399	Keji	23
Kela	393	Zhuohe	22
Daisi	369	Ani	18
Li	350	Funi	18
Banxi	295	Kang	18
Yang	284	Qijia	18
Lüxi	281	Tu'e	12
Diga	261	Mengyong	10
Gesi	260	Dazhuba	9
Ahei	246	Hong	8
Hei	243	Laluo	8

Name	Population	Name	Population
Longren	8	Cang	1
Masha	8	Fuduo	1
Micha	8	Gucong	1
Bendizu	7	La	1
Chaoxian	7	Laba	1
Gaoshan	6	Li (alternate character)	1
Lie	6	Limin	1
Fan	5	Lishi	1
Gaoli	5	Luoyi	1
Gui	5	Meng (alternate character)	1
Jia	5	Mianren	1
Naxi (alternate character)	5	Moluo	1
Shang	5	Nahua	1
Wu	5	Nama	1
Baiyi	4	Nayi	1
Dongchuan	4	Nibo'er	1
Donglan	4	Qiang	1
Jiangxi	4	Riben	1
Punan	4	Ri'erman	1
Shoutou	4	Sanni	1
Zeheng	4	Shan	1
Banyi	3	Shanyihong	1
"Unclear minzu" (buming minzu)	3	Shi	1
Laowu	3	Shu	1
Misi	3	Wu'ersiwei	1
Akuo	2	Xiang	1
Douyi	2	Yishan	1
Hanhui	2	Yishi	1
Huahong	2	Bairen	n/a
Kejia	2	Illegible	n/a
Malimasha	2	Mingji	n/a
Manzi	2	Naxiang	n/a
Tu (alternate character)	2	Qiu	n/a
Aluo	1	Minorities	5,625,082
Boluo	1	Total Population	17,257,237

SOURCE: Yunnan sheng renmin zhengfu minzu shiwu weiyuanhui yanjiushi, "*Yunnan shao-shu minzu renkou tongjibiao (xuanweihui cailiao)* [Population Chart for the Minority Na-tionalities of Yunnan (Electoral Commission Materials)]," YNPA, Quanzong 2152, Index 1, File 48 (August 25, 1954).

Classification Squads, Phases One and Two

Research Squads in Phase One (June 2 to July 21, 1954)[a]

Wenshan-Funing Squad	Tujia Squad	Shiping Squad	Mojiang County Hani Squad	Kunming-Lunan-Mile-Yunlong Squad	Bailangzu Squad	Lemo Squad	Achang-Benren Squad
Lin Yaohua	Liu Yaohan	Wang Furen	Wang Xiaoyi	Yang Kun	Fu Maoji	Fang Guoyu	Yang Yucai
Zhou Yaowen	Lü Guangtian	Zhan Kailong	Chang Hongen	Shen Jiaju	Zhang Fengqi	Liu Lu	Chen Fengxian
Shi Lianzhu	Zhu Jiapin			Na Xun	Zhang Yaqing	Zhou Rucheng	Zhou Wenyu
Huang Shupin	An Rong			Lu Changding		Wang Enqing	Wan Wentao
Liu Enliang	Huang Wenbin			Xue Jian		Pi Li	Gong Rongxing
Zhao Dafu	Wang Liangzhi			Zou Fengxiang		Liu Chuanlin	Zhang Jingmeng
Sun Yuesu	Li Hongchang			Bi Xide			
	Yin Peizhang			Zhou Wenyu			
	Yang Jinxian						

Research Squads in Phase Two (August 15 to September 29, 1954)[b]

Dali-Lijiang Squad	Xinping Squad	Wenshan-Mengzi-Gejiu Squad	Kunming Squad
Lin Yaohua	Wang Xiaoyi	Yan Ruxian	Fu Maoji
Wang Furen	Shi Lianzhu	Zhang Fengqi	Fang Guoyu
Yang Yucai	Chen Fengxian	Huang Wenbin	Xiao Qingwen
An Rong	Chang Hongen	Lü Guangtian	Xu Lin
Wang Liangzhi	Shen Jiaju		Zhou Yaowen
Wan Wentao			Liu Lu
Huang Shupin			Zhang Ronghua

[a] Specific dates refer to the research schedule of team member Wang Xiaoyi, compiled from interviews with Wang Xiaoyi on January 3, 2003 and January 27, 2003.

[b] Certain researchers did not participate in both phases of the Classification, which accounts for changes in the lists of names here.

Population Sizes of Groups Researched during Phase One and Phase Two

Population of Target Groups	Number of Groups	Number Researched during Phase One (June 2 to July 21, 1954[a])	Number Researched during Phase Two (August 15 to September 29, 1954)
Over 100,000	3	3 (100%)	0 (0%)
10,000 to 100,000	18	13 (72%)	5 (28%)
1,000 to 10,000	20	4 (20%)	16 (80%)
Under 1,000	15	1 (7%)	14 (93%)
Total	56	21 (37.5%)	35 (62.5%)
	plus two whose populations were not given	plus two whose populations were not given	

[a]Specific dates refer to the research schedule of team member Wang Xiaoyi, compiled from interviews with Wang Xiaoyi on January 3, 2003 and January 27, 2003. During the Classification project, Professor Wang maintained a remarkably detailed daily journal, which he recited to me during our oral history sessions.

NOTES

INTRODUCTION

Epigraphs, p. 1: http://shequ.qihoo.com/q/feeling/991352.html?f=1 (accessed August 7, 2008).

1. These fifty-five include the Zhuang, Manchu, Hui, Miao, Uighur, Tujia, Yi, Mongol, Tibetan, Buyi, Dong, Yao, Korean, Bai, Hani, Kazakh, Li, Dai, She, Lisu, Gelao, Dongxiang, Gaoshan, Lahu, Shui, Wa, Naxi, Qiang, Tu, Mulao, Xibo, Kyrgyz, Daur, Jingpo, Maonan, Sala, Bulang, Tajik, Achang, Pumi, Ewenke, Nu, Jing, Jinuo, De'ang, Bao'an, Russian, Yugu, Uzbek, Menba, Oroqen, Dulong, Tatar, Hezhe, and Luoba. Fei Xiaotong, *Zhonghua minzu duoyuan yiti geju* [The Plurality and Organic Unity of the Zhonghua Minzu] (Beijing: Zhongyang renmin xueyuan chubanshe, 1989). This concept of plural singularity has since been picked up and advanced by a new generation of Chinese ethnologists and anthropologists. For a more contemporary instantiation of this argument, see Zhang Haiyang, *Zhongguo de duoyuan wenhua yu Zhongguo ren de rentong* (Beijing: Minzu chubanshe, 2006). In texts designed for a wider audience, this approach is even more standardized. For an example of how authors emphasize both the unity and diversity of the People's Republic for both a domestic and an international audience, see Ma Yin, ed., *China's Minority Nationalities* (Beijing: Foreign Languages Press, 1989).

2. John Fitzgerald, "The Nationless State: The Search for a Nation in Modern Chinese Nationalism," *Australian Journal of Chinese Affairs* 33 (January 1995): 75–104.

3. Jane Caplan and John Torpey, eds., *Documenting Individual Identity: The Development of State Practices in the Modern World* (Princeton: Princeton University Press, 2001), 3.

4. Thomas Heberer, "Nationalities, Conflict, and Ethnicity in the People's Republic of China, with Special Reference to the Yi in the Liangshan Yi Autonomous Prefecture," in *Perspectives on the Yi of Southwest China*, ed. Stevan Harrell (Berkeley: University of California Press, 2001), 218.

5. David Bradley, "Language Policy for the Yi," in *Perspectives on the Yi*, 195.

6. Nicholas Tapp, "In Defense of the Archaic: A Reconsideration of the 1950s Ethnic Classification Project in China," *Asian Ethnicity* 3 (2002): 67.

7. Gregory Guldin, *The Saga of Anthropology in China: From Malinowski to Mao* (Armonk, NY: M. E. Sharpe, 1994), 131.

8. Huang Guangxie, *Zhongguo de minzu shibie* [Ethnic Classification in China], (Beijing: Minzu chubanshe, 1995). The Classification has remained virtually absent from English-language scholarship on Chinese ethnicity. For example, whereas many have examined Communist-era ethnopolitics, scholars have typically started their stories with the officially recognized minzu of China, rather than with the process by which they were first categorized. In her classic analysis of Communist ethnopolitics, for example, June Dreyer does not address the Classification at all. Colin Mackerras dedicates a mere three pages to the project in his 1994 work, and no attention at all in either his preceding or following publications. June Dreyer, *China's Forty Millions* (Cambridge, MA: Harvard University Press, 1976); Colin Mackerras, *China's Minorities: Integration and Modernization in the Twentieth Century* (Oxford: Oxford University Press, 1994); Colin Mackerras, *China's Minority Cultures* (New York: St. Martin's Press, 1995); Colin Mackerras, *China's Ethnic Minorities and Globalisation* (London: RoutledgeCurzon, 2003). In anthropology, the project has also remained unexamined. Whereas many have discussed how non-Han communities in China operate within the fifty-six-minzu framework, and in certain instances have expressed opposition to their official designations, the history of the project whereby these categories of minzu identities were first articulated remains uncharted territory. One important exception is the work of Melissa Brown, whose work on the classification of the Tujia has been enlightening. See Melissa J. Brown, "Ethnic Classification and Culture: The Case of the Tujia in Hubei, China," *Asian Ethnicity* 2, no. 1 (2001): 55-72.

9. David I. Kertzer and Dominique Arel, "Censuses, Identity Formation, and the Struggle for Political Power," in *Census and Identity: The Politics of Race, Ethnicity, and Language in National Censuses*, ed. David I. Kertzer and Dominique Arel (Cambridge: Cambridge University Press, 2002), 1-42.

10. Lorraine Daston, "The Coming Into Being of Scientific Objects," in *Biographies of Scientific Objects*, ed. Lorraine Daston (Chicago: University of Chicago Press, 2000), 6.

11. These sites include: the National Library of China (Beijing), Central University of Nationalities (Beijing), Chinese Academy of Social Sciences (Beijing), Southwest University of Nationalities (Chengdu), Sichuan University (Chengdu), Sichuan Provincial Archives (Chengdu), Yunnan Provincial Archives (Kunming), Worcestershire Record Office (Worcester, England), and the Royal Geographic Society. I began to use these sources in my earlier published works on the Classification—see Thomas S. Mullaney, "Ethnic Classification Writ Large: The 1954 Yunnan Province Ethnic Classification Project and its Foundations in Republican-Era Taxonomic Thought," *China Information* 18, no. 2 (July 2004): 207-41; Thomas S. Mullaney, "55 + 1 = 1 or the Strange Calculus of Chinese Nationhood," *China Information* 18, no. 2 (July 2004): 197-205; Thomas S. Mullaney, "Coming to Terms with the Nation: Ethnic Classification and Scientific Statecraft in Modern China, 1928–1954" (PhD diss., Columbia University, 2006).

12. Yunnan sheng minzu shibie yanjiuzu [Yunnan Province Ethnic Classification Re-

search Team], "*Yongsheng Shuitian, Luoluo, Zhili, Ziyi, Lang'e, Talu deng minzu de yuyan* [The Languages of the Shuitian, Luoluo, Zhili, Ziyi, Lang'e, and Talu Minzu of Yongsheng County]," YNPA, Quanzong 2152, Index 3, File 78 (October 1954): 74–77; Yunnan Province Ethnic Classification Research Team, "*Yongsheng xian 'Liming' zu qingkuang diaocha baogao* [Report on the Investigation into the Situation of the 'Liming' Minzu of Yongsheng County]," YNPA, Quanzong 2152, Index 3, File 78 (1954): 1–12; Yunnan Province Ethnic Classification Research Team, "*Yongsheng di'er qu Lude xiang 'Liude' zu fangwen jilü* [Transcript of the Visitation with the 'Liude' Minzu of Lude Village in the Second Area of Yongsheng County]," YNPA, Quanzong 2152, Index 3, File 78 (September 1954): 88–97; Yunnan Province Ethnic Classification Research Team, "*Xinping xian 'Mili' zu diaocha cailiao* [Materials from the Investigation of the 'Mili' Minzu of Xinping County]," YNPA, Quanzong 2152, Index 3, File 18 (1954): 86–100.

13. Pamela Kyle Crossley, "Nationality and Difference in China: The Post-Imperial Dilemma," in *The Teleology of the Modern Nation-State: Japan and China*, ed. Joshua Fogel (Philadelphia: University of Pennsylvania Press, 2005); Magnus Fiskesjö, "Rescuing the Empire: Chinese Nation-Building in the Second Half of the Twentieth Century," *European Journal of East Asian Studies* 5, no. 1 (2006): 15–44; James Townshend, "Chinese Nationalism," in *Chinese Nationalism*, ed. Jonathan Unger (Armonk, NY: M. E. Sharpe, 1996), 1–30.

14. Joseph W. Esherick, "How the Qing Became China," in *Empire to Nation: Historical Perspectives on the Making of the Modern World*, ed. Joseph W. Esherick, Hasan Kayali, and Eric Van Young (Lanham, MD: Rowman & Littlefield, 2006).

15. Liu Xiaoyuan, *Frontier Passages: Ethnopolitics and the Rise of Chinese Communism, 1921–1945* (Stanford: Stanford University Press, 2004).

16. Carol Lee Hamrin and Timothy Cheek, eds., *China's Establishment Intellectuals* (Armonk, NY: M. E. Sharpe, 1986).

17. Partha Chatterjee, "Whose Imagined Community?" in *Nationalism: Critical Concepts in Political Science*, vol. 3, ed. John Hutchinson and Anthony D. Smith (London: Routledge, 2000), 940–45.

18. See Bernard Cohn, *Colonialism and its Forms of Knowledge: The British in India* (Princeton: Princeton University Press, 1996); Nicholas B. Dirks, *Castes of Mind: Colonialism and the Making of Modern India* (Princeton: Princeton University Press, 2001); Timothy Mitchell, *Colonising Egypt* (Berkeley: University of California Press, 1991); Timothy Mitchell, *Rule of Experts: Egypt, Techno-Politics, Modernity* (Berkeley: University of California Press, 2002); Kevin M. Doak, "Building National Identity through Ethnicity: Ethnology in Wartime Japan and After," *Journal of Japanese Studies* 27, no. 1 (Winter 2001).

19. Joseph Stalin, *Marxism and the National and Colonial Question* (San Francisco: Proletarian Publishers, 1975).

20. Dru Gladney, *Muslim Chinese: Ethnic Nationalism in the People's Republic* (Cambridge, MA: Harvard University Press, 1991).

21. Louisa Schein, *Minority Rules: The Miao and the Feminine in China's Cultural Politics* (Durham: Duke University Press, 2000), 3–4. Ralph Litzinger, *Other Chinas: The Yao and the Politics of National Belonging* (Durham: Duke University Press, 2000).

22. James Millward, "The Qing Frontier," in *Remapping China: Fissures in Historical Terrain*, ed. Gail Hershatter (Stanford: Stanford University Press, 1996), 119.

23. For example, in his seminal work Frank Dikötter refers to a conference held in 1962 wherein PRC leadership decided to abandon any official usage of terms like *tribe* and *clan*, as had been used by the Soviet Union, and to employ the term *minzu* in all situations. While my understanding of the matter does not deviate from this, the meeting in the early 1960s should be seen not as the formulation of a new policy, but simply an officialization of one that had already been in place since at least 1954. The timing of this conference, it seems to me, had less to do with China's changing viewpoint on ethnicity than with the deteriorating condition of Sino-Soviet relations. See Frank Dikötter, *The Discourse of Race in Modern China* (London: Hurst, 1992).

24. Melissa J. Brown, "On Becoming Chinese," in *Negotiating Ethnicities in China and Taiwan*, ed. Melissa J. Brown (Berkeley: Institute of East Asian Studies, University of California Press, 1997), 37–74; Mette Hansen, *Lessons in Being Chinese: Minority Education and Ethnic Identity in Southwest China* (Seattle: University of Washington Press, 1999). In her path breaking study on the Soviet Union, Francine Hirsch uncovered a similar process that she terms "double assimilation." Hirsch defines this concept as "the assimilation of a diverse population into nationality categories and, simultaneously, the assimilation of those nationally categorized groups into the Soviet state and society." As we will see in the closing chapters of the book, this definition is highly useful for understanding Chinese "nationality work" in the post-Classification period. Francine Hirsch, *Empire of Nations: Ethnographic Knowledge and the Making of the Soviet Union* (Ithaca: Cornell University Press, 2005), 14.

25. Geoffrey Bowker and Susan Leigh Star, *Sorting Things Out: Classification and Its Consequences* (Cambridge, MA: MIT Press 1999).

26. James C. Scott, *Seeing Like a State: How Certain Schemes to Improve the Human Condition Have Failed* (New Haven: Yale University Press, 1998).

27. In Alain Dessaint's *Minorities of Southwest China*, for example, the author provides readers with a table in which we learn that the Yi designation for Lisu is "Lipo," the Lisu name for Yi is "Lolo," and so forth. See Alain Y. Dessaint, *Minorities of Southwest China: An Introduction to the Yi (Lolo) and Related Peoples and an Annotated Bibliography* (New Haven, CT: HRAF Press, 1980), 6–7.

28. Alain Desrosières, "How to Make Things which Hold Together: Social Science, Statistics and the State," in *Discourses on Society. The Shaping of the Social Science Disciplines*, ed. Peter Wagner (Dordrecht: Kluwer Academic Publishers, 1991), 199.

29. Nelson Goodman, Mary Douglas, and David L. Hull, *How Classification Works: Nelson Goodman among the Social Sciences* (Edinburgh: Edinburgh University Press, 1992); Mary Douglas, "Rightness of Categories," in *How Classification Works: Nelson Goodman Among the Social Sciences*, ed. Mary Douglas (Edinburgh: Edinburgh University Press, 1992), 239–71; Paul K. Feyerabend, *Against Method* (London: Verso, 1988); Bruno Latour, *Science in Action: How to Follow Scientists and Engineers through Society* (Cambridge, MA: Harvard University Press, 1987); Ian Hacking, "Making Up People," in *The Science Studies Reader*, ed. Mario Biagiolo (New York: Routledge, 1999), 161–71. Bowker and Star, *Sorting Things Out*.

30. Bowker and Star, *Sorting Things Out*, 42.

31. Walker S. Connor, *Ethnonationalism: The Quest for Understanding* (Princeton: Princeton University Press, 1994). Outside of political science, the discipline of anthropology is

another site in which scholars have vigorously engaged each other in debates over the proper definition of ethnicity, ethnic group, and so forth. Since I approach this question as a historian, however, my interest in definitional orthodoxy is different. I am concerned with understanding how the historical actors in this period attempted to develop and disseminate their own definition of, for example, minzu. I am uninterested in trying to arrive at a standard definition myself. For more on competing definitions of key terms such as ethnicity, ethnic group, etc., see Michael Moerman, "Ethnic Identification in a Complex Civilization: Who Are the Lue?" *American Anthropologist* 67, no. 5 (1965): 1215–30; Fredrik Barth, "Introduction," in *Ethnic Groups and Boundaries,* ed. Fredrik Barth (Oslo: Universitetsforlaget, 1969), 9–38; Charles Keyes, "Towards a New Formulation of the Concept of Ethnic Group," *Ethnicity* 3 (1976): 202–13; Thomas Eriksen, *Ethnicity and Nationalism* (London: Pluto Press, 1993). In comparison with these approaches, my work is more in-line with that of Frank Dikötter, whose efforts have long been to trace the conceptual mutations over time of such central terms as *race* and *nation*. See Frank Dikötter, *The Discourse of Race in Modern China* (London: Hurst, 1992); Frank Dikötter, "Culture, 'Race' and Nation: The Formation of National Identity in Twentieth Century China," *Journal of International Affairs* 49, no. 2 (1996): 590–605; Frank Dikötter, "Racial Discourse in China: Continuities and Permutations," in *The Construction of Racial Identities in China and Japan,* ed. Frank Dikötter (Hong Kong: Hong Kong University Press, 1997), 12–33. In China, the history of the concept of minzu has also begun to receive more attention. See Peng Yingming, "*Guanyu wo guo minzu gainian lishi de chubu kaocha* [Preliminary Research on the History of the Concept of Minzu in China]," *Minzu yanjiu* 2 (1985): 5–11.

CHAPTER 1

Epigraph, p. 18: Mao Zedong, "On the Ten Major Relationships," in *Selected Works of Mao Tse-tung,* Volume 5 (Beijing: Foreign Languages Press, 1977).

1. For an overview of early PRC administrative policies, and particularly the formation of autonomous administrative areas, see Henry Schwarz, *Chinese Policies Towards Minorities: An Essay and Documents* (Bellingham: Western Washington State College Program in East Asian Studies, 1971).

2. Deng Xiaoping, "*Guanyu 'Zhonghua Renmin Gongheguo quanguo renmin daibiao dahui xuanjufa' cao'an de shuoming* [Explanation of the Draft 'Election Law for the All-Country People's Representative Congress of the People's Republic of China']," in *Minzu zhengce wenxuan* (Urumqi: Xinjiang renmin chubanshe, 1985), 201.

3. Ibid. If the county were home to one hundred thousand citizens, a proportionally small minority group would receive one delegate in the county-level People's Congress for every five hundred persons while the Han Chinese in the same county would receive one delegate for every one thousand. For minority groups whose populations exceeded 10 percent of the population of the administrative unit, the system of proportional representation was calculated exactly the same as for the local Han. This proviso was added to prevent counties and provinces with large minority populations from having a disproportionate number of non-Han delegates in their respective People's Congresses.

4. Zhongyang renmin zhengfu minzu shiwu weiyuanhui [Central People's Government Nationalities Affairs Commission], *Zhongguo shaoshu minzu jianbiao—buchong ben* [Simple Chart of the Minorities of China—Supplementary Edition] (Beijing: Nationalities Affairs Commission, 1951).

5. For this list of minzu, see appendix A. Yunnan sheng minzhengting minzu shiwu weiyuanhui [Yunnan Province Civil Affairs Department Nationalities Affairs Commission], *Yunnan xiongdi minzu zhuyao fenbu diqu jiantu* [Simple Map of the Main Distribution Regions of Brother Nationalities in Yunnan], YNPA, Quanzong 2152, Index 3, File 3 (July 20, 1951): 5.

6. For this list of minzu, see appendix B. Yunnan Province Nationalities Affairs Commission, *Yunnan sheng xiongdi minzu fenbu lüetu* [Outline Distribution Map of Brother Nationalities in Yunnan Province], YNPA, Quanzong 2152, Index 3, File 4 (1953): 1.

7. See appendices A and B for the complete list of ethnonyms in each source. Note: the total number of groups does not add up to 125, on account that some groups are listed without population data.

8. *"Yunnan sheng xuanju gongzuo baogao—chugao* [Report on Election Work in Yunnan Province—Preliminary Draft]," YNPA, Quanzong 14, Index 2, File 84. Previous mainland regimes had attempted direct enumerations, but in each case failed to carry them out. See Chen Ta, "The Beginnings of Modern Demography," *American Journal of Sociology* 52 (1947): 7–16. Chen outlines two failed attempts at empire- and nationwide enumerations, the first planned by late Qing reformers but aborted by the 1911 Revolution; the second scheduled to be held in 1947, but ultimately abandoned.

9. John S. Aird, *The Size, Composition, and Growth of the Population of Mainland China* (Washington, DC: U.S. Government Printing Office, 1961); "La Recensement de la Chine: Méthodes et Principaux Resultats," *Population* 11, no. 4 (October–December 1956), 734. For a detailed look at the evolution of the modern Chinese census, see Ping-ti Ho, *Studies on the Population of China 1368–1953* (Cambridge, MA: Harvard University Press, 1959).

10. Marc S. Abramson, *Ethnic Identity in Tang China* (Philadelphia: University of Pennsylvania Press, 2008); Hoyt Tillman, "Proto-Nationalism in Twelfth-Century China? The Case of Ch'en Liang," *Harvard Journal of Asiatic Studies* 39, no. 2 (1979): 403–28. For interesting perspectives on this debate, see Pamela Kyle Crossley, "Thinking about Ethnicity in Early Modern China," *Late Imperial China* 11, no. 1 (1990): 1–35; Mark C. Elliott, "Ethnicity in the Qing Eight Banners," in *Empire at the Margins: Culture, Ethnicity, and Frontier in Early Modern China*, ed. Pamela Kyle Crossley, Helen F. Siu, and Donald S. Sutton (Berkeley: University of California Press, 2006), 27–57.

11. She Yize, *Zhongguo tusi zhidu* [China's Native Chieftain System] (Chongqing: Zhengzhong shuju, 1944).

12. Peter Perdue, *China Marches West: The Qing Conquest of Central Eurasia* (Cambridge, MA: Harvard University Press, 2005).

13. Mark C. Elliott, *The Manchu Way: The Eight Banners and Ethnic Identity in Late Imperial China* (Stanford: Stanford University Press, 2001). For more on Qing colonial administration in the north, see James Millward, *Beyond the Pass: Economy, Ethnicity, and Empire in Qing Central Asia, 1759–1864* (Stanford: Stanford University Press, 1998); Nicola Di Cosmo, "Qing Colonial Administration in Inner Asia," *International Historical Review* 20, no. 2 (June 1998): 287–309; Peter Perdue, "Empire and Nation in Comparative Perspective:

Frontier Administration in Eighteenth-Century China," *Journal of Early Modern History* 5, no. 4 (November 2001): 282–304; Perdue, *China Marches West*.

14. Pamela Crossley, *A Translucent Mirror: History and Identity in Qing Imperial Ideology* (Berkeley: University of California Press, 1999).

15. Evelyn Rawski, "Presidential Address: Reenvisioning the Qing: The Significance of the Qing in Chinese History," *Journal of Asian Studies* 55 (November 1996).

16. Nicola Di Cosmo, "Qing Colonial Administration in Inner Asia," *International Historical Review* 20, no. 2 (June 1998): 287–309; James Millward, *Beyond the Pass: Economy, Ethnicity, and Empire in Qing Central Asia, 1759–1864* (Stanford: Stanford University Press, 1998); Peter Perdue, *China Marches West: The Qing Conquest of Central Eurasia* (Cambridge, MA: Harvard University Press, 2005).

17. C. Patterson Giersch, *Asian Borderlands: The Transformation of Qing China's Yunnan Frontier* (Cambridge, MA: Harvard University Press, 2006).

18. John E. Herman, "Empire in the Southwest: Early Qing Reforms to the Native Chieftain System," *Journal of Asian Studies* 56, no. 1 (February 1997): 47–74.

19. Giersch, *Asian Borderlands*, 45. See also Louisa Schein, *Minority Rules: The Miao and the Feminine in China's Cultural Politics* (Durham: Duke University Press, 2000). See also Dai Yingcong, "The Rise of the Southwestern Frontier under the Qing, 1640–1800" (PhD diss., University of Washington, 1996).

20. Giersch, *Asian Borderlands*, 61–62.

21. Ibid., chapter 4.

22. Ibid., 190. For more on Qing policy in the southwest, and particularly its concern over the potentially destabilizing effect of Han in-migration, see David Bello, "To Go Where No Han Could Go for Long: Malaria and the Qing Construction of Ethnic Administrative Space in Frontier Yunnan," *Modern China* 31, no. 3 (July 2005): 283–317.

23. David Atwill, *The Chinese Sultanate: Islam, Ethnicity, and the Panthay Rebellion in Southwest China, 1856–1873* (Stanford: Stanford University Press, 2005), 67–68. When viewed alongside Atwill's account, the work of Donald Sutton helps provide an even broader context for understanding the ethnic dimensions of late imperial violence along the Qing frontier. See Donald S. Sutton, "Violence and Ethnicity on a Qing Colonial Frontier," *Modern Asian Studies* 37, no. 1 (2003): 41–80.

24. Atwill, *The Chinese Sultanate*, 70–76.

25. Kai-wing Chow, "Imagining Boundaries of Blood: Zhang Binglin and the Invention of the Chinese Race in Modern China," in *Racial Identities in East Asia*, ed. Barry Sautman (Hong Kong: Hong Kong University of Science and Technology, 1995); Dru Gladney, *Muslim Chinese: Ethnic Nationalism in the People's Republic* (Cambridge, MA: Harvard University Press, 1991); Prasenjit Duara, *Rescuing History from the Nation: Questioning Narratives of Modern China* (Chicago: University of Chicago Press, 1995).

26. These processes, it bears reminding, are not synonymous with sinicization, a point illuminated by Evelyn Rawski. See Rawski, "Presidential Address"; Ping-ti Ho, "In Defense of Sinicization: A Rebuttal of Evelyn Rawski's 'Reenvisioning the Qing,'" *Journal of Asian Studies* 57 (February 1998). Beyond Confucian and Chinese practice, the Manchu had positioned themselves as patrons of their other imperial subjects as well, including the Mongolians and Tibetans. See Harold L. Kahn, *Monarchy in the Emperor's Eyes: Image and Real-*

ity in the Ch'ien-lung Reign (Cambridge, MA: Harvard University Press, 1971); David M. Farquhar, "Emperor as Bodhisattva in the Governance of the Ch'ing Empire," *Harvard Journal
of Asiatic Studies* 38, no. 1 (1978): 5-34.

27. For an examination of turn-of-the-century Han-Manchu relations, see Edward J. M.
Rhoads, *Manchus and Han: Ethnic Relations and Political Power in Late Qing and Early Re-
publican China, 1861–1928* (Seattle: University of Washington Press, 2001). On the complexity
of the nationalist and anti-Manchu thought of Zhang Binglin, see Kauko Laitinen, *Chinese
Nationalism in the late Qing Dynasty: Zhang Binglin as an Anti-Manchu Propagandist* (Lon-
don: Curzon Press, 1990). See also Young-tsu Yong, *Search for Modern Nationalism: Zhang
Binglin and Revolutionary China, 1869–1936* (Hong Kong: Oxford University Press, 1989).
Interestingly, the ambivalence of Zhang's anti-Manchu thought is a question that was taken
up earlier by Joshua Fogel when he was still a graduate student at Columbia University. See
Joshua A. Fogel, "Race and Class in Chinese Historiography: Divergent Interpretations of
Zhang Bing-lin and Anti-Manchuism in the 1911 Revolution," *Modern China* 3, no. 3 (July
1977): 346–75. For more information on late imperial anti-Manchuism itself, see Peter
Zarrow, "Historical Trauma: Anti-Manchuism and Memories of Atrocity in Late Qing
China," *History and Memory* 16, no. 2 (Fall/Winter 2004): 67–107; Ishikawa Yoshihiro, "Anti-
Manchu Racism and the Rise of Anthropology in Early 20th Century China," *Sino-Japanese
Studies* 15 (April 2003): 19–26; Ishikawa Yoshihiro, *Racialism during the Revolution of 1911
and the Rise of Chinese Anthropology* (Beijing: Central Literature Press, 2002). For one of the
caustic examples of contemporary anti-Manchu propaganda, see Tsou Jung, *The Revolutionary Army: A Chinese Nationalist Tract of 1903,* trans. John Lust (The Hague: Mouton,
1969). For more on the introduction of Darwinist and Social Darwinist theories to China,
see James Reeve Pusey, *China and Charles Darwin* (Cambridge, MA: Harvard University
Press, 1983).

28. Chow, "Imagining Boundaries of Blood," 157. For more on the discursive centrality
of "zu" and "minzu" in the articulation of an anti-Manchu position, see Kai-wing Chow, "Narrating Nation, Race and National Culture: Imagining the Hanzu Identity in Modern China,"
in *Constructing Nationhood in Modern East Asia,* ed. Kai-wing Chow, Kevin Doak, and Poshek
Fu (Ann Arbor: University of Michigan Press, 2001), 47–83.

29. Ibid.

30. Rhoads, *Manchus and Han,* 291. This subversive discourse of minzu found its way
into late Qing native-place textbooks as well. For a fascinating recent study, see May-bo Ching,
"Classifying Peoples: Ethnic Politics in late Qing Native-Place Textbooks and Gazetteers," in
The Politics of Historical Production in Late Qing and Republican China, ed. Tze-ki Hon and
Robert Culp (Leiden: Brill, 2007), 55–78.

31. Edward J. M. Rhoads, *Manchus and Han: Ethnic Relations and Political Power in Late
Qing and Early Republican China, 1861–1928* (Seattle: University of Washington Press, 2000).

32. Joseph W. Esherick, "How the Qing Became China," in *Empire to Nation: Historical
Perspectives on the Making of the Modern World,* ed. Joseph W. Esherick, Hasan Kayali, and
Eric Van Young (Lanham, MD: Rowman & Littlefield, 2006), 243–45.

33. Elliott, *The Manchu Way.* For a more concise overview of the Banner System and its
place in the formulation of Manchu identity, see Elliott, "Ethnicity in the Qing Eight Banners." Beyond Elliott's account, see also Ning Chia, "The Lifanyuan and the Inner Asian Rit-

uals in the Early Qing (1644–1795)," *Late Imperial China* 14, no. 1 (June 1993): 60–92; Evelyn S. Rawski, *The Last Emperors: A Social History of Qing Imperial Institutions* (Berkeley: University of California Press, 1998); Crossley, *A Translucent Mirror;* Peter Perdue, "Empire and Nation in Comparative Perspective."

34. For more on this troubled transition from empire to nation-state, see Pamela Crossley, "Nationality and Difference: The Post-Imperial Dilemma," *Late Imperial China* 11, no. 1 (1990): 1–35.

35. Esherick, "How the Qing Became China," 248–52.

36. For an in-depth look at Mongolia in the first half of the twentieth-century, see Xiaoyuan Liu, *Reins of Liberation: An Entangled History of Mongolian Independence, Chinese Territoriality, and Great Power Hegemony, 1911–1950* (Stanford: Stanford University Press, 2006).

37. Lin Hsiao-ting, *Tibet and Nationalist China's Frontier: Intrigues and Ethnopolitics, 1928–49* (Vancouver: University of British Columbia Press, 2006).

38. *Wuzu gonghe* has also been translated as "Five Races." Although the translation "race" does a fine job of capturing the idea of essentialism, it obscures the premodern origins of the *wuzu* formulation and its relationship with, for example, categories within the Qing banner system. To use the term *race* implies a clean break with the past, of a novel formulation based on modernist, Darwinian concept. "Five Peoples" avoids this modernist bias. Another attractive alternative is "Five Lineages," as suggested most recently by James Leibold. See James Leibold, "Competing Narratives of Racial Unity in Republican China: From the Yellow Emperor to Peking Man," *Modern China* 32, no. 2 (April 2006): 181–220.

39. John Fitzgerald, *Awakening China: Politics, Culture, and Class in the Nationalist Revolution* (Stanford: Stanford University Press, 1988), 183; James Leibold, "Positing 'minzu' within Sun Yat-sen's Discourse of 'Minzuzhuyi,'" *Journal of Asian History* 38, nos. 1–2: 163–213. In some respects, the transition from empire to nation-state brought with it similar challenges in the case of Japan as well. Having inherited the territories of the Tokugawa, territories managed according to the very different frontier logic, the Meiji Japanese state opted to extend undifferentiated sovereignty over a historically other and excluded part of the Japanese imperial domain. See David L. Howell, "Ainu Ethnicity and the Boundaries of the Early Modern Japanese State," *Past and Present* 142 (February 1994): 69–93.

40. D. K. Lieu, "The 1912 Census of China," *Bulletin de l'Institut International de Statistique* 26, no.2 (1931): 85–109.

41. Soviet leaders urged the Chinese Communists to extend the cause of national liberation to the border regions. By speaking through the CCP, they attempted to pressure the Guomindang into granting semiautonomous status to minority groups along the border, a policy which would have facilitated continued Soviet influence in Mongolia and Xinjiang. See Xiaoyuan Liu, *Frontier Passages: Ethnopolitics and the Rise of Chinese Communism, 1921–1945* (Stanford: Stanford University Press, 2004).

42. Herold J. Wiens, *China's March Toward the Tropics: A Discussion of the Southward Penetration of China's Culture, Peoples, and Political Control in Relation to the Non-Han-Chinese Peoples of South China and in the Perspective of Historical and Cultural Geography* (Hamden, CT: Shoe String Press, 1954), 151–52.

43. Liu, *Frontier Passages,* 23–24.

44. Frank Dikötter, *The Discourse of Race in Modern China* (London: Hurst, 1992).

45. Patricia Stranahan, *Underground: The Shanghai Communist Party and the Politics of Survival, 1927–1937* (Lanham, MD: Rowman & Littlefield, 1998).

46. Chiang Kai-shek, *Zhongguo zhi mingyun* [China's Destiny], 2nd rev. ed. (1943; 1947; reprint, Taipei: Zhongzheng shuju, 1986), 73; Liu, *Frontier Passages*, 73.

47. "Constitution of the Soviet Republic" (November 7, 1931), in Schwarz, *Chinese Policies Towards Minorities*.

48. Chiang, *China's Destiny*; Liu, *Frontier Passages*, 71–72. "Constitution of the Soviet Republic" (November 7, 1931), in Schwarz, *Chinese Policies Towards Minorities*, 49.

49. Harrison E. Salisbury, *The Long March* (New York: Harper and Row, 1985), 107–8.

50. Gladney, *Muslim Chinese*, 87. Beyond Gladney's account, see also Lin Huaming, "Hongjun changzheng yu minzu gongzuo [Nationality Work and the Red Army's Long March]," in *Changzheng dashidian bianweihui*, vol. 2, ed. Changzheng dashidian (Guiyang: Guizhou renmin chubanshe, 1996): 2046–51.

51. Liu, *Frontier Passages*, 80.

52. Leibold, "Competing Narratives of Racial Unity in Republican China."

53. Chiang, *China's Destiny*, 13. This quote appears in the 1947 version, not the 1943 original. In most cases, in fact, the 1947 version is much more openly assimilationist and monogenic than the original.

54. Elliott, *The Manchu Way*.

55. Chiang, *China's Destiny*, 20–21.

56. The progenitor myth of the Yellow Emperor has been treated masterfully by James Leibold. See Leibold, "Competing Narratives of Racial Writing in Republican China: From the Yellow Emperor to Peking Man," *Modern China* 32, no. 2 (2006): 181–220.

57. David Michael Deal, "National Minority Policy in Southwest China, 1911–1965" (PhD diss., University of Washington, 1971), 56.

58. Minzu wenti yanjiuhui [Nationalities Question Research Society], ed., *Huihui minzu wenti* [The Question of the Huihui Nationality] (Beijing: Minzu chubanshe, 1980).

59. Ibid., 67.

60. Ibid., 69. Communist theoretician and propagandist Chen Boda also mounted a critique against Chiang Kai-shek's manifesto *China's Destiny*. See Chen Boda, "Ping 'Zhongguo zhi mingyun'" [Critique of 'China's Destiny'], in *Minzu wenti wenxian huibian*, ed. Zhonggong zhongyang tongzhanbu (Beijing: Zhonggong zhongyang dangxiao chubanshe, 1991).

61. Matsumoto Masumi, *Chūgoku minzoku seisaku no kenkyū: Shinmatsu kara 1945-nen made no 'minzokuron' o chūshin ni* [A Study of the Ethnic Policies of China: Focusing on "Ethnic Theories" from the Late Qing until 1945] (Tokyo: Taga Shuppan, 1999). Wang Jianmin, *Zhongguo Minzuxue Shi, shang* [The History of Ethnology in China, vol. 1] (Kunming: Yunnan Education Publishing House, 1997), 228.

62. Chen Lianzhen and Huang Caoliang, *Kangzhan zhong de Zhongguo minzu wenti* [The National Question in Wartime China] (Hankou: Liming shuju, 1938), 8.

63. Ibid.

64. See Walker S. Connor, *The National Question in Marxist-Leninist Theory and Strategy* (Princeton: Princeton University Press, 1984).

65. Chen and Huang, *Kangzhan zhong de Zhongguo minzu wenti*, 44.

66. Deal, "National Minority Policy in Southwest China," 59–60.

67. Schwarz, *Chinese Policies Towards Minorities*, 52–53.

68. Ibid.

69. Huang Guangxue, ed., *Dangdai Zhongguo de minzu gongzuo (shang)* [Ethnicity Work in Contemporary China, vol. 1] (Beijing: Dangdai zhongguo congshu bianji weiyuanhui, 1993), 66.

70. John DeFrancis, "National and Minority Policies," *Annals of the American Academy of Political and Social Science* 277 (1951), 154. In the early Communist period, efforts of state integration and consolidation extended beyond ethnopolitical administration, of course. For a broader look at the administration of Yunnan in the early People's Republic, see Dorothy J. Solinger, *Regional Government and Political Integration in Southwest China, 1949–1954: A Case Study* (Berkeley: University of California Press, 1977).

71. John Herman, "The Cant of Conquest: Tsui Offices and China's Political Incorporation of the Southwestern Frontier," in *Empire at the Margins: Culture, Ethnicity, and Frontier in Early Modern China*, ed. Pamela Kyle Crossley, Helen F. Siu, and Donald S. Sutton (Berkeley: University of California Press, 2006), 135–70; John Huang, *Dangdai Zhongguo de minzu gongzuo (shang)*, 46.

72. For a fascinating study of the early Soviet censuses, and Soviet nationalities categories, see Francine Hirsch, *Empire of Nations: Ethnographic Knowledge and the Making of the Soviet Union* (Ithaca: Cornell University Press, 2005). For more on the 1939 Soviet Census as a model for China's 1953–54 census, see Lawrence Krader and John Aird, "Sources of Demographic Data on Mainland China," *American Sociological Review* 24, no. 5 (October 1959): 623–30.

73. Huang, *Zhongguo de minzu shibie*, 147. This is also a four-character idiomatic expression derived from the longer passage "*shiwu yi zhuren suo cheng zhi ming wei ming*" (see glossary for characters).

74. The phrase "*ming cong zhuren*" is sometimes glossed as "names follow their bearer's will," as Stéphane Gros does in the special edition of *China Information* for which I served as guest editor. See Stéphane Gros, "The Politics of Names: The Identification of the Dulong (Drung) of Northwest Yunnan," *China Information* 18 (July 2004). For those under the age of eighteen, minzu status was selected by one's parents. In these cases, another possible gloss is "names shall be chosen by head-of-household *(zhuren)*."

75. Theodore Shabad, "Counting 600 Million Chinese," *Far Eastern Survey* (April 1956): 60–61. In betrothal adoption, wealthy families served as the caretakers for orphan girls with the intention of marrying them to their sons. For a detailed look at betrothal adoption, see Arthur P. Wolf and Chieh-shan Huang, *Marriage and Adoption in China, 1845–1945* (Stanford: Stanford University Press, 1980).

76. Shabad, "Counting 600 Million Chinese," 60.

77. "La Recensement de la Chine: Méthodes et Principaux Resultats," 731–32.

78. Shabad, "Counting 600 Million Chinese," 59–60. In addition to the problem of double-counting, there was also the issue of mobile populations, such as boat dwellers. It was decided that their official place of residence should be the port of call where their vessel was registered. In cases of unregistered vessels, individuals would have to document their vessels as part of the census process. In this way, the census and voter registration was also in-

strumental in the sedentarization of the population, and thus, the further consolidation of Communist state power.

79. Central Office of Investigation and Registration (*Zhongyang diaocha dengji ban-gongshi*), 1953.

80. Katherine Palmer Kaup, *Creating the Zhuang: Ethnic Politics in China* (Boulder, CO: Lynne Rienner Publishers, 2000), 55–56.

81. Ibid.

82. "*Yunlong xian jiceng puxuan gongzuo zongjie* [Summary of Grassroot Voting Work in Yunlong County," YNPA, Quanzong 2183, Index 1, File 38 (April 1954): 193.

83. "Yongsheng County Report on the Voter Registration/Census of 1953–1954," YNPA, Quanzong 2183, Index 1, File 13 (July 16, 1954).

84. "*Yunnan sheng Kunming shi renkou diaocha dengji gongzuo zongjie* [Summary of Population Investigation and Registration Work in Kunming City, Yunnan Province]," YNPA, Quanzong 83, Index 1, File 32 (July 24, 1954): 7.

85. The literature on the 1953–54 census and the Classification frequently cites Yunnan as having over 260 distinct *nyms* in the inaugural census. See Fei Xiaotong, *Toward a People's Anthropology* (Beijing: New World Press, 1981). According to my own analysis of census tabulations from each county within Yunnan, it appears that census officials recorded somewhere in the order of 200 ethnic names, not the 260-plus often cited by Fei and others. The remaining fifty-odd groups, if they were indeed recorded at all, seem to have been collapsed into the miscellaneous category of "other minzu" *(qita minzu)*. By virtue of the fact that their ethnonyms had not been recorded, these fifty names could not have been submitted for review to the Classification team, and thus stood no chance of being officially recognized by the state.

86. It should be noted that two "groups" disappeared from our history as soon as they entered: the "unclear minzu" (population three) and the "other minzu" (population 38,148). By virtue of the fact that the names of the component groups were not recorded, they stood no chance of being officially recognized by the state.

87. James C. Scott, *Seeing Like a State: How Certain Schemes to Improve the Human Condition Have Failed* (New Haven: Yale University Press, 1998).

88. We cannot dismiss this possibility outright—as linguists have documented, there can and do exist "last peoples." For a thought-provoking study of "last speakers," see Lenore A. Grenoble and Lindsay J. Whaley, *Endangered Languages: Language Loss and Community Response* (Cambridge: Cambridge University Press, 1998). However, the default usage of the term *group* when describing those names that appears in the inaugural census demands reconsideration.

89. Dissemination of information regarding Communist minority policies constituted one of the major objectives in a series of early pre-Classification PRC campaigns led by the "Nationalities Visitation Teams" *(minzu fangwentuan)*. See Zhongyang minzu fangwentuan, "Xinan minzu fangwentuan shuji," (Beijing, 1951).

90. As outlined by Chen, the inaugural NPC was scheduled to host 1,200 delegates. See Chen Ta, "New China's Population Census of 1953 and its Relations to National Reconstruction and Demographic Research," *Bulletin de l'Institut International de Statistique* 36, no. 2 (1957): 263.

91. "La Recensement de la Chine: Méthodes et Principaux Resultats," 745.

92. Prior to 1954, the *Common Program* served as the working constitution of the PRC. Article 53 reads: "Article 53. All national minorities shall have freedom to develop their dialects and languages, to preserve or reform their traditions, customs and religious beliefs. The People's Government shall assist the masses of the people of all national minorities to develop their political, economic, cultural and educational construction work" (Schwarz, *Chinese Policies Towards Minorities*, 52–53).

93. Fang Fuqi, *Fang Guoyu zhuan* [Biography of Fang Guoyu] (Kunming: Yunnan daxue chubanshe, 2001), 141. Fang Fuqi cites May 15 as the official formulation. Given the chronology of Classification research, which began in April, this date appears now to be inaccurate— except if we treat May 15 as the day when the team was made official.

94. A passage by Ralph Litzinger provides a case in point: "The new revolutionary regime," Litzinger writes, "asked minorities to step forward and register the names by which they wished to be identified. By 1955, more than four hundred different ethnic groups had taken up the call." See Ralph Litzinger, *Other Chinas: The Yao and the Politics of National Belonging* (Durham: Duke University Press, 2000), 7. Louisa Schein adopts the term *groups* as well, reflecting a trend that is widespread in our understanding of the 1953–54 census. See Schein, *Minority Rules*, 84.

CHAPTER 2

Epigraph, page 42: Ding Su, "*Xinan minzu de fenlei fenbu ji yidong* [Categories, Distributions, and Migrations of Ethnic Groups in the Southwest]," *Renwen kexue xuebao* 1, no. 1 (1941): 137.

1. Lin Yueh-hwa [Lin Yaohua], *The Golden Wing, A Sociological Study of Chinese Familism* (London: Kegan Paul Trench Trubner, 1947); Lin Yueh-hua [Lin Yaohua], *The Lolo of Liangshan* (New Haven: HRAF Press, 1961).

2. Yanjing-Tsinghua-Peking University Summer 1950 Inner Mongolia Work and Research Team, ed., *Neimenggu Hunameng minzu diaocha baogao* [Report on Ethnological Investigation in Hunameng, Inner Mongolia] (Hohhot: Inner Mongolia Nationalities Press, 1997).

3. Zhaona Situ (Junast) and Li Hengpu, *Dangdai Zhongguo minzu yuyanxuejia* [Contemporary Chinese Minority Linguists] (Xining: Qinghai renmin chubanshe, 1989), 302–5.

4. Wang Xiaoyi, Interview, Beijing, February 19, 2003.

5. Wang Xiaoyi, Interview, Beijing, January 21, 2003, citing his journal from the 1954 lecture on "The Utility of Language in the Course of Investigations *[Yuyan zai diaocha li de zuoyong]*."

6. Luo Changpei and Fu Maoji, "*Guonei shaoshuminzu yuyan wenzi de qingkuang* [The Situation of Linguistic Scripts for Domestic Minority Nationalities]," *Zhongguo yuwen* (March 1954): 21–26.

7. Worcestershire Records Office (hereafter WRO) Bulk Accession 5571 Reference 705:385 Parcel 1.

8. WRO Bulk Accession 9015 Reference 705:385 Parcel 1.

9. Pushto (Pashto) and Persian are two prominent languages in Afghanistan. Hindus-

tani (Urdu) was the language of colonial administration in British India. For more on British colonial language policy, see Bernard Cohn, "The Command of Language and the Language of Command," in *Subaltern Studies IV*, ed. Ranajit Guhat (Delhi: Oxford University Press, 1987): 276–329. For the relationship between Hindustani, Hindi, and Urdu, see David Lelyveld, "Colonial Knowledge and the Fate of Hindustani," *Comparative Studies in Society and History* 35, no. 4 (October 1993): 665–82.

10. WRO Bulk Accession 9015 Reference 705:385 Parcel 1.

11. The passes in question, eight in all, were constructed in the Ming by Chen Yongbin (1547–1617) following the sixteenth century war between the Ming and the Taungoo dynasty (1486–1752). See Yingcong Dai, "A Disguised Defeat: The Myanmar Campaign of the Qing Dynasty," *Modern Asian Studies* 38, no. 1 (2004): 145–89.

12. Henry Rodolph Davies, *Yün-nan, the Link Between India and the Yangtze* (Cambridge: Cambridge University Press, 1909), 98–99.

13. Ibid., 27.

14. Ibid., 53.

15. Archibald R. Colquhoun, *The "Overland" to China* (London: Harper, 1900); A. R. Colquhoun, "On the Aboriginal and Other Tribes of Yunnan and the Shan Country," *Journal of the Anthropological Institute of Great Britain and Ireland* 13 (1884): 3–4.

16. Samuel R. Clarke, *Among the tribes in South-west China* (Taipei: Ch'eng Wen Publishing, 1970), xx.

17. A. F. Legendre, *Au Yunnan et dans le Massif du Kin-ho* (Paris: Fleuve d'or, 1913).

18. Joseph Francis Charles Rock, *Studies in Na-khi Literature* (Hanoi: Bulletin de l'École Française d'Extrême-Orient, 1938); Joseph Francis Charles Rock, *The Ancient Na-khi Kingdom of Southwest China* (Cambridge, MA: Harvard University Press, 1947); Joseph Francis Charles Rock, M. Harders-Steinhäuser, and Georg Jayme, *The Life and Culture of the Na-khi Tribe on the China-Tibet Borderland* (Wiesbaden: Verzeichnis der orientalischen Handschriften in Deutschland, 1963).

19. Cen Jiawu, *Cen Jiawu minzu yanjiu wenji* [Ethnological Writings of Cen Jiawu] (Beijing: Minzu chubanshe, 1992), 135.

20. Alain Desrosières, "How to Make Things which Hold Together: Social Science, Statistics and the State," in *Discourses on Society: The Shaping of the Social Science Disciplines*, ed. Peter Wagner (Dordrecht: Kluwer Academic Publishers, 1991), 212.

21. James C. Scott, *Seeing Like a State: How Certain Schemes to Improve the Human Condition Have Failed* (New Haven: Yale University Press, 1998), 1.

22. Jane Caplan and John Torpey, eds., *Documenting Individual Identity: The Development of State Practices in the Modern World* (Princeton: Princeton University Press, 2001), 1.

23. Nicholas B. Dirks, *Castes of Mind: Colonialism and the Making of Modern India* (Princeton: Princeton University Press, 2001), 43–45.

24. WRO Bulk Accession 5301 Reference 705:385 Parcel 1.

25. "Review of 'Yunnan, the Link between India and the Yangtze,'" *Bulletin of the American Geographical Society* 41 (1909): 652.

26. For an economical but in-depth overview of French and British colonial interests in the region, see John L. Christian, "Anglo-French Rivalry in Southeast Asia: Its Historical Geography and Diplomatic Climate," *Geographical Review* 31, no. 2 (April 1941): 272–82.

27. Davies, *Yün-nan,* 114.

28. Ibid.

29. WRO Bulk Accession 4351 Reference 705:385 Parcel 1.

30. Ibid.

31. Ibid. As with many other amateur philologists, it is unclear what sort of training Davies received in phonetic transcription. It is possible that he received training in phoneticization at Eton as part of his language training. See WRO Bulk Accession 9015 Reference 705:385 Parcel 1. Special thanks to David Willis, Joseph Salmons, and Martha Ratliff for their assistance in this question about amateur linguistics.

32. Quoted in Dell Hymes, "Notes Toward a History of Linguistic Anthropology," *Anthropological Linguistics* 5, no. 1 (January 1963): 65.

33. Davies, *Yün-nan,* 353–54. See R. L. Trask, *The Dictionary of Historical and Comparative Linguistics* (Edinburgh: Edinburgh University Press, 2000), 39.

34. Dell Hymes, *Essays in the History of Linguistic Anthropology—Amsterdam Studies in the Theory and History of Linguistic Science III Studies in the History of Linguistics,* vol. 25 (Amsterdam: John Benjamin, 1983), 64–67. See also George A. Grierson, *Linguistic Survey of India* (Delhi: Motilal Banarsidass, 1967), 4–13.

35. Abbé Desgodin, "Mots principaux des langues de certaines tribus," *Bulletin de la Société de Géographie* 5 (January–June 1873): 144.

36. Holt S. Hallett, "Exploration Survey for a Railway Connection between India, Siam, and China," *Proceedings of the Royal Geographical Society and Monthly Record of Geography* 8, no. 1 (January 1886): 1–20; Paul Vial, *De la Langue et de l'Écriture Indigenes au Yün-nân* (Paris: Ernest Leroux, 1890); Henri d'Orléans, "From Yun-nan to British India," *The Geographical Journal* 7, no. 3 (March 1896): 300–309; R. F. Johnson, *From Peking To Mandalay: A Journey From North China To Burma Through Tibetan Szechuan And Yunnan* (Bangkok: White Lotus, 2001).

37. Hymes, *Essays in the History of Linguistic Anthropology,* 69–72.

38. Desgodin, "Mots Principaux," 144.

39. Worcester Record Office BA 4351 Rec 705:385 Parcel 1.

40. Ibid.

41. Geoffrey Sampson, *Schools of Linguistics* (Stanford: Stanford University Press, 1980), 18. On importance of Schleicher and his centrality to history of linguistics see Otto Jespersen, *Language: Its Nature, Development and Origin* (London: Allen & Unwin, 1922), 71; R. H. Robins, *A Short History of Linguistics* (Bloomington: Indiana University Press, 1967); John Waterman, *Perspectives in Linguistics* (Chicago: University of Chicago Press, 1970), 31–32; John Peter Maher, "More on the History of the Comparative Methods: The Tradition of Darwinism in August Schleicher's Work," *Anthropological Linguistics* 8 (1966): 1–12; A. Schleicher, *Darwinism Tested by the Science of Language,* trans A. V. W. Bikkers (London: John Camden Hotten, 1869), 13–14; Henry M. Hoeningswald, "On the History of the Comparative Method," *Anthropological Linguistics* 5, no. 1 (1963): 1–11; Lisa Taub, "Evolutionary Ideas and 'Empirical' Methods: The Analogy between Language and Species in Works by Lyell and Schleicher," *British Journal for the History of Science* 26, no. 2 (June 1993): 171–93; Linda Dowling "Victorian Oxford and the Science of Language," *Publication of the Modern Language Association* 97, no. 2 (1982): 160–78; A. Schleicher, *A Compendium of the Compara-*

tive Grammar of Indo-European, Sanskrit, Greek, and Latin Languages, trans. H. Bendall (London: Teubnee, 1874); E. F. K. Koerner, "Towards a Historiography of Linguistics: 19th and 20th Century Paradigm," in *History of Linguistic Thought and Contemporary Linguistics,* ed. Herman Parret (Berlin: Walter de Gruyter, 1976); Hymes, *Studies in the History of Linguistics.*

42. Bernard Cohn, *Colonialism and Its Forms of Knowledge: The British in India* (Princeton: Princeton University Press, 1996), 54.

43. Cohn, *Colonialism and Its Forms of Knowledge,* 55. David Lelyveld also phrased it well when he described the contemporary British linguistics as an "ideology of languages as separate, autonomous objects of the world which could be classified, arranged and deployed as media of exchange." See Lelyveld, "Colonial Knowledge and the Fate of Hindustani," *Comparative Studies in Society and History* 35, no. 4 (October 1993): 669.

44. Cited in Taub, "Evolutionary Ideas and 'Empirical' Methods," 161, 181; J. W. Burrow, "The Uses of Philology in Victorian England"; Hilary Henson, *British Social Anthropologists and Language: A History of Separate Development* (Oxford: Clarendon, 1974); M. Silverstein, "Encountering Language and Languages of Encounter in North American Ethnohistory," *Journal of Linguistic Anthropology* 6, no. 2 (1994): 126–44; A. J. Schutz, *The Voices of Eden: A History of Hawaiian Language Studies* (Honolulu: University of Hawai'i Press, 1994); A. M. Davies, *Nineteenth-Century Linguistics,* vol. 4, *History of Linguistics Series,* ed. G. Lepschy (London: Longman, 1998); Johannes Fabian, *Language and Colonial Power: The Appropriation of Swahili in the Former Belgian Congo, 1880–1938* (Berkeley: University of California Press, 1986); F. J. Newmeyer, *The Politics of Linguistics* (Chicago: University of Chicago Press, 1986).

45. Burrow, "The Uses of Philology in Victorian England."

46. Peter Penner, *Robert Needham Cust, 1821–1909: A Personal Biography* (New Delhi: Chanakya Publications, 1987). See also Grierson, *Linguistic Survey of India.*

47. For an analysis of Gallatin, see Robert E. Bieder, *Science Encounters the Indian, 1820–1880: The Early Years of American Ethnology* (Norman: University of Oklahoma Press, 1986).

48. J. W. Powell. "Indian Linguistic Families North of Mexico," *Bureau of American Ethnology* 7 (1891): 1–142.

49. Frederick W. Hodge, ed., *Handbook of American Indians* (Washington, DC: Bureau of American Ethnology Bulletin 30, 1907, 1911).

50. A. L. Kroeber, quoted in Hymes, "Notes Toward a History of Linguistic Anthropology," 82.

51. Quoted in Hymes, *Essays in the History of Linguistic Anthropology,* 135.

52. Davies, *Yün-nan,* 1.

53. Ibid., 369.

54. Ibid., 224–25.

55. Michel Foucault, *The Order of Things: An Archaeology of the Human Sciences* (New York: Vintage Books, 1970), 135.

56. Ibid., 132.

57. Ibid.

58. WRO Bulk Accession 4238 Reference 705:3885 Parcel 3.

59. H. R. Davies, "Reviewed work(s): In Farthest Burma by F. Kingdon Ward," *Geographical Journal* 58, no. 3 (September 1921): 230–32. H. R. Davies and David Prain, "From the Yangtze to the Irrawaddy: Discussion," *Geographical Journal* 62, no. 1 (July 1923): 18–20.

H. R. Davies, "Review: The Tibetan Border," *Geographical Journal* 63, no. 3 (March 1924): 247–49. (This last citation is a review of *The Mystery Rivers of Tibet by F. Kingdon Ward and To the Alps of Chinese Tibet* by J. W. Gregory and C. J. Gregory.)

60. Reference to this lecture is made in Ding Wenjiang, *Cuanwen congke* (Shanghai: Zhongyang yanjiuyuan lishi yuyan yanjiusuo zhuankan, 1935), 1. For more on Ding Wenjiang, see Charlotte Furth, *Ting Wen-chiang: Science and China's New Culture* (Cambridge, MA: Harvard University Press, 1970).

61. Li Ji, *The Formation of the Chinese People: An Anthropological Inquiry* (New York: Russell and Russell, 1967), 254.

62. Cen, *Cen Jiawu minzu yanjiu wenji*, 137.

63. Peter Becker, "The Standardized Gaze: The Standardization of the Search Warrant in Nineteenth-Century Germany," in *Documenting Individual Identity: The Development of State Practices in the Modern World.*, ed. Jane Caplan and John Torpey (Princeton: Princeton University Press, 2001), 139–63.

64. Guoli zhongyang yanjiuyuan [Academia Sinica], "*Guoli zhongyang yanjiuyuan zongbaogao 1932* [Summary Report of the Academia Sinica, 1932]," 323.

65. Ling Chunsheng, "*Yunnan minzu de dili fenbu* [The Geographic Distribution of Ethnic Groups in Yunnan]," *Dili xuebao* 3 (1936). Laura Hostetler, *Qing Colonial Enterprise: Ethnography and Cartography in Early Modern China* (Chicago: University of Chicago Press, 2001), 136, 148.

66. Ling, "*Yunnan minzu de dili fenbu.*"

67. The other three included Taiweisi, Tanweisi, and Deweishi. This last name is the one which appears on Davies' passport which he used during his travels. WRO Bulk Accession 5571 Reference 705:385 Parcel 1.

68. Edward R. Tufte, *Envisioning Information: The Visual Display of Quantitative Information* (Chesire, CT: Graphics Press, 1990), 33.

69. Geoffrey Bowker and Susan Leigh Star, *Sorting Things Out: Classification and Its Consequences* (Cambridge, MA: MIT Press, 1999), 44.

70. For an overview of Gu Jiegang's place within the history of scholarship on the northwest, see Laurence A. Schneider, *Ku Chieh-kang and China's New History: Nationalism and the Quest for Alternative Traditions* (Berkeley: University of California Press, 1971); Tze-ki Hon, "Ethnic and Cultural Pluralism: Gu Jiegang's Vision of a New China in His Studies of Ancient History," *Modern China* 22 (1996): 315–40; and Jonathan Lipman, *Familiar Strangers: A History of Muslims in Northwest China* (Seattle: University of Washington Press, 1997), 17.

71. Chang-tai Hung, *Going to the People: Chinese Intellectuals and Folk Literature, 1918–1937* (Cambridge, MA: Harvard University Press, 1985), 171–72. See also Chow Tse-tsung, *The May Fourth Movement: Intellectual Revolution in Modern China* (Stanford: Stanford University Press, 1967); Vera Schwarcz, *The Chinese Enlightenment: Intellectuals and the Legacy of the May Fourth Movement of 1919* (Berkeley: California University Press, 1986).

72. Wu Wenzao, "*Xiandao shequ shidi yanjiu de yiyi he gongyong,*" in *Renleixue Shehuixue yanjiu wenji* (Beijing: Minzu Chubanshe, 1990), 147.

73. Bruno Latour, *Science in Action: How to Follow Scientists and Engineers through Society* (Cambridge, MA: Harvard University Press, 1987), 232.

74. Ling, "*Yunnan minzu de dili fenbu,*" 533.

75. In a conference held in Dali, Yunnan, in August 2007, a group of commentators suggested that these adjustments might be best thought of as the localization or "sinification" of Western theories, assuming that the motivation of these changes must be tied to an anxiety over the Euro-American origins of the Davies model. Whereas sinification is important elsewhere in the history of Chinese ethnology (see the works by Gregory Guldin and Wang Jianmin, among others), I think this interpretation needs to be reconsidered. Ling, Ma, Ding, and others were not worried about "sinifying" the Davies model so much as *ethnologizing* it—that is, transforming it from one expressly connected to language to one that, at least putatively, is concerned with ethnic identity. The anxiety of these scholars stems not from the Western origins of the Davies model, but from its *linguistic* origins.

76. Here we have further corroboration of the point in note 75. Tao Yunkui recognized the anxiety among his colleagues for what it was: a concern with ethnologizing what was unquestionably a model of *language*. Tao Yunkui, "*Jige Yunnan tuzu de xiandai dili fenbu ji qi renkou zhi guji* [The Present Geographic Distribution of a Few Local Yunnanese Ethnic Groups and the Ancient Traces of their Populations]," *Guoli zhongyang yanjiuyuan lishi yuyan yanjiusuo renleixue jikan* 7 (1938): 422.

77. Gregory Guldin, *The Saga of Anthropology in China: From Malinowski to Mao* (Armonk, NY: M. E. Sharpe, 1994), 57.

78. Tsuin-chen Ou, "Education in Wartime China," in *Nationalist China during the Sino-Japanese War, 1937-1945*, ed. Paul K. T. Sih (Hicksville, NY: Exposition Press, 1977), 99. This figure, furthermore, does not account for those institutions that were already located in the interior.

79. The year 1938 was a landmark one. In April, Peking University, Tsinghua University, and Nankai University relocated to Kunming to form the Southwest Associated University (*Xinan Lianhe Daxue* or "Lianda"). Also in 1938, Central University relocated to Chongqing (Sichuan), Guangzhou's Zhongshan University relocated to Dengjiang (Yunnan), Wuhan University relocated to Leshan (Sichuan), and Jinlu University relocated to Chengdu to form part of the amalgamated Huaxi Xiehe University. Soon thereafter, Wuchang Huazhong University relocated to Yunnan and Shanghai's Fudan University relocated to Chongqing. That autumn, the Academia Sinica Institute of History and Philology relocated to Longquan, Yunnan, and Zhongshan University relocated to Chengjiang, Yunnan. See Ou, "Education in Wartime China," 117. See also Wang Jianmin, *Zhongguo minzuxue shi, shang*, 216-20. Fei Xiaotong, *Earthbound China: A Study of Rural Economy in Yunnan* (Chicago: University of Chicago Press, 1945), xiii. In 1940, Fei Xiaotong was appointed head of the research station after Wu Wenzao relocated to Chongqing, Sichuan. See Lin Yaohua and Yu Xiangwen, *Liangshan Yi jia* [The Lolo of Liangshan] (Taipei: Nantian shuju, 1978), 116.

80. Wang, *Zhongguo minzuxue shi, shang*, 217.

81. Lin and Yu, *Liangshan Yi jia*, 116.

82. Wang, *Zhongguo minzuxue shi, shang*, 402.

83. Wu Zelin, *Minzu yanjiu wenji* (Beijing: Minzu chubanshe, 1991), 1.

84. Fei Xiaotong, *Toward a People's Anthropology* (Beijing: New World Press, 1981), 9.

85. Fei, *Earthbound China*, 9.

86. Karin Knorr Cetina, *Epistemic Cultures: How the Sciences Make Knowledge* (Cambridge, MA: Harvard University Press, 1999), 26.

87. Ibid.

88. Knorr Cetina, *Epistemic Cultures*, 27.

89. Ibid.

90. Luo Changpei and Xing Qinglan, *Lianshan Baiyi yuwen chutan* [A Preliminary Investigation of the Baiyi Language of Lianshan] (Beijing: Beijing daxue chubanshe, 1950).

91. Luo Changpei, "*Cong yuyan shang lun Yunnan minzu de fenlei* [On the Categorization of Yunnanese Ethnic Groups from the Perspective of Language]," *Bianzheng gonglun* 1 (March 1942).

92. Taiweisi [H. R. Davies], *Yunnan ge Yizu ji qi yuyan yanjiu* [Research on the Barbarians of Yunnan and their Languages], trans. Zhang Junmai (Shanghai: Shangwu yinshuguan, 1939). Note that the title is different from the 1909 original, on account that Zhang only translated the appendix of Davies' text. H. R. Davies, *Shina minzokuron* [On the minzu of China], trans. Suyama Taku (Tokyo: Keiyou Shobou, 1940).

93. Taiweisi [H. R. Davies], *Yunnan ge Yizu ji qi yuyan yanjiu*. Zhou was also a member of the Bai minority group and is perhaps most well known in China for being the man whose calligraphy is prominently featured in the Stone Forest in Yunnan.

94. Luo Changpei, "*Cong yuyan shang lun Yunnan minzu de fenlei*," 45.

95. Ling Chunsheng, "*Yunnan minzu de dili fenbu*," 539.

96. Ling Chunsheng, "*Tang dai Yunnan de wuman yu baiman kao* [Reflections on the Wuman and Baiman of Tang Dynasty Yunnan]," *Renleixue jikan* 1, no. 1 (1938). Ma Changshou, "*Sichuan gudai minzu lishi kaodeng*," *Zhongguo qingnian jikan* 2 (January 1941).

97. Ding Su, "*Xinan minzu de fenlei fenbu ji yidong*"; Wei Huilin, "*Zhongguo minzu fenlei lunlüe* [On the Categorization of Chinese Ethnic Groups]," *Bianjiang yanjiu tongxun* 1 (March 1942); Rui Yifu, "*Zhonghua minzu de zhipai ji qi fenbu* [Branches of the Zhonghua Minzu and their Distribution]," *Zhongguo minzu xuehui shi zhounian jinian lunwenji* [Selected Essays in Commemoration of the Tenth Year Anniversary of the Chinese Ethnological Association] (December 1944); Rui Yifu, "*Xinan bianmin yu Miandian renmin* [The Border Peoples of the Southwest and the People of Burma]," *Bianzheng gonglun* 4 (January 1945); Rui Yifu, "*Zai lun zhonghua minzu de zhipai ji qi fenbu* [Once More on the Branches of the Zhonghua Minzu and their Distribution]," *Minzuxue yanjiu jikan* 5 (April 1946); Lin Yaohua, "Social Life of Aboriginal Groups In and Around Yunnan," *Journal of the West China Border Research Society* 15 (1944); Cen Jiawu, "*Lun minzu yu zongzu* [On ethnicity and lineage]," *Bianzheng gonglun* 3 (April 1944).

98. Huang Wenshan, "*Cen zhu 'Xinan minzu wenhua luncong' xu* [Preface to Cen's 'Theses on the Culture of the Ethnic Groups of the Southwest']," *Shehui xuexun* 5 (1947): 9.

99. Ding, "*Xinan minzu de fenlei fenbu ji yidong*," 137. Interestingly, the linguistic paradigm in Chinese ethnotaxonomy seems to have taken hold among foreign scholars at this time as well. In his 1942 essay "Ethnographic Investigations of China," S. M. Shirokogoroff argued that the study of ethnic groups of China required

preliminary work of distinction of groups from some point of view. Since the language is perhaps the easiest and the most simple character, it may be put at the basis of the map which at least will show the approximate territorial limits of groups which are distinct at least in respect to the spoken language . . . We may expect from such an investigation that there will be revealed groups speaking not only Chinese dialects with sometimes undefinable boundaries, but also non-Chinese languages, and an ethnical map, the first important result of inquiry, will be ready. If we have such a map we may not rely upon trying village after village, but proceed with our investigation of ethnical units where it will be possible to distinguish easily common elements from the accidental.

See S. M. Shirokogoroff, "Ethnographic Investigations of China," *Folklore Studies* 1 (1942): 1–2.

100. Wang, *Zhongguo minzuxue shi, xia*, 64.

101. These seven scholars included Zhou Yaowen, An Rong, Xu Lin, Chang Hongen, Tong Wei, Liu Lu, and Fu Maoji. See Xu Lin, "*Cangshan erhai lian yulong xueshan qing*," *Dali wenhua* 1 (1992). Luo Changpei and Fu Maoji, "*Guonei shaoshuminzu yuyan wenzi de qingkuang.*"

102. Author's interview with the late Xu Lin, wife of Fu Maoji and participant in both the 1952 linguistic survey and the 1954 Ethnic Classification Project. See also Xu, "*Cangshan erhai lian yulong xueshan qing.*"

103. Yunnan Province Nationalities Affairs Commission, "*Yunnan xiongdi minzu zhuyao fenbu diqu jiantu* [Simplified Map of the Main Regional Distributions of Brother Nationalities in Yunnan]," YNPA, Quanzong 2152, Index 3, File 3 (1951): 5; Yunnan Province Nationalities Affairs Commission, "*Yunnan sheng xiongdi minzu fenbu lüetu* [Preliminary Distribution Map of Brother Nationalities in Yunnan Province]," YNPA, Quanzong 2152, Index 3, File 4 (1953).

104. Yunnan Province Nationalities Affairs Commission, "*Yunnan sheng shaoshu minzu tongzu yicheng fenlei biao (caogao)* [Chart of Yunnan Minorities Who Are the Same but Have Different Names—Draft]" (Kunming: Yunnan Province Nationalities Affairs Commission, 1953).

105. WRO Bulk Accession 9015 Reference 705:385 Parcel 1.

106. Liu Geping, May 11, 1951 speech delivered at the eighty-fourth government administration meeting of the Government Administration Council in the "Summary Report on the Central Nationalities Visitation Team's Visits to the Nationalities of the Southwest (*Zhongyang minzu fangwentuan fangwen xinan ge minzu de zongjie baogao*)."

107. Yang Yucai, "*Yunnan sheng jige zhuyao shaoshu minzu de dili fenbu* [The Geographic Distribution of a Few Main Minority Nationalities in Yunnan Province]," *Dili zhishi* (September 1954).

CHAPTER 3

Epigraph, p. 69: Lin Yaohua, "*Guanyu minzu shibie wenti de yijian* [Opinions Regarding the Problem of Ethnic Classification]," YNPA, Quanzong 2152, Index 1, File 46 (1954): 47.

1. April 30, 1954. Chen Yongling's address, as recorded in the diary of Wang Xiaoyi. Wang Xiaoyi, Interview, Beijing, January 23, 2003.

2. Q. C. Jing, "Development of Psychology in China," *International Journal of Psychology* 29, no. 6 (1994): 667–75; Ambrose Yeo-Chi King and Wang Tse-Sang, "The Development

and Death of Chinese Academic Sociology: A Chapter in the Sociology of Sociology," *Modern Asian Studies* 12, no. 1 (1978): 37–58.

3. Fang Fuqi, *Fang Guoyu zhuan* [Biography of Fang Guoyu] (Kunming: Yunnan daxue chubanshe, 2001), 141; Wang Xiaoyi, Interview, Beijing, January 3, 2003.

4. Jiang was not an official member of the Yunnan Province Ethnic Classification research team, but did serve as an advisor.

5. Wang Jianmin, *Zhongguo minzuxue shi: Shang, 1903–1949* [The History of Ethnology in China: Part 1, 1903–1949] (Kunming: Jiaoyu chubanshe, 1997), 379.

6. Wang, *Zhongguo minzuxue shi: shang*, 406.

7. Xin Liu, "Past and Present: Two Moments in the History of Chinese Anthropology," in *The Making of Anthropology in East and Southeast Asia*, ed. Shinji Yamashita, Joseph Bosco, Bosco Yamashita, and J. S. Eades (Oxford: Berghahn Books, 2004).

8. Wang, *Zhongguo Minzuxue shi: shang*, 385.

9. Xu Jiahua, ed., *Li Qunjie wenji* [The Writings of Li Qunjie] (Kunming: Yunnan minzu chubanshe, 2001), 1–7, 575.

10. For more on Zhang Chong, see Li Qiao, *Yizu jiang Zhang Chong zhuanji* [A Biography of the Yi General Zhang Chong] (Chengdu: Sichuan wenyi chubanshe, 1989); Xie Benshu, *Zhang Chong zhuan 1901–1980* [A Biography of Zhang Chong, 1901–1980] (Chengdu: Sichuan renmin chubanshe, 1993).

11. Yunnan sheng minzu shiwu weiyuanhui yanjiushi, *Yunnan minzu shibie cankao ziliao* [Reference Material from the Ethnic Classification Project in Yunnan] (Kunming: Yunnan sheng minzu shiwu weiyuanhui yanjiushi, 1955).

12. Ibid.

13. Special thanks to Steve Harrell for helping me distinguish between issues of existence and composition here.

14. Wang Xiaoyi, Interview, Beijing, January 23, 2003.

15. See chapter 2.

16. Joseph Stalin, *Marxism and the National and Colonial Question* (San Francisco: Proletarian Publishers, 1975).

17. Francine Hirsch, "The Soviet Union as a Work-in-Progress: Ethnographers and the Category Nationality in the 1926, 1937, and 1939 Censuses," *Slavic Review* 56, no. 2 (Summer 1997): 251–78, 257.

18. Francine Hirsch, *Empire of Nations: Ethnographic Knowledge and the Making of the Soviet Union* (Ithaca: Cornell University Press, 2005), 123–30.

19. YNPA, Quanzong 2152, Index 1, File 44 (May 20, 1954): 13.

20. Gregory Guldin, *The Saga of Anthropology in China: From Malinowski to Mao* (Armonk, NY: M. E. Sharpe, 1994), 30.

21. Cai Yuanpei, "*Shuo minzuxue* [On Ethnology]," in *Cai Yuanpei xuanji* [Selected Writings of Cai Yuanpei] (Hangzhou: Zhejiang renmin chubanshe, 1993); Wang Mingming, "The Third Eye: Towards a Critique of 'Nativist Anthropology,' " *Critique of Anthropology* 22 (2002): 149.

22. Cai, "*Shuo minzuxue*"; James Leibold, "Competing Narratives of Racial Unity in Republican China: From the Yellow Emperor to Peking Man," *Modern China* 32, no. 2 (2006): 208–9.

23. Yang Kun, "*Minzuxue yu renleizue* [Ethnology and Anthropology]," *Guoli Beijing daxue xuebao* 1 (1935).

24. YNPA, Quanzong 11, Index 8, File 12.

25. Ibid.

26. Ibid. In his work on Guizhou, Siu-woo Cheung had uncovered a very similar ban on ethnonyms issued at roughly the same time. See Siu-woo Cheung, "Miao Identities, Indigenism and the Politics of Appropriation in Southwest China during the Republican Period," *Asian Ethnicity* 4, no. 1 (February 2003): 111.

27. Jiang Yingliang, *Kangzhanzhong de xinan minzu wenti* [The Question of Southwest Ethnic Groups in Wartime] (Chongqing: Zhongshan Bureau of Culture and Education, 1938).

28. Ibid., 14.

29. Ibid., 15.

30. Ibid., 6.

31. Ibid., 10.

32. Ibid.

33. Ibid., 9.

34. Louisa Schein, "Gender and Internal Orientalism in China," *Modern China* 23, no. 1 (January 1997): 69–98.

35. Wu Wenzao, "*Bianzhengxue Fafan,*" reprinted in *Renleixue shehuixue yanjiu wenji* [Selected Readings on Anthropology and Sociology] (Beijing: Minzu chubanshe, 1990), 264–65.

36. Ibid.

37. Cen Jiawu, "*Kangzhan yu bianjiang minzu wenhua yundong* [The War of Resistance and the Cultural Movement of Border Ethnic Groups]," *Gengsheng pinglung* 3 (1938): 8.

38. YNPA, Quanzong 11, Index 8, File 13.

39. Ibid.

40. Selçuk Esenbel, "Japan's Global Claim to Asia and the World of Islam: Transnational Nationalism and World Power, 1900–1945," *American Historical Review* 109 (October 2004): 1154–64, 1167.

41. Jiang Yingliang, *Jiang Yingliang minzu yanjiu wenji* [Selected Ethnological Writings of Jiang Yingliang] (Beijing: Minzu chubanshe, 1992), 40, referring to J. Edkins's study "The Miao-tsi Tribes" and Terrien de Lacouperie, *The Languages of China Before the Chinese* (Osnabrück: Otto Zeller, 1969). See also Albert Terrien de Lacoupérie, *Western Origin of the Early Chinese Civilisation from 2,300 B.C. to 200 A.D.* (Osnabrück: Otto Zeller, 1966).

42. Jiang, *Jiang Yingliang minzu yanjiu wenji*, 40–41.

43. Interestingly, the same arguments were being made by Japanese ethnologists operating in China. As outlined by Prasenjit Duara, Torii Ryūzō expressed concern over leaving the ethnology of China to foreigners, citing examples of theories of the Persian origin of people in Chinese Turkestan. Like Jiang Yingliang and others, Torii believed that Western anthropologists were laying the ideological justification for the extension of European influence among groups of supposed Indo-European extraction living in the territory of China. Prasenjit Duara, "Ethnics (*minzoku*) and Ethnology (*minzokushugi*) in Manchukuo" (Asia Research Institute Working Paper Series 74, September 2006), 11.

44. Cen Jiawu, "*Kangzhan yu bianjiang minzu wenhua yundong,*" 8.

45. Cen Jiawu, "*Xinan zhongzu yanjiu zhi huigu yu qianzhan* [Reflections on and Future Development of Research into the Races of the Southwest]," *Zhongguo qingnian jikan* 1 (1940): 233.

46. We find further examples of this accommodationist strategy in the work of Gu Jiegang. See Gu Jiegang, "*Zhonghua minzu shi yige*" [The Zhonghua nation is one], reprinted in *Gu Jiegang juan*, ed. Gu Chao and Gu Hong (Shijiazhuang: Hebei jiaoyu chubanshe, 1996), 777–78. For a further discussion of how Gu and others often amended their ethnopolitical outlooks in negotiation with the GMD, see Leibold, "Competing Narratives," 181–220; and James Leibold, *Reconfiguring Chinese Nationalism: How the Qing Frontier and Its Indigenes Became Chinese* (New York: Palgrave Macmillian, 2007).

47. Zhang Yanxiu, "*Zai lun Yi Han tongyuan* [Once More on the Common Origins of the Yi and Han]," *Xinan bianjiang* 6 (May 1939). It is important to note that not all social scientists were pressing against the official line of the Guomindang state. A number of anthropologists aligned themselves with the GMD, as examined by James Leibold. See Leibold, *Reconfiguring Chinese Nationalism*, 138–44.

48. Consequently, these reforms technically increased the number of scholars professionally identified as ethnologists. According to Arkush, Fei Xiaotong would have in fact preferred to contribute to New China as a sociologist, through research into social and economic issues, particularly in rural areas. Sociology was disbanded over the 1951–52 period, however, leaving ethnology as Fei's only option. R. David Arkush, *Fei Xiaotong and Sociology in Revolutionary China* (Cambridge, MA: Harvard University Press, 1981), 225–28.

49. Gregory Guldin, "Anthropology by Other Names: The Impact of Sino-Soviet Friendship on the Anthropological Sciences," *Australian Journal of Chinese Affairs* 27 (January 1992): 135.

50. Lin Yaohua, "*Guanyu minzu shibie wenti de yijian* [Opinions Regarding the Problem of Ethnic Classification]," YNPA, Quanzong 1, Index 2152, File 46 (1954): 39–56. See also Lin Yaohua, "*Youguan minzu shibie ji ge mingci de jieshi* [Explanations of Certain Terms Related to Ethnic Classification]," in *Yunnan shaoshu minzu shehui lishi diaocha (san)* [Social History Investigation of Minority Nationalities in Yunnan (Three)], ed. Yunnan sheng bianji zu (Kunming: Yunnan minzu chubanshe, 1987). Three years later, Lin Yaohu and Fei Xiaotong provided a more in-depth look at many of the issues first broached in Lin and Fu's 1954 work. See Fei Xiaotong, "*Dangqian minzu gongzuo tigei minzuxue de ji ge renwu* [A Few Responsibilities That Current and Future Nationalities Work has Given to Ethnology]," *Zhongguo minzu wenti yanjiu jikan* 6 (January 1957).

51. Lin, "*Guanyu minzu shibie wenti de yijian*," 47.

52. Ibid., 44. Interestingly, Mao himself expressed doubt over the Soviet distinction even before the advent of Classification, arguing in 1953 that "the scientific analysis [of groups] is permissible but, politically speaking, we should not go about making distinctions between which groups are nationalities *(minzu)* and which are tribes *(buzu)*." Huang Guangxue, ed., *Dangdai Zhongguo de minzu gongzuo—shang* [Nationality Work in Contemporary China, volume 1] (Beijing: Dangdai zhongguo congshu bianji weiyuanhui, 1993). Lin Yaohua made no references to these comments by Mao.

53. Lin, "*Guanyu minzu shibie wenti de yijian*," 45.

54. Ibid., 44–45.

55. Ibid., 45.

56. Ibid., 44. See also in Lin, "*Youguan minzu shibie ji ge mingci de jieshi*," 55.

57. Lin, "*Youguan minzu shibie ji ge mingci de jieshi*," 55.

58. Lin, "*Guanyu minzu shibie wenti de yijian*," 48.

59. Yunnan Province Nationalities Affairs Commission Research Office, "*Yunnan sheng shaoshu minzu zhixi xishu yanjiu gaikuang he cunzai wenti* [Overall Situation of Research into the Branches of Minority Nationalities in Yunnan Province along with Existing Problems]," YNPA, Quanzong 2152, Index 1, File 47 (May 12, 1954): 26-38.

60. "*Shangcong Yunnan sheng shaoshuminzu yanjiu zu diaocha jihua—fujian* [Investigation Plan Submitted by the Yunnan Province Ethnic Classification Research Team—Appendix]," YNPA, Quanzong 2152, Index 1, File 44 (June 7, 1954): 25.

61. "*Shangcong Yunnan sheng shaoshuminzu yanjiu zu diaocha jihua—fujian*," 27-28.

62. Yunnan Province Nationalities Affairs Commission Research Office, "*Yunnan sheng shaoshu minzu zhixi xishu yanjiu gaikuang he cunzai wenti*," 36.

63. Ibid., 37.

64. Ibid., 36.

65. Wang Xiaoyi, Interview, Beijing, January 23, 2003.

66. Guizhou Province Nationalities Affairs Commission, "*Fu youguan ni sheng Sha zu (Buyi) mingcheng zhi yijian* [Responding with Opinions Regarding the Name of the Sha Minzu (Buyi) in Your Province]," YNPA, Quanzong 2152, Index 1, File 44 (June 20, 1954): 67.

67. Ibid.

68. Stevan Harrell identifies a similar problem along the Yunnan-Tibet border, wherein an otherwise coherent Prmi ethnic group was divided into two separate minzu categories: Zang in Tibet and Pumi in Yunnan. See Stevan Harrell, "The Nationalities Question and the Prmi Problem," in *Negotiating Ethnicities in China and Taiwan*, ed. Melissa J. Brown (Berkeley: Institute for East Asian Studies, University of California, 1996), 274-96.

69. For a closer look at the Tujia elsewhere in China, see Melissa J. Brown, "Local Government Agency: Manipulating Tujia Identity," *Modern China* 28, no. 3 (July 2002): 362-95. See also Melissa J. Brown, "Ethnic Classification and Culture: The Case of the Tujia in Hubei, China," *Asian Ethnicity* 2, no. 1 (March 2001): 55-72.

70. YNPA, Quanzong 2152, Index 2, File 19 (1954): 103-5. This report was presented in 1954 by the Yunnan Province Nationalities Affairs Commission some time prior to June 25.

71. Yunnan Province Nationalities Affairs Commission Research Office, "*Yunnan sheng shaoshu minzu zhixi xishu yanjiu gaikuang he cunzai wenti*."

72. Ibid., 36.

73. Ibid., 39.

74. Ibid., 37.

75. Prasenjit Duara, *Rescuing History from the Nation*, 17.

76. My findings complement the insights of Dorothy Solinger in her examination of Chinese Communist ethnopolitics in Yunnan. As she argues, the Communists varied their approaches to different ethnic groups depending upon the perceived "assimilability" of each. My main revision would be this: Solinger's concept of "assimilability" presupposes the existence and coherence of the groups to be assimilated, which, as we have seen, was no by no means always the case. Rather, the Classification team was acutely concerned with formu-

lating particular ethnonational configurations that it would be plausible for the state to realize in the post-Classification period. When considered in conjunction with the concept of "ethnic potential" outlined earlier, then, I believe that Solinger's concept of "assimilability" remains extremely useful. See Dorothy J. Solinger, "Minority Nationalities in China's Yunnan Province: Assimilation, Power, and Policy in a Socialist State," *World Politics* 30, no. 1 (October 1977).

77. Stéphane Gros, "The Politics of Names: The Identification of the Dulong (Drung) of Northwest Yunnan," *China Information* 18, no. 2 (2004): 275–302. Anyone who has had the pleasure of discussing matters of minzu with cabdrivers in Beijing will appreciate how appropriate Gros's usage of the term "common sense" truly is. One would be hard-pressed to identify many other countries in the world in which the average person seem as familiar with their nation's precise number of official minorities as, for example, the average American is familiar with the precise number of American states.

CHAPTER 4

Epigraphs, p. 92: Yunnan sheng minzu shibie yanjiuzu [Yunnan Province Ethnic Classification Research Team], "*Yingjiang Achang zu gaikuang* [Situation of the Achang Minzu of Yingjiang]," YNPA, Quanzong 2152, Index 3, File 65 (1954): 22. Research Interviews conducted June 21–24, 1954.

1. Yunnan sheng minzu shibie yanjiuzu [Yunnan Province Ethnic Classification Team], "*Jianbao*[Brief Report]," YNPA, Quanzong 2152, Index 1, File 44 (1954): 34–37. For a complete list of squads and squad members, see appendix D.

2. Wang Xiaoyi, Interview, Beijing, January 3, 2003.

3. Shi Lianzhu, Interview, Beijing, January 27, 2003.

4. Wang Xiaoyi, Interview, Beijing, January 3, 2003; Shi Lianzhu, Interview, Beijing, January 27, 2003.

5. Wang Xiaoyi, Interview, Beijing, January 3, 2003. Yunnan sheng minzu shibie yanjiuzu [Yunnan Province Ethnic Classification Research Team], "*Mojiang xian 'Hani' zu shehui diaocha cailiao* [Materials from the Social Investigation into the 'Hani' Minzu of Mojiang County]," YNPA, Quanzong 2152, Index 3, File 34 (1954): 14–37.

6. Shi Lianzhu, Interview, Beijing, January 27, 2003.

7. Wang Xiaoyi, Interview, Beijing, January 3, 2003.

8. Nicholas Tapp, "In Defense of the Archaic: A Reconsideration of the 1950s Ethnic Classification Project in China," *Asian Ethnicity* 3 (2002): 67.

9. Wang Xiaoyi, Interview, Beijing, January 3, 2003. Similar preferences were discussed by Shi Lianzhu (Shi Lianzhu, Interview, Beijing, January 27, 2003).

10. Wang Xiaoyi, Interview, Beijing, January 3, 2003.

11. In Chinese: "*Nimen shi yi jia ma?* "; "*Nimen guoqu shi yi jia de ma?* "; "*Nimen shi yige zuxian chuan xia lai de ma?* " Wang Xiaoyi, Interview, Beijing, January 3, 2003; Shi Lianzhu spoke on this issue as well. Interview, Beijing, January 27, 2003.

12. Shi Lianzhu, Interview, Beijing, January 27, 2003; Wang Xiaoyi, Interview, Beijing, January 3, 2003.

13. Wang Xiaoyi, Interview, Beijing, January 3, 2003.

14. Mao Zedong, *Report from Xunwu,* trans. Roger R. Thompson (Stanford: Stanford University Press, 1990), 3.

15. Ibid., 23–24.

16. Mao Zedong, "Oppose Book Worship," Marxists.org, www.marxists.org/reference/archive/mao/selected-works/volume-6/mswv6_11.htm#s3.

17. Mao, "Oppose Book Worship."

18. Mao, *Report from Xunwu,* 25; Mao, "Oppose Book Worship."

19. Mao, "Oppose Book Worship."

20. Yung-chen Chiang, *Social Engineering and the Social Sciences in China, 1919–1949* (Cambridge: Cambridge University Press, 2001), 155.

21. Mao, *Report from Xunwu,* 19.

22. Ibid., 5.

23. Mao, "Rectify the Party's Style of Work," www.marxists.org/reference/archive/mao/selected-works/volume-3/mswv3_06.htm.

24. Mao, "In Opposition to Party Formalism," quoted in Ross Terrill, *Mao: A Biography*(Stanford: Stanford University Press, 1999), 198.

25. William Theodore de Bary and Richard John Lufrano, eds., *Sources of Chinese Tradition: From 1600 through the Twentieth Century* (New York: Columbia University Press, 1999), 476.

26. Mao Zedong, "Preface and Postscript to *Rural Surveys,*" Marxists.org, www.marxists.org/reference/archive/mao/selected-works/volume-3/mswv3_01.htm (accessed July 17, 2007).

27. Mao, *Report from Xunwu,* 25.

28. Mao "The Methods of Leadership" (June 1, 1943) quoted in Mark Selden, *The Yenan Way in Revolutionary China* (Cambridge, MA: Harvard University Press, 1971), 274.

29. "*Jiangcheng xian Hani zu Yi zu zizhiqu shouweihui tiaozheng minzu zhixi baogao—gaoyao* [Report on the Rectification of National Branches of the Hani and Yi Minzu of Jiangcheng County by the Autonomous Region Shouweihui—Draft]," YNPA, Quanzong 2152, Index 1, File 44 (June 20, 1953): 66.

30. Ibid.

31. Yunnan sheng minzu shibie yanjiuzu [Yunnan Province Ethnic Classification Research Team], *Yunnan sheng minzu shibie yanjiu di yi jieduan chubu zongjie* [Preliminary Summary of the First Phase of Ethnic Classification Research in Yunnan Province] (Kunming: Yunnan sheng minzu shibie yanjiuzu, 1954), 3. Readers will notice that this population differs dramatically from the "Tulao" featured in the census results of 1953–54. Again, this derives from the highly flexible term *Tu* which forms the basis of the ethnonym (see chapter 3).

32. Yunnan sheng minzu shibie yanjiuzu, *Yunnan sheng minzu shibie yanjiu di yi jieduan chubu zongjie,* 1–4.

33. Wang Xiaoyi, Interview, Beijing, January 23, 2003.

34. Stevan Harrell, "The History of the History of the Yi," in *Cultural Encounters on China's Ethnic Frontiers,* ed. Stevan Harrell (Seattle: University of Washington Press, 1995), 7.

35. Yunnan sheng minzu shibie yanjiuzu [Yunnan Province Ethnic Classification Re-

search Team], " *'Tulao' zu shibie xiaojie* [Brief Summary of the Classification of the 'Tulao' Minzu]," YNPA, Quanzong 2152, Index 1, File 45 (1954): 25.

36. Ibid.

37. Yunnan sheng minzu shibie yanjiuzu [Yunnan Province Ethnic Classification Research Team], *"Funing 'Heiyi' zu shehui qingkuang diaocha* [Research into the social conditions of the 'Heiyi' Minzu of Funing]," YNPA, Quanzong 2152, Index 3, File 31 (1954): 123–31. Report describes research interview conducted on July 10, 1954.

38. Yunnan sheng minzu shibie yanjiuzu [Yunnan Province Ethnic Classification Research Team], *"Funing 'Tu' zu shehui qingkuang diaocha* [Investigation into the Social Conditions of the 'Tu' Minzu of Funing]," YNPA, Quanzong 2152, Index 3, File 31 (1954): 78.

39. Yunnan sheng minzu shibie yanjiuzu [Yunnan Province Ethnic Classification Research Team], " *'Tulao' zu shibie xiaojie* [Brief Summary of the Classification of the 'Tulao' Minzu]," YNPA, Quanzong 2152, Index 1, File 45 (1954): 21. The term *yunniang,* translated here as "deliberate," can also mean to "brew" or "ferment," as with liquor. This term gives one a vivid sense of the idea of potentiality and fulfillment.

40. Eric J. Hobsbawm, *Nations and Nationalism: Programme, Myth, Reality* (Cambridge: Cambridge University Press, 1992), 52–54. See also Paul V. Kroskrity, ed., *Regimes of Language: Ideologies, Polities, and Identities* (Sante Fe, New Mexico: School of American Research Press, 2008).

41. Hobsbawm, *Nations and Nationalism,* 52.

42. Ibid., 54.

43. Shi Lianzhu, Interview, Beijing, January 27, 2003.

44. See the census statistics in chapter 1.

45. Yunnan sheng minzu shibie yanjiuzu [Yunnan Province Ethnic Classification Research Team], *"Xinping xian 'Mili' zu diaocha* [Investigation into the 'Mili' Minzu of Xinping County]," YNPA, Quanzong 2152, Index 3, File 18 (1954): 100.

46. Yunnan sheng minzu shibie yanjiuzu [Yunnan Province Ethnic Classification Research Team], *"Yingjiang xian Husa Lasa Achang zu gaikuang* [Situation of the Achang Minzu of Husalasa in Yingjiang County]," YNPA, Quanzong 2152, Index 3, File 65 (1954): 56.

47. Yunnan sheng minzu shibie yanjiuzu [Yunnan Province Ethnic Classification Research Team], *"Lianghe Achang qingkuang* [Situation of the Achang of Lianghe]," YNPA, Quanzong 2152, Index 3, File 65 (1954): 95; interview conducted June 8–9, 1954.

48. Ibid.

49. Ibid.

50. Yunnan sheng minzu shibie yanjiuzu, *"Lianghe Achang qingkuang,"* 224. When differentiating between local and metropolitan epistemologies, I follow Bruno Latour in my dissatisfaction with binaries such as "scientific versus unscientific" or "objective versus subjective." We should not assume that state-cum-social scientific modes of knowledge are somehow "universal," in the sense of being universally shared. The worldviews of both the Achang representative and the Ethnic Classification researchers are similarly local and even parochial, insofar as each is tied to and advanced by particular communities of practice, and each is opaque and unintelligible to uninitiated outsiders. The primary differences involve methods and scales of data accumulation, and the vastly dissimilar levels of aggressiveness with which

the two communities of practice attempted to extend and propagate their particular knowledge at the expense of other forms. When differentiating these two different modes of knowledge, to quote Latour, "it is not at the cognitive differences we should marvel, but at this general mobilisation of the world" that enabled Chinese taxonomists to make the social world "revolve around the mind" instead of vice versa. See Latour, *Science in Action: How to Follow Scientists and Engineers through Society* (Cambridge, MA: Harvard University Press, 1987), 225.

51. Yunnan sheng minzu shibie yanjiuzu [Yunnan Province Ethnic Classification Research Team], "*Achang zu shibie xiaozu* [Summary Report on the Classification of the Achang Minzu]," YNPA, Quanzong 2152, Index 1, File 45 (1954): 5.

52. Yunnan sheng minzu shibie yanjiuzu [Yunnan Province Ethnic Classification Research Team], "*Yingjiang Achang zu gaikuang* [Situation of the Achang Minzu of Yingjiang]," YNPA, Quanzong 2152, Index 3, File 65 (1954): 22.

53. Ibid., 21–22.

54. Wang Xiaoyi, Interview, Beijing, January 3, 2003. See appendix D for complete list of researchers delegated to each squad.

55. Fang Guoyu, "*Qing queding Yunnan ge minzu mingcheng baoqing zhongyang zhengshi gongbao* [Please Confirm the Names of All Minzu in Yunnan and Then Submit Them to the Center for Formal Promulgation]," YNPA, Quanzong 2165, Index 3, File 157.

56. Ibid.

57. Thomas S. Kuhn, *The Structure of Scientific Revolutions* (Chicago: University of Chicago Press, 1962).

58. Li Qunjie, "*Tigong wo sheng jige ge gezu ge cheng de zhengming chubu yijian de baogao*," YNPA, Quanzong 2152, Index 1, File 44 (1954): 74–75.

59. Ibid., 74–78.

60. Ibid., 76–77.

61. YNPA Quanzong 2152, Index 1, File 45 (1954): 70.

62. Ibid., 71.

63. Ibid., 70.

64. Ibid., 70–71.

65. Ibid., 70.

66. Ibid., 66.

67. "Summary Report" (1953) reprinted in "Guanyu Guizhou sheng Zhongjia (Buyi) zu tongyi minzu mingcheng ji Jiangcheng xian tiaozheng minzu zhixi tongbao," YNPA, Quanzong 2152, Index 1, File 44 (June 20, 1953): 63.

68. Ibid.

69. "Summary Report" (1953) reprinted in "Guanyu Guizhou sheng Zhongjia (Buyi) zu tongyi minzu mingcheng ji Jiangcheng xian tiaozheng minzu zhixi tongbao," 65.

70. Circa 1956, the Yi were reported to have 3.25 million people, making them the fourth largest group in China after the Zhuang, Uighur, and Hui. The next largest group was the Tibetans, with 2.77 million people.

71. For a detailed look at the question of "slave society" in Liangshan, see Ann Maxwell Hill, "Captives, Kin, and Slaves in Xiao Liangshan," *Journal of Asian Studies* 60, no. 4 (November 2001): 1033–49.

72. Yunnan sheng minzu shibie yanjiuzu [Yunnan Province Ethnic Classification Research Team], "*Yongsheng Shuitian, Luoluo, Zhili, Ziyi, Lang'e, Talu deng minzu de yuyan* [The Languages of the Shuitian, Luoluo, Zhili, Ziyi, Lang'e, and Talu Minzu of Yongsheng County]," YNPA, Quanzong 2152, Index 3, File 78 (1954): 79.

73. For example, the team justified its choice of the Shuitian by citing linguistic reasons. First, the team had recorded a larger list of Shuitian vocabulary words than for other groups, the report explained, thereby facilitating more complete comparison. Second, the Shuitian language was less influenced by Chinese, the team argued, than other groups in the region. Although not cited expressly, I strongly suspect that there are additional historical and political justifications for choosing the Shuitian—perhaps simply that, unlike the aforementioned Langsu, Tagu, and Liude, the Shuitian representatives did not regard the Yi of Liangshan with the same enmity. Yunnan sheng minzu shibie yanjiuzu, "*Yongsheng Shuitian, Luoluo, Zhili, Ziyi, Lang'e, Talu deng minzu de yuyan*," 75.

74. Ibid., 98–104.

75. Ibid.

76. Ibid.

77. Ibid.

78. Yunnan sheng minzu shibie yanjiuzu [Yunnan Province Ethnic Classification Research Team], "*Yongsheng Shuitian, Luoluo, Zhili, Ziyi, Lang'e, Talu deng minzu de yuyan* [The Languages of the Shuitian, Luoluo, Zhili, Ziyi, Lang'e, and Talu Minzu of Yongsheng County]," YNPA, Quanzong 2152, Index 3, File 78 (October 1954): 74–77.

79. Yunnan sheng minzu shibie yanjiuzu, "Yongsheng Shuitian, Luoluo, Zhili, Ziyi, Lang'e, Talu deng minzu de yuyan," 75; Yunnan sheng minzu shibie yanjiuzu, "Yongsheng 'Luo' 'Shuitian' 'Zhili' 'Ziyi' 'Liming' shibie xiaojie," 100; Yunnan sheng minzu shibie yanjiuzu [Yunnan Province Ethnic Classification Research Team], "*Xinping xian 'Ache' diaocha cailiao* [Research Materials on the 'Ache' of Xinping County]," YNPA, Quanzong 2152, Index 3, File 18 (1954): 45–54; Yunnan sheng minzu shibie yanjiuzu [Yunnan Province Ethnic Classification Research Team], "*Yongsheng xian 'Lang'e' qingkuang diaocha* [Research into the Situation of the 'Lang'e' of Yongsheng County]," YNPA, Quanzong 2152, Index 3, File 78 (1954): 26–41; Yunnan sheng minzu shibie yanjiuzu [Yunnan Province Ethnic Classification Research Team], "*Yongsheng xian 'Liming' zu qingkuang diaocha baogao* [Report on the Investigation into the Situation of the 'Liming' minzu of Yongsheng County]," YNPA, Quanzong 2152, Index 3, File 78 (1954): 1–12; Yunnan sheng minzu shibie yanjiuzu [Yunnan Province Ethnic Classification Research Team], "*Yongsheng di'er qu Lude xiang 'Liudu' zu fangwen jilü* [Transcript of the Visitation with the 'Liude' minzu of Lude Village in the Second Area of Yongsheng County]," YNPA, Quanzong 2152, Index 3, File 78 (1954): 88–97; Yunnan sheng minzu shibie yanjiuzu [Yunnan Province Ethnic Classification Research Team], "*Xinping xian 'Luowu' zu gaikuang* [Overall Situation of the 'Luowu' Minzu of Xinping County]," YNPA, Quanzong 2152, Index 3, File 18 (1954): 60–85. Yunnan sheng minzu shibie yanjiuzu [Yunnan Province Ethnic Classification Research Team], "*Xinping xian wu qu Pingzhang xiang 'Menghua' zu diaocha ziliao* [Research materials on the 'Menghua' minzu of Pingzhang Village in the Fifth Area of Xinping County]," YNPA, Quanzong 2152, Index 3, File 70 (1954): 76–87. Yunnan sheng minzu shibie yanjiuzu [Yunnan Province Ethnic Classification Research Team], "*Xinping xian wu qu Pingzhang xiang 'Micha' zu qingkuang cailiao* [Materials on the

Situation of the 'Micha' minzu of Pingzhang Village in the Fifth Area of Xinping County]," YNPA, Quanzong 2152, Index 3, File 20 (1954): 95–109. Yunnan sheng minzu shibie yanjiuzu [Yunnan Province Ethnic Classification Research Team], "*Xinping xian 'Mili' zu diaocha cailiao* [Materials from the Investigation of the 'Mili' Minzu of Xinping County]," YNPA, Quanzong 2152, Index 3, File 18 (1954): 86–100. Yunnan sheng minzu shibie yanjiuzu [Yunnan Province Ethnic Classification Research Team], "*Yunnan sheng Jingdong xian 'Mili' zu qingkuang diaocha chubu zongjie* [Preliminary Summary of the Investigation into the Situation of the 'Mili' Minzu of Jingdong County in Yunnan Province]," YNPA, Quanzong 2152, Index 3, File 34 (1954): 1–13; Yunnan sheng minzu shibie yanjiuzu [Yunnan Province Ethnic Classification Research Team], "*Muji shibie xiaojie* [Summary on the Classification of the Muji]," YNPA, Quanzong 2152, Index 3, File 30 (1954): 193–97; Yunnan sheng minzu shibie yanjiuzu [Yunnan Province Ethnic Classification Research Team], "*Yongsheng xian di'er qu 'Nazha' 'Talu' diaocha cailiao* [Materials from the Investigation of the 'Nazha' and 'Talu' of the Second Area of Yongsheng County]," YNPA, Quanzong 2152, Index 3, File 78 (1954): 117–31; Yunnan sheng minzu shibie yanjiuzu [Yunnan Province Ethnic Classification Research Team], "*Yongsheng xian di'er qu 'Tagu' zu diaocha* [Investigation of the 'Tagu' Minzu of the Second Area of Yongsheng County]," YNPA, Quanzong 2152, Index 3, File 78 (1954): 18–25; Yunnan sheng minzu shibie yanjiuzu [Yunnan Province Ethnic Classification Research Team], "*Yongsheng 'Zhili' zu qingkuang diaocha fu Ziyi zu qingkuang* [Investigation into the Situation of the 'Zhili' Minzu of Yongsheng with an addendum on the Situation of the 'Ziyi' Minzu]," YNPA, Quanzong 2152, Index 3, File 78 (1954): 58–73; Yunnan sheng minzu shibie yanjiuzu [Yunnan Province Ethnic Classification Research Team], "*Xinping xian 'Chesu' zu gaikuang* [The General Situation of the 'Chesu' Minzu of Xinping County]," YNPA, Index 2152, Quanzong 3, File 18 (1954): 26–37; Yunnan sheng minzu shibie yanjiuzu [Yunnan Province Ethnic Classification Research Team], "*Wenshan Mengzi Gejiu 'Pu' zu he 'Muji' zu diaocha baogao* [Report on the Investigation of the 'Pu' and 'Muji' Minzu in Wenshan, Mengzi, and Gejiu Counties]," YNPA, Quanzong 2152, Index 3, File 30 (1954): 92–156. This report also contains specific analyses of the Tulaopo (123), Azha (129–30), and Zuoke (134–35). Yunnan sheng minzu shibie yanjiuzu [Yunnan Province Ethnic Classification Research Team], "*Xinping xian Yi zu fangwen cailiao* [Materials from the Visitation of the Yi Minzu of Xinping County]," YNPA, Quanzong 2152, Index 3, File 19 (1954): 72–95; Yunnan sheng minzu shibie yanjiuzu, "*Yongsheng 'Luo' zu he 'Shuitian' zu qingkuang diaocha* [Investigation into the Situation of the 'Luo' and 'Shuitian' Minzu of Yongsheng County]," YNPA, Quanzong 2152, Index 3, File 78 (1954): 42–57.

CHAPTER 5

Epigraphs, page 120: "*Jiemi 'Zhonghua wei shibie minzu'* [Exposing the 'Yet-To-Be-Classified Minzu of China']," http://blog.sina.com.cn/s/blog_48c9a3a501000b5t.html, August 27, 2007 (accessed August 15, 2008). Stevan Harrell, *Perspectives on the Yi of Southwest China*, (Berkeley: University of California Press, 2001), 8.

1. Zhonghua renmin gongheguo diyi jie quanguo renmin daibiao dahui diyi ci huiyi mishuchu, ed., *Zhonghua renmin gongheguo diyi jie quanguo renmin daibiao dahui diyi ci huiyi lukan* [Record of the First Meeting of the First Plenum of the All-Country National

People's Congress of the People's Republic of China] (Beijing: Zhonghua renmin gongheguo diyi jie quanguo renmin daibiao dahui diyi ci huiyi mishuchu, 1955), 11. The one exception was Taiwan, which was listed as "temporarily absent."

2. Ibid., 26–27.

3. Ibid., 599–600.

4. Henry G. Schwarz, *Chinese Policies towards Minorities: An Essay and Documents* (Bellingham: Western Washington State College Program in East Asian Studies, 1971), 63.

5. Ibid.

6. Nationality Work Editorial Board, ed., *Minzu gongzuo shouce* [Handbook for Nationality Work] (Kunming: Yunnan People's Press, 1985), 31–32.

7. "*Guanyu Zhongguo gongmin queding minzu chengfen de guiding* [Regulations Concerning the Verification of Minzu Status for Chinese Citizens]," May 10, 1990. Issued jointly by the Nationalities Affairs Commission, Public Security Bureau, and the Guowuyuan Fourth Census Leading Small Group, www.gd.xinhuanet.com/newscenter/ztbd/2007–11/13/content_11657918.htm (accessed July 7, 2008).

8. Jin Xinghua, ed., *Zhongguo minzu yuwen gongzuo* [Minority Language Work in China] (Beijing: Minzu chubanshe, 2005). Researchers were also part of the larger process of creating written scripts for minority languages that were entirely oral.

9. Zhongguo kexueyuan minzu yanjiusuo Yunnan shehui lishi diaochazu [Chinese Academy of Social Sciences Yunnan Social History Investigation Team], ed., *Wazu jianshi jianzhi hebian (chugao)* [Concise History and Gazetteer of the Wa Nationality (draft)] (Beijing: Chinese Academy of Social Sciences Institute of Ethnology, 1963). Zhongguo kexueyuan minzu yanjiusuo Yunnan shehui lishi diaochazu, ed., *Benglongzu jianshi jianzhi hebian (chugao)* [Concise History and Gazetteer of the Benglong Nationality (draft)] (Beijing: Chinese Academy of Social Sciences Institute of Ethnology, 1963); Zhongguo kexueyuan minzu yanjiusuo Yunnan shehui lishi diaochazu, ed. *Baizu jianshi jianzhi hebian (chugao)* [Concise History and Gazetteer of the Bai Nationality (draft)] (Beijing: Chinese Academy of Social Sciences Institute of Ethnology, 1963); Zhongguo kexueyuan minzu yanjiusuo Yunnan shehui lishi diaochazu, ed., *Naxizu jianshi jianzhi hebian (chugao)* [Concise History and Gazetteer of the Naxi Nationality (draft)] (Beijing: Chinese Academy of Social Sciences Institute of Ethnology, 1963); Zhongguo kexueyuan minzu yanjiusuo Yunnan shehui lishi diaochazu, ed., *Daizu jianshi jianzhi hebian (chugao)* [Concise History and Gazetteer of the Dai Nationality (draft)] (Beijing: Chinese Academy of Social Sciences Institute of Ethnology, 1964); Zhongguo kexueyuan minzu yanjiusuo Sichuan shehui lishi diaochazu, ed., *Yizu jianzhi (chugao)* [Concise Gazetteer of the Yi Nationality (draft)] (Beijing: Chinese Academy of Social Sciences Institute of Ethnology, 1963); Zhongguo kexueyuan minzu yanjiusuo Guangxi shehui lishi diaochazu, ed., *Zhuangzu jianshi (chugao)* [Concise History of the Zhuang Nationality (draft)] (Beijing: Chinese Academy of Social Sciences Institute of Ethnology, 1964); Zhongguo kexueyuan minzu yanjiusuo Guizhou shehui lishi diaochazu, ed., *Miaozu jianshi jianzhi hebian (chugao)* [Concise History and Gazetteer of the Miao Nationality (draft)] (Beijing: Chinese Academy of Social Sciences Institute of Ethnology, 1963).

10. Michel-Rolph Trouillot, *Silencing the Past: Power and the Production of History* (Boston: Beacon Press, 1995).

11. Siu-woo Cheung, "Representation and Negotiation of Ge Identities in Southeast

Guizhou," in *Negotiating Ethnicities in China and Taiwan,* ed. Melissa J. Brown (Berkeley: Institute for Asian Studies, University of California, 1996), 245; see also Adrienne M. Dwyer, "The Texture of Tongues: Language and Power in China," in *Nationalism and Ethnoregional Identities in China,* ed. William Safran (London: Frank Cass, 1998), 68–85.

12. The series includes one study for each group. For example: Li Jinqun and Wang Chengquan, *Naxizu* [The Naxi Nationality] (Beijing: Minzu chubanshe, 2004); Li Jincan, *Lahuzu* [The Lahu Nationality] (Beijing: Minzu chubanshe, 2004).

13. Yang Guanghai, ed., *Zhongguo shaoshu minzu shehui lishi kexue jilu yingpian juben xuanbian* [Selection of Scripts from the Chinese Minority Nationalities Social History Scientific Documentary Film project—Volume 1] (Beijing: Chinese Academy of Social Sciences Ethnological Research Institute, 1981); "*Yang Guanghai ji qi zuopin* [Yang Guanghai and His Works]," *Zhongguo minzu bao* (December 21, 2007).

14. These anthropological films predate, but in many ways anticipate, later Chinese films in their representation of Chinese minorities. See Paul Clark, "Ethnic Minorities in Chinese Films: Cinema and the Exotic," *East-West Film Journal* 1, no. 2 (1987): 15–32.

15. Dru Gladney, *Muslim Chinese: Ethnic Nationalism in the People's Republic* (Cambridge, MA: Harvard University Press, 1991), 203; Merle Goldman, "Religion in Post-Mao China," *Annals of the American Academy of Political and Social Science* 483, no. 1 (1986): 145–56; Erik Mueggler, *The Age of Wild Ghosts: Memory, Violence, and Place in Southwest China* (Berkeley: University of California Press, 2001), chapter 8; Roderick MacFarquhar and Michael Schoenhals, *Mao's Last Revolution* (Cambridge, MA: Harvard University Press, 2006), 258; Mette Hansen, *Lessons in Being Chinese: Minority Education and Ethnic Identity in Southwest China* (Seattle: University of Washington Press, 1999), 57–60; Schein, *Minority Rules: The Miao and the Feminine in China's Cultural Politics* (Durham: Duke University Press, 2000), 86–88.

16. Ralph A. Litzinger, "Memory Work: Reconstituting the Ethnic in Post-Mao China," *Cultural Anthropology* 13, no. 2 (May 1998): 224–55.

17. Timothy S. Oakes, "Ethnic Tourism in Rural Guizhou: Sense of Place and the Commerce of Authenticity," in *Tourism, Ethnicity, and the State in Asian and Pacific Societies,* ed. Michel Picard and Robert E. Wood (Honolulu: University of Hawai'i Press, 1987). See also Bai Zhihong, "The Discourse of Tourism Development in the Construction of a Bai Cultural and Historic City," *Thai-Yunnan Project Bulletin* 2 (2001).

18. Eric Hobsbawm and Terence Ranger, eds., *The Invention of Tradition* (Cambridge: Cambridge University Press, 1983).

19. Dru Gladney, "Representing Nationality in China: Refiguring Majority/Minority Identities," *Journal of Asian Studies* 53, no. 1 (February 1994): 97.

20. Susan D. Blum, "Margins and Centers: A Decade of Publishing on China's Ethnic Minorities," *Journal of Asian Studies* 61, no. 4 (November 2002): 1287–310.

21. Ibid., 1289.

22. Library of Congress Authorities and Vocabularies, http://id.loc.gov/authorities/sh8 5045253#concept (accessed January 2, 2010).

23. "*56 ge minzu shuang baotai 10 yue panju Beijing* [Twins from the Fifty-Six Minzu Prepare to Gather in Beijing in October]," August 12, 2005, http://sym2005.cass.cn/file/ 2005082136006.html (accessed August 7, 2008).

24. "56 ge minzu yingjie aoyun daoji 56 tian zhuti wanhui," www.bjyouth.gov.cn/jcxx/
dx/196979.shtml (accessed August 7, 2008). Six days later, on June 22, 2008, a group of calligraphers, again one from each of the fifty-six minzu, convened to plan an elaborate demon-
stration of multiethnic harmony. In July 2008, the calligraphers gathered atop the Great Wall
at Mutian and each produced, in their own minority's script, the word "wealth" *(fu)*. See
www.shufa.com/Html/x/2008-6/2008623105428.shtml (accessed August 7, 2008).

25. See http://2008.sohu.com/20080419/n256397368.shtml (accessed August 7, 2008).

26. To this list, numerous other examples could be added. Barry Sautman recounts, for
example, China's presentation to the United Nations a tripod adorned with fifty-six dragons,
meant to bring together both sides of unified multinationalism. As Sautman notes, this gift
(meant to symbolize, as the Chinese media noted, "the Chinese nation as descendants of dragons") disregarded the origin myths of many of China's official minzu, for whom it is not the
dragon, but the wolf, dog, monkey, snake, or other animals that serve as the mythical progenitor. See "Bronze 'century tripod' cast for United Nations," September 6, 1995, cited in
Barry Sautman, "Myths of Descent, Racial Nationalism and Ethnic Minorities in the People's
Republic of China," in *The Construction of Racial Identities in China and Japan,* ed. Frank
Dikötter (Hong Kong: Hong Kong University Press, 1997), 77.

27. See http://bbs.6.cn/t.php?tid=265355 (accessed August 7, 2008).

28. Zhang Fengqi, *Yunnan sheng minzu shibie zonghe baogao* [Summary Report on Ethnic Classification in Yunnan] (Kunming: Yunnan sheng minzu shibie yanjiuzu, 1960), 1.

29. Ibid., 1.

30. Ibid., 4. The 1960 Classification report notes that the Donglan, Longjiang, and Tusi
were lumped into the Zhuang just prior to the expedition, initiated by the local party committee as part of the establishment of the Wenshan Autonomous Prefecture. With regards
to the Zheyuan, the 1954 team had originally categorized it as a subset of the Han. The 1960
switched this designation, moving them from the Han to the Zhuang category.

31. In only two cases did the team express doubt over subcategorization, with regards to
Laomian (a newly encountered ethnonymic group in Lancang and Ximeng); and the Tu'e of
Hushui and Lanping counties. For the prior, the team debated over whether to categorize
them as a standalone group, or as a subset of either the Lahu or Yi. As for the Tu'e, the team
expressed doubt over whether to categorize them as Nu or Yi.

32. Zhang Fengqi, *Yunnan sheng minzu shibie zonghe baogao,* 1–9.

33. Dru C. Gladney, *Ethnic Identity in China: The Making of a Muslim Minority Nationality* (Fort Worth: Harcourt Brace College Publishers, 1998), 14–15.

34. "*56 ge minzu zhiwai hao you na xie meiyou bei renke de minzu?*" http://ks.cn.yahoo
.com/question/1307110802309_1.html (accessed Aug 13, 2008). Subsequent discussions appear on http://tieba.baidu.com/f?kz=370121923 (accessed August 13, 2008) and http://ks.cn
.yahoo.com/question/1407110902122.html (accessed Aug 13, 2008).

35. See www.pkucn.com/chenyc/post.php?action=reply&fid=1&tid=7948 (accessed Aug
13, 2008).

36. Susan Leigh Star, "Orphans of Infrastructure" (paper presented at Stanford Seminar
on Science, Technology, and Society, Stanford University, December 8, 2006).

37. Zhang Fengqi, *Yunnan sheng minzu shibie zonghe baogao,* 9.

38. Ibid.

39. Ibid., 6–7.

40. Paul Hattaway, *Operation China: Introducing All the Peoples of China* (Carlisle, UK: Piquant, 2000).

41. Many such groups are listed as well in James S. Olson, *An Ethnohistorical Dictionary of China* (Westport, CT: Greenwood Press, 1998).

42. Hattaway, *Operation China*, 470. Yunnan sheng renmin zhengfu minzu shiwu weiyuanhui yanjiushi, "*Yunnan shaoshu minzu renkou tongjibiao (xuanweihui cailiao)*," (Yunnan Provincial Archives, 1954), 166–67.

43. Ibid., 166–67.

44. Yunnan sheng renmin zhengfu minzu shiwu weiyuanhui yanjiushi, "*Yunnan shaoshu minzu renkou tongjibiao (xuanweihui cailiao)*," (Kunming: Yunnan Provincial Archives, 1954), 104–5.

45. Hattaway, *Operation China*, 57.

46. Yunnan sheng renmin zhengfu minzu shiwu weiyuanhui yanjiushi, "*Yunnan shaoshu minzu renkou tongjibiao (xuanweihui cailiao)*," (Kunming: Yunnan Provincial Archives, 1954), 145–47; Hattaway, *Operation China*.

47. Yunnan sheng renmin zhengfu minzu shiwu weiyuanhui yanjiushi, "*Yunnan shaoshu minzu renkou tongjibiao (xuanweihui cailiao)*," (Kunming: Yunnan Provincial Archives, 1954), 45–47.

48. Jamin R. Pelkey, "Yunnan's Myriad 'Yi': Profiles on the Peoples Classified as 'Yi' in Yunnan Province" (unpublished manuscript provided by the author, 1999); Hattaway, *Operation China*, 269.

49. Pelkey, "Yunnan's Myriad 'Yi' " 118; Hattaway, *Operation China*, 491.

50. Hattaway, *Operation China*, 319.

51. Jamin R. Pelkey, "Initial Investigative Report on the Yi Peoples of Honghe Prefecture" (unpublished manuscript provided by the author, n.d.), 8; Hattaway, *Operation China*, 377.

52. Vladimir Li, "Some Approaches to the Classification of Small Ethnic Groups in South China," *Thai-Yunnan Project Newsletter* 20 (March 1993); Hattaway, *Operation China*, 501; Pelkey, "Yunnan's Myriad Yi"; Yunnan sheng renmin zhengfu minzu shiwu weiyuanhui yanjiushi, "Yunnan shaoshu minzu renkou tongjibiao (xuanweihui cailiao)," (Kunming: Yunnan Provincial Archives, 1954), 112.

53. In all, this series, overseen by the renowned Chinese linguist Sun Hongkai, contains at least thirty different studies by this point, a number of which describe as "newly discovered" languages and language-speaking groups whose existence was already known, but who were subordinated beneath other minzu categories. See Li Yunbing, *Laji yu yanjiu* [Research on the Laji Language] (Beijing: Minzu chubanshe, 2000); Chen Guoqing, *Kemu yu yanjiu* [Research on the Kemu Language] (Beijing: Minzu chubanshe, 2002); Dai Qingxia, *Langsu yu yanjiu* [Research on the Langsu Language] (Beijing: Minzu chubanshe, 2005).

54. Sha Like, " '*Zuqun*' *yu* '*minzu*' *de guoji duihua* [The International Dialogue about 'Zuqun' and 'Minzu']," *Minzu wenti yanjiu* 12, no. 7 (2001).

55. Stevan Harrell, *Ways of Being Ethnic in Southwest China* (Seattle: University of Washington Press, 2001), 244.

CONCLUSION

1. Stevan Harrell, "Languages Defining Ethnicity in Southwest China," in *Ethnic Identity: Creation, Conflict, and Accommodation*, ed. Lola Romanucci-Ross and George DeVos (Walnut Creek, CA: Altamira Press, 1995), 97–114.

2. Colin Mackerras, *China's Minorities: Integration and Modernization in the Twentieth Century* (Hong Kong: Oxford University Press, 1994), 144.

3. Ibid., 143–44; Siu-Woo Cheung, "Representation and Negotiation of Ge Identities in Southeastern Guizhou," in *Negotiating Ethnicities in China and Taiwan*, ed. Melissa J. Brown (Berkeley: Institute of East Asian Studies, University of California, 1996), 240–73.

4. Jonathan Lipman, *Familiar Strangers: A History of Muslims in Northwest China* (Seattle: University of Washington Press, 1997), xxiv.

5. Kevin Caffrey, "Who 'Who' Is, and Other Poetics of National Policy: Yunnan *Minzu Shibie* and Hui in the Process," *China Information* 18 (July 2004).

CHARACTER GLOSSARY

Abu 阿布

Achang 阿昌

Ache 阿車

Ahei 阿黑

Aka 阿卡

Ake 阿克

Akuo 阿括

Alu 阿魯

Aluo 阿罗

Ami 阿迷

Amo 阿模

Amu 阿木

Ani 阿尼

Asu 阿蘇

Asuo 阿梭

Axi 阿細, 阿西

Axian 阿霰

Aza 阿杂

Azha 阿札

Azhe 阿哲, 阿者

Ao 傲

Bajia 八甲

Bai 白

Baijia 白家, 百家

Baike 白壳

Bailang 擺偂, 擺瑯, 白朗

Bairen 白人

Baiyi 白衣, 白邑, 白僰

Baizi 百子

Banxi 班喜

Banyi 班依

Baoshan benren 保山本人

bei Zhuang 北僮

Ben 本

Bendi 本地

Benren 本人

Benglong 崩龍

Biyue 碧約

Bo 僰

Boluo 波罗, 颇罗

185

Bowa 泼哇

Bubang 補蚌

Budu 布都

Bujiao 補角

Bukong 布孔

Bulang 布朗

buluo 部落

buming minzu 不明民族

Buwa 补哇

Buxia 補夏, 布夏

Buyi 佈依

buzu 部族

Canyi 参义

Cang 沧

Chabo 岔钵

Chaman 岔满

Chashan 茶山

Chaoxian 朝鲜

Chesu 車蘇

da houfang 大后方

Dalao 大佬

Dali Tujia 大理土家

Datou 大頭

Dazhuba 大助巴

da Zhongguo zhuyi 大中国主义

Dai 岱, 傣

Daisi 代司

Daiweisi 戴维斯

Dan 蜑

Danren 蛋人

Deweishi 德威施

Deng 等

Diga 底嘎

diaochahui 调查会

Dingge 定格

Dongchuan 东川

Donglan 东兰

Dongshu 東屬

Douyi 都夷

Douyun 都勻

Douyundou 都勻都

Du 独

Duota 墮塔, 墮塔

Fan 番

feng ma niu bu xiangji 风马牛不相及

Fuduo 伏多

Funi 伏尼

Ganniu 干纽

Gaoli 高礼

Gaomian 高棉

Gaoshan 高山

Gesi 格斯

Gucong 古聪

Gui 贵

Guola 过拉

guozu 国族

Guomindang 国民党

Hani 哈尼

Hasake 哈萨克

Han 漢

Hanhui 漢回

Hanjian 漢奸

Haoni 豪尼

Hei 黑

Heihua 黑話

Heipu 黑莆, 黑浦, 黑甫

Heisu 黑傈

Heiyi 黑衣

Hong 洪

Huahong 花红

Huasu　花傈

Huayao　花腰

Huanyang　歡養

huangdi　黄帝

Hui　回

Huimin haishi Hanmin?　回民还是汉民?

Huijian　回奸

Jia　戛

Jiazhou　甲洲

jianshi　简史

Jiangxi　江西

Jingdong　景东

Jingpo　景颇

Kabie　卡别

Kadan　卡妲

Kadu　卡都

Kaduo　卡墮

Kakang　卡康

Kamu　卡目

Kana　卡納

Kawa　卡瓦

Kang　亢

Keji　克机

Kejia　客家

Kela　克按

Kelao　克佬

Kongge　空格

Kucong　苦聰, 苦葱

La　腊

Laba　拉扒

Lahu　拉祜

Laji　拉基

Lalu　臘魯

Laluo　腊傈

Lama　拉马

Lami　腊迷, 臘密, 腊咪, 腊米

Laniao　拉鳥

Lawu　拉乌

Laxi　拉西

Lazi　辣子

Lang'e　莨莪

Langsu　浪速

Lao　佬

Laopin　老品

Lemo　勒墨

Li　俐, 黎, 傈

Lijiang Tujia　麗江土家

Limi　哩迷, 哩咪

Limin　利民

Liming　黎明

Lishi　黎仕

Lisu　栗粟, 傈僳

Liangshan　梁山

Lie　猎

Liude　六得

Liutou　六頭

Long'an　隆安

Longren　龙人

Lude　禄德

Luzu　璐族

Lüxi　侣喜

Luo　倮

Luohei　倮黑, 儸黑

Luoluo　倮倮

Luomian　羅勉

Luowu　羅婺, 羅武

Luoyi　倮夷

Mahei　麻黑

Malimasha　馬麗馬沙

Masha　马沙

Mata　骂他

Man　滿

Manzi　蛮子

Meng　蒙, 孟

Menggu　蒙古

Menghua　蒙化

Mengjian　蒙奸

Mengwu　孟武

Mengyong　蒙庸

Micha　密岔

Mili　米里, 迷俐, 咪哩

Misi　米司

Miyi　密義

Mian　緬

Mianren　缅人

Miao　苗

Minjia　民家

Minlang　民郎

minzu　民族

minzu chubanshe　民族出版社

minzu fangwentuan　民族访问团

minzu gongzuo　民族工作

minzu jituan　民族集团

minzu kapian　民族卡片

minzu mingcheng　民族名称

minzu shibie　民族识别

minzu wawa　民族娃娃

minzu zijue　民族自决

ming cong zhuren　名从主人

Mingji　明機

Mosu　莫苏

Moxie　麼些

Muhua　沐花

Muji　侔儶, 母机

Nahua　纳华

Nalu　那路

Nama　那马

Naniao　那鳥

Naxi　纳喜, 纳西

Naxiang　纳香

Nayi　哪夷

Naza　纳杂

Nazha　納渣

Nanjing　南京

Nanni　南尼

nan Zhuang　南僮

Nibo'er　尼泊尔

Nong　儂

Nu　怒

Nuobi　糯比

Paijiao　排角

Pin　品

Polapei　泼拉培

Pu　普

Pu'er　普洱, 普耳

Pu'er benren　普洱本人

Pula　撲拉, 普拉

Puman　蒲滿, 蒲曼

Qi　棲

Qidi　奇地

Qidian　七甸

Qijia　七甲

Qima　奇馬

qita minzu　其他民族

Qianji　黔记

Qiang　羌

Qing　青

Qiu　俅

Qu　曲

Riben　日本

Ri'erman 日耳曼

Ruanke 阮可

Sa 撒

Sani 撒尼

Sanda 三達

Sanmin 散民

Sanni 散尼

Sansu 三蘇

Santuohong 三妥紅

Sha 沙

Shan 善

Shanhou 山后

Shansu 山蘇

Shantou 山頭

Shanyihong 山夷紅

Shang 尚

shangceng renshi 上层人士

Shi 仕

shiwu yi zhuren suo cheng zhi ming wei ming 事物以主人所称之名为名

shizu 氏族

Shoutou 手头

Shu 黍, 述

Shui 水

Shuihu 水戶

Shuitian 水田

Shuiyi 水彝

shuofu gongzuo 说服工作

Silang 斯郎

Suobi 所比, 梭比

tacheng 他称

Tagu 他谷

Talu 他魯

Tamiao 他苗

Taiweisi 台维斯

Taiyi 台邑

Tanweisi 谭维斯

Tanglang 儻俍

tese minzu fuzhuang 特色民族服装

Tianbao 天保

tongcheng 统称

tongyi de duo minzu guojia 统一的多民族国家

tongzhong er yiming 同种而异名

Tu 土, 突

Tu'e 兔莪, 吐莪

Tujia 土家

Tulapa 图拉帕

Tulao 土佬, 土老

Tuli 土里

Tusi 土司

Wei shibie minzu 未识别民族

Woni 窝尼

Wu 乌

Wu'ersiwei 吾尔斯维

wuzu gonghe 五族共和

xifan 西番, 西蕃

Ximoluo 西抹羅, 西摩羅, 西摩洛

xinan minzu 西南民族

Xiang 象

Xiangtang 湘儻, 湘堂, 香堂

Xie 些

Yang 秧

Yao 傜, 瑶

Yi 彝, 夷

yihua zhihua 以华治华

Yishan 义山

Yishi 夷施

yi zhong mingcheng ji zhong xiefa 一种名称几种写法

yi zhong minzu ji zhong mingcheng　一种民族几种名称

yizu wenti　彝族问题

Yongbai　永白

youdi fangshi　有的放矢

Youle　攸樂

Yue　越

Yuenan　越南

Yunnan tongzhi　云南通志

yunniang　酝酿

Zaiqi haishi Hanmin?　在旗还是汉民?

Zang　藏

Zeheng　则恒

Zhemin　蔗民

Zhili　支理

zhixi　支系

Zhong　重

Zhonghua minzu　中华民族

Zhongjia　仲家

zhongzu　种族

Zhuang　僮, 壮

Zhuohe　卓核

Zi　子

zicheng　自称

Zijun　子君

Ziyi　子彝

zizhi　自治

Zong　棕

Zuoke　昨柯

BIBLIOGRAPHY

ARCHIVES

Sichuan sheng dang'an guan (Sichuan Provincial Archives), Chengdu, China
Worcestershire Records Office, Worcestershire, United Kingdom
Yunnan sheng dang'an guan (Yunnan Provincial Archives), Kunming, China

PERIODICALS

Bianjiang yanjiu tongxun
Bianzheng gonglun
Bulletin de la Société de Géographie
Bulletin of the American Geographical Society
Bureau of American Ethnology Annual Report
Dili xuebao
Dili zhishi
Folklore Studies
Gengsheng pinglung
Geographical Journal
Guoli beijing daxue xuebao
Guoli zhongyang yanjiuyuan lishi yuyan yanjiusuo renleixue jikan
Guoli zhongyang yanjiuyuan zongbaogao
Journal of the West China Border Research Society
Lishi yanjiu
Minzuxue yanjiu jikan
Qingnian zhongguo jikan
Renleixue jikan
Renwen kexue xuebao

Shehui xuexun
Xinan bianjiang
Zhongguo minzu wenti yanjiu jikan
Zhongguo minzu xuehui shi zhounian jinian lunwenji
Zhongguo yuwen

PRIMARY SOURCES

"*56 ge minzu shuang baotai 10 yue panju Beijing* [Twins from the Fifty-Six Minzu Prepare to Gather in Beijing in October]." August 12, 2005. http://sym2005.cass.cn/file/200508213 6006.html (accessed August 7, 2008).

Cai Yuanpei. "*Shuo minzuxue* [Something about Ethnology]." In *Cai Yuanpei Xuanji* [Selected Writings of Cai Yuanpei]. Hangzhou: Zhejiang renmin chubanshe, 1993.

Cen Jiawu. "*Kangzhan yu bianjiang minzu wenhua yundong* [The War of Resistance and the Cultural Movement of Border Ethnic Groups]." *Gengsheng pinglung* 3, no. 10 (1938).

———. "*Xinan zhongzu yanjiu zhi huigu yu qianzhan* [Retrospective and Future Prospects for Research of the Southwestern Races]." *Qingnian zhongguo jikan* 1, no. 4 (1940).

———. "*Lun minzu yu zhongzu* [On Ethnicity and Race]." *Bianzheng gonglun* 3, no. 4 (1944): 1–10.

———. *Cen Jiawu minzu yanjiu wenji* [Ethnological Writings of Cen Jiawu]. Beijing: Minzu chubanshe, 1992.

Chen Boda. "Ping 'Zhongguo zhi mingyun' [Critique of 'China's Destiny']." In *Minzu wenti wenxian huibian, 7/1921–9/1949*. Edited by Zhonggong zhongyang tongzhanbu. Beijing: Zhonggong zhongyang dangxiao chubanshe, 1991.

Chen Kehan. *Mofan kangri genjudi Jin-Cha-Ji bianqu*. Chongqing: Xinhua ribao guan, 1939.

Chen Lianzhen and Huang Caoliang. *Kangzhan zhong de Zhongguo minzu wenti*. Hankou: Liming shuju, 1938.

Chiang Kai-shek. *Zhongguo zhi mingyun* [China's Destiny]. Taipei: Zhongzheng shuju, 1986.

Clarke, Samuel R. *Among the Tribes in South-west China*. Taipei: Ch'eng Wen Publishing, 1970.

Colquhoun, Archibald R. *The "Overland" to China*. London: Harper, 1900.

Davies, Henry Rodolph. *Yün-nan, the Link Between India and the Yangtze*. Cambridge: Cambridge University Press, 1909.

———. "Review: In Farthest Burma by F. Kingdon Ward." *Geographical Journal* 58, no. 3 (September 1921): 230–32.

———. "Review: The Tibetan Border." *Geographical Journal* 63, no. 3 (March 1924): 247–49.

———. *Shina minzokuron* [On the minzu of China]. Translated by Suyama Taku. Tokyo: Keiyou Shobou, 1940.

Davies, Henry Rodolph, and David Prain. "From the Yangtze to the Irrawaddy: Discussion." *Geographical Journal* 62, no. 1 (July 1923): 18–20.

Deng Xiaoping. "*Guanyu 'Zhonghua Renmin Gongheguo quanguo renmin daibiao dahui xuanjufa' cao'an de shuoming* [Explanation of the Draft 'Election Law for the All-Country People's Representative Congress of the People's Republic of China' (February 11, 1953)]". In *Minzu zhengce wenxuan*. Urumqi: Xinjiang renmin chubanshe, 1985.

Desgodin, Auguste. "Mots Principaux des Langues de Certaines Tribus." *Bulletin de la So-ciété de Géographie* 144 (January–June 1873): 144–50.

Ding Su. "*Xinan minzu de fenlei fenbu ji yidong* [Categories, Distributions, and Migrations of Ethnic Groups in the Southwest]." *Renwen kexue xuebao* 1, no. 1 (1941).

Ding Wenjiang. *Cuanwen congke.* Shanghai: Shangwu yinshuguan/Zhongyang yanjiuyuan lishi yuyan yanjiusuo zhuankan, 1935.

Fang Guoyu. "*Qing queding Yunnan ge minzu mingcheng baoqing zhongyang zhengshi gong-bao* [Please confirm the names of all nationalities in Yunnan and submit them to the cen-ter for formal promulgation]." YNPA, Quanzong 3, Index 2165, File 157 (August 12, 1954).

Fei Xiaotong. *Earthbound China: A Study of Rural Economy in Yunnan.* Chicago: University of Chicago Press, 1945.

———. "*Dangqian minzu gongzuo tigei minzuxue de ji ge renwu* [A Few Responsibilities that Current and Future Nationalities Work Has Given to Ethnology]." *Zhongguo minzu wenti yanjiu jikan* 6 (1957).

Grierson, George A. *Linguistic Survey of India.* Delhi: Motilal Banarsidass, 1967.

Gu Jiegang. "*Zhonghua minzu shi yige* [The Zhonghua Nation is One]." In *Gu Jiegang juan.* Edited by Gu Chao and Gu Hong. Shijiazhuang: Hebei jiaoyu chubanshe, 1996.

"*Guanyu Guizhou sheng Zhongjia (Buyi) zu tongyi minzu mingcheng ji Jiangcheng xian tiao-zheng minzu zhixi tongbao.*" YNPA, Quanzong 2152, Index 1, File 44 (June 20, 1953): 62–66.

"*Guanyu jumin shenfenzheng shiyong minzu wenti he minzu chengfen tianxie wenti de tongzhi* [Notification Regarding the Use of Minority Script and Filling Out Nationality Identity on Residency Identification Cards]." www.mzb.com.cn/onews.asp?id=18007 (accessed August 6, 2008).

"*Guanyu Sui-Meng gongzuo de jueding* [Decision on Our Work among the Mongols of Sui-yuan Province]." In *Minzu wenti wenxian huibian: 7/1921–9/1949* [Collection of Docu-ments on the National Question, July 1921–September 1949]. Edited by Zhonggong zhongyang tongzhanbu. Beijing: Zhonggong zhongyang dangxiao chubanshe, 1991.

"*Guanyu Zhongguo lingnei shaoshu minzu wenti de jueyi'an* [Draft Resolution on the National Minority Question in China]." In *Minzu wenti wenxian huibian: 7/1921–9/1949* [Col-lection of Documents on the National Question, July 1921–September 1949]. Edited by Zhonggong zhongyang tongzhanbu. Beijing: Zhonggong zhongyang dangxiao chuban-she, 1991.

Guizhou Province Nationalities Affairs Commission. "*Fu youguan ni sheng Sha zu (Buyi) ming-cheng zhi yijian* [Responding with Opinions Regarding the Name of the Sha Minzu (Buyi) in Your Province]." YNPA, Quanzong 2152, Index 1, File 44 (June 20, 1954): 67–73.

Guoli zhongyang yanjiuyuan [Academia Sinica]. "*Guoli zhongyang yanjiuyuan zongbaogao 1932* [Summary Report of the Academia Sinica, 1932]." Edited by Guoli zhongyang yan-jiuyuan, 1932.

———. "*Guoli zhongyang yanjiuyuan zongbaogao 1935* [Summary Report of the Academia Sinica, 1935]." Edited by Guoli zhongyang yanjiuyuan, 1935.

Hallett, Holt S. "Exploration Survey for a Railway Connection between India, Siam, and China." *Proceedings of the Royal Geographical Society and Monthly Record of Geography, New Monthly Series* 8, no. 1 (January 1886): 1–20.

Hodge, Frederick W., ed. *Handbook of American Indians.* 2 vols. Washington, D.C.: Bureau of American Ethnology, 1907 and 1911.

Huang Wenshan. *"Cen zhu 'Xinan minzu wenhua luncong' xu* [Preface to Cen's 'Collected Treatises on the Culture of the Southwestern Ethnic Groups']." *Shehui xuexun* 5 (1947).

Jiang Yingliang. *Kangzhan zhong de xinan minzu wenti* [The Question of Southwest Ethnic Groups in Wartime]. Chongqing: Zhongshan Bureau of Culture and Education, 1938.

———. *Jiang Yingliang minzu yanjiu wenji* [Collected Ethnological Research of Jiang Yingliang]. Beijing: Minzu chubanshe, 1992.

"Jiangcheng xian Hani zu Yi zu zizhiqu shouweihui tiaozheng minzu zhixi baogao (gaoyao) [Report on the Rectification of National Branches of the Hani and Yi Minzu of Jiang-cheng County by the Autonomous Region Shouweihui—Draft]." YNPA, Quanzong 2152, Index 1, File 44 (March 23, 1954): 66.

Johnson, R. F. *From Peking To Mandalay: A Journey From North China To Burma Through Tibetan Szechuan and Yunnan.* Bangkok: White Lotus, 2001.

Li Jincan. *Lahuzu* [The Lahu Nationality]. Beijing: Minzu chubanshe, 2004.

Li Jinqun and Wang Chengquan. *Naxizu* [The Naxi Nationality]. Beijing: Minzu chubanshe, 2004.

Lin Yaohua. "Social Life of Aboriginal Groups In and Around Yunnan." *Journal of the West China Border Research Society* 15 (1944).

———. *"Guanyu minzu shibie wenti de yijian* [Opinions Regarding the Problem of Ethnic Classification]." YNPA, Quanzong 2152, Index 1, File 46: 39–56 (May 15, May 22, 1954).

———. *"Guanyu 'minzu' yi ci de shiyong he yiming de wenti* [About the Use and Translation of the Term 'minzu']." *Lishi yanjiu* 2 (1963): 171–90.

———. *"Youguan minzu shibie ji ge mingci de jieshi* [Explanations of Certain Terms Related to Ethnic Classification]." In *Yunnan shaoshu minzu shehui lishi diaocha (san)* [Social History Investigation of Ethnic Minorities in Yunnan (Three)]. Edited by Yunnan sheng bian-jizu. Kunming: Yunnan minzu chubanshe, 1987.

Lin Yaohua and Yu Xiangwen. *Liangshan Yi jia* [The Lolo of Liangshan]. Taipei: Nantian shuju, 1978.

Ling Chunsheng. *"Yunnan minzu de dili fenbu* [The Geographic Distribution of Ethnic Groups in Yunnan]." *Dili xuebao* 3, no. 3 (1936).

———. *"Tang dai Yunnan de wuman yu baiman kao* [Investigation of the Wuman and Baiman of Tang Dynasty Yunnan]." *Renleixue jikan* 1, no. 1 (1938).

Liu Geping. *"Zhongyang fangwentuan fangwen xinan ge minzu de zongjie baogao* [Summary Report on the Central Visitation Team's Visit to the Nationalities of the Southwest]." Beijing, 1951.

Luo Changpei. *"Cong yuyan shang lun Yunnan minzu de fenlei* [On the Categorization of Yunnanese Ethnic Groups from the Perspective of Language]." *Bianzheng gonglun* 1, no. 7–8 (1942).

———. *"Guonei shaoshuminzu yuyan xishu he wenzi qingkuang."* *Renmin ribao,* March 31, 1951.

Luo Changpei and Fu Maoji. *"Guonei shaoshuminzu yuyan wenzi de qingkuang* [The Situation of Linguistic Scripts for Domestic Minority Nationalities]." *Zhongguo yuwen* (1954).

Luo Changpei and Xing Qinglan. *Lianshan Baiyi yuwen chutan* [A Preliminary Investigation of the Baiyi Language of Lianshan]. Beijing: Beijing daxue chubanshe, 1950.

Ma Changshou. "*Sichuan gudai minzu lishi kaodeng.*" *Qingnian zhongguo jikan* 2, no. 2 (1941).

Mao Zedong. "Oppose Book Worship," www.marxists.org/reference/archive/mao/selected-works/volume-6/mswv6_11.htm#s3

———. "On the Ten Major Relationships." In *Selected Works of Mao Tse-tung*, vol. 5. Beijing: Foreign Languages Press, 1977.

———. *Report from Xunwu*. Translated by Roger R. Thompson. Stanford: Stanford University Press, 1990.

Minzu wenti yanjiushi, ed. *Huihui minzu wenti* [The Question of the Huihui Nationality]. Beijing: Minzu chubanshe, 1980.

Orléans, Henri d'. "From Yun-nan to British India." *Geographical Journal* 7, no. 3 (March 1896): 300–9.

Powell, J. W. "Indian Linguistic Families North of Mexico." *Bureau of American Ethnology Annual Report* 7 (1891): 1–142.

"Review of 'Yunnan, the Link between India and the Yangtze.'" *Bulletin of the American Geographical Society* 41, no. 10 (1909): 651–52.

Rock, Joseph Francis Charles. *Studies in Na-khi Literature*. Hanoi: Bulletin de l'École Française d'Extrême-Orient, 1938.

———. *The Ancient Na-khi Kingdom of Southwest China*. Cambridge, MA: Harvard University Press, 1947.

Rock, Joseph Francis Charles, M. Harders-Steinhäuser, and Georg Jayme. *The Life and Culture of the Na-khi Tribe on the China-Tibet Borderland*. Wiesbaden: Verzeichnis der orientalischen Handschriften in Deutschland, 1963.

Rui Yifu. "*Zhonghua guozu jie* [Explication of the Chinese Nation-Race]." *Renwen kexue xuebao* 1, no. 2 (1942).

———. "*Zhonghua minzu de zhipai ji qu fenbu* [The Branches of the Zhonghua Minzu and their Distributions]." *Zhongguo minzu xuehui shi zhounian jinian lunwenji* (1944): 3–13.

———. "*Xinan bianmin yu Miandian renmin* [The Border Peoples of the Southwest and the People of Burma]." *Bianzheng gonglun* 4, no. 1 (1945).

———. "*Zai lun zhonghua minzu de zhipai ji qi fenbu* [Once More on the Branches of the Zhonghua Minzu and their Distributions]." *Minzuxue yanjiu jikan* 5 (1946): 29–40.

Schleicher, August. "Darwinism Tested by the Science of Language." Translated by Max Müller. *Nature* 1, no. 10 (1870): 256–59.

———. *A Compendium of the Comparative Grammar of Indo-European, Sanskrit, Greek, and Latin Languages*. Translated by Herbert Bendall. London: Trubner, 1874.

"Shenzhen: 3,000 Municipal Citizens Unable to Exchange ID Cards Because of 'Lengpizi'; Police Urge Prudence When Naming Newborns." *Renmin ribao*, November 3, 2004.

Shirokogoroff, S. M. *Anthropology of Northern China*. Shanghai: Kelly & Walsh, 1923.

———. "Ethnographic Investigations of China." *Folklore Studies* 1 (1942): 1–8.

Siguret, J. *Territoires et Populations des Confins du Yunnan*. Peiping: Editions Henri Vetch, 1937.

Stalin, Joseph. *Marxism and the National-Colonial Question*. San Francisco: Proletarian Publishers, 1975.

Taiweisi [H. R. Davies]. *Yunnan ge Yizu ji qi yuyan yanjiu* [Research on the Barbarians of Yunnan and their Languages]. Translated by Zhang Junmai. Shanghai: Shangwu yinshuguan, 1939.

Tao Yunkui. *"Jige Yunnan tuzu de xiandai dili fenbu ji qi renkou zhi guji* [The Present Geographic Distribution of a Few Local Yunnanese Ethnic Groups and the Ancient Traces of their Populations]." *Guoli zhongyang yanjiuyuan lishi yuyan yanjiusuo renleixue jikan* 7, no. 4 (1938): 419–47.

Tsou Jung [Zou Rong]. *The Revolutionary Army: A Chinese Nationalist Tract of 1903.* Translated by John Just. The Hague: Mouton, 1968.

Ulanfu. "Report on the General Program for the Implementation of Regional Autonomy for Minorities (August 8, 1952)." In *Chinese Policies Towards Minorities: An Essay and Documents.* Edited by Henry G. Schwarz. Bellingham: Western Washington State College Program in East Asian Studies, 1952.

Vial, Paul. *De la Langue et de l'Écriture Indigenes au Yün-nân.* Paris: Ernest Leroux, 1890.

Wei Huilin. *"Zhongguo minzu fenlei lunlüe."* *Bianjiang yanjiu tongxun* 1, no. 2 (1942).

Wu Wenzao. *"Bianzhengxue fafan."* Reprinted in *Renleixue shehuixue yanjiu wenji.* Beijing: Minzu chubanshe, 1990.

Xu Jiahua, ed. *Li Qunjie wenji* [The Writings of Li Qunjie]. Kunming: Yunnan minzu chubanshe, 2001.

Yanjing-Tsinghua-Peking University Summer 1950 Inner Mongolia Work and Research Team, ed. *Neimenggu Hunameng minzu diaocha baogao* [Report on Ethnological Investigation in Hunameng, Inner Mongolia]. Hohhot: Inner Mongolia Nationalities Press, 1997.

Yang Kun. *"Minzuxue yu renleixue* [Ethnology and Anthropology]." *Guoli beijing daxue xuebao* 1, no. 4 (1935).

———. *"Wo guo minsuxue yundong shibei* [Overview History of the Folklore Movement in China]." In *Yang Kun minzu yanjiu wenji* [Collected Works of Ethnological Research by Yang Kun]. Beijing: Minzu chubanshe, 1991.

Yang Yucai. *"Yunnan sheng jige zhuyao shaoshu minzu de dili fenbu* [The Geographic Distribution of a Few Main Minority Nationalities in Yunnan Province]." *Dili zhishi* (September 1954).

"Yongsheng County Report on the Voter Registration/Census of 1953–4." YNPA, Quanzong 1, Index 2183, File 13 (July 16, July 22, 1954).

"Yuanyang xian puxuan renkou diaocha zonghe zongjie [Comprehensive summary report on registration and population investigation of Yuanyang County]." YNPA, Quanzong 1, Index 218, File 13.

"Yunlong xian jiceng puxuan gongzuo zongjie [Summary of Grassroot Voting Work in Yunlong County]." YNPA, Quanzong 83, Index 1, File 38 (April 1954).

Yunnan Province Nationalities Affairs Commission. *"Yunnan xiongdi minzu zhuyao fenbu diqu jiantu* [Simplified Map of the Main Regional Distributions of Brother Nationalities in Yunnan]." YNPA, Quanzong 2152, Index 3, File 3 (1951): 5.

———. *"Yunnan sheng xiongdi minzu fenbu lüetu* [Preliminary Distribution Map of Brother Nationalities in Yunnan Province]." YNPA, Quanzong 2152, Index 3, File 4 (1953).

———. *"Yunnan sheng shaoshu minzu renkou tongji biao (xuanweihui cailiao)* [Chart of the

Population Statistics of Minorities in Yunnan Province (Electoral Commission Materials)." YNPA, Quanzong 2152, Index 1, File 48 (1954): 1–167.

Yunnan Province Nationalities Affairs Commission Research Office. "*Yunnan sheng shaoshu minzu zhixi xishu yanjiu gaikuang he cunzai wenti* [Overall Situation of Research into the Branches of Minority Nationalities in Yunnan Province along with Existing Problems]." YNPA, Quanzong 2152, Index 1, File 47 (May 12, 1954): 26–38.

"*Yunnan sheng Kunming shi renkou diaocha dengji gongzuo zongjie* [Summary of Population Investigation and Registration Work in Kunming City, Yunnan Province]." YNPA, Quanzong 83, Index 1, File 32 (July 24, 1954): 7.

Yunnan sheng minzu shibie yanjiuzu [Yunnan Province Ethnic Classification Research Team]. "*Achang zu gaikuang* [Situation of the Achang Minzu of Yingjiang]." YNPA, Quanzong 2152, Index 5, File 65 (1954): 1–22.

——. "*Achang zu shibie xiaozu* [Summary Report on the Classification of the Achang Minzu]." YNPA, Quanzong 2152, Index 1, File 45 (1954): 1–5.

——. "*Funing 'Heiyi' zu shehui qingkuang diaocha* [Research into the Social Conditions of the 'Heiyi' Minzu of Funing]." YNPA, Quanzong 2152, Index 3, File 31 (1954): 123–31.

——. "*Jianbao* [Brief Report]." YNPA, Quanzong 2152, Index 1, File 44 (1954): 34–37.

——. "*Lianghe Achang qingkuang* [Situation of the Achang of Lianghe]." YNPA, Quanzong 2152, Index 3, File 65 (June 8–9, 1954): 84–95.

——. "*Mojiang xian 'Hani' zu shehui diaocha cailiao* [Materials from the Social Investigation into the 'Hani' Minzu of Mojiang County]." YNPA, Quanzong 2152, Index 3, File 34 (1954): 14–37.

——. "*Muji shibie xiaojie* [Small Summary on the Classification of the Muji]." YNPA, Quanzong 2152, Index 3, File 30 (1954): 193–97.

——. "*Shangcong Yunnan zheng shaoshu minzu shibie yanjiuzu diaocha jihua* [Investigation Plan Submitted by the Yunnan Province Ethnic Classification Research Team]." YNPA, Quanzong 2152, Index 1, File 44 (June 7, 1954): 23–33.

——. " '*Tulao' zu shibie xiaojie* [Brief Summary of the Classification of the 'Tulao' Minzu]." YNPA, Quanzong 2152, Index 1, File 45 (1954): 21–26.

——. "*Wenshan Mengzi Gejiu 'Pu' zu he 'Muji' zu diaocha baogao* [Report on the Investigation of the 'Pu' and 'Muji' Minzu in Wenshan, Mengzi, and Gejiu Counties]." YNPA, Quanzong 2152, Index 3, File 30 (1954): 92–156.

——. "*Wenshan Puzu ('Pula') shibie xiaojie* [Summary Report of the Classification of the Pu Minzu ('Pula') of Wenshan]." YNPA, Quanzong 2152, Index 1, File 45 (July 10, 1954): 9–13.

——. "*Wenshan zhuanqu Nong zu shibie xiaojie* [Summary Report of the Classification of the Nong Minzu of Wenshan Special Area]." YNPA, Quanzong 2152, Index 1, File 45 (1954): 33–38.

——. "*Xinping xian 'Ache' diaocha cailiao* [Research Materials on the 'Ache' of Xinping County]." YNPA, Quanzong 2152, Index 3, File 18 (1954): 45–54.

——. "*Xinping xian 'Chesu' zu gaikuang* [The General Situation of the 'Chesu' Minzu of Xinping County]." YNPA, Quanzong 2152, Index 3, File 18 (1954): 26–37.

——. "*Xinping xian 'Luowu' zu gaikuang* [Overall Situation of the 'Luowu' Minzu of Xinping County]." YNPA, Quanzong 2152, Index 3, File 18 (September 1954): 60–85.

———. *"Xinping xian 'Mili' zu diaocha* [Investigation into the 'Mili' Minzu of Xinping County]." YNPA, Quanzong 2152, Index 3, File 18 (1954): 86–100.

———. *"Xinping xian wu qu Pingzhang xiang 'Menghua' zu diaocha ziliao* [Research Materials on the 'Menghua' Minzu of Pingzhang Village in the Fifth Area of Xinping County]." YNPA, Quanzong 2152, Index 3, File 70 (1954): 76–87.

———. *"Xinping xian wu qu Pingzhang xiang 'Micha' zu qingkuang cailiao* [Materials on the Situation of the 'Micha' Minzu of Pingzhang Village in the Fifth Area of Xinping County]." YNPA, Quanzong 2152, Index 3, File 20 (1954): 95–109.

———. *"Xinping xian 'Mili' zu diaocha cailiao* [Materials from the Investigation of the 'Mili' Minzu of Xinping County]." YNPA, Quanzong 2152, Index 3, File 18 (1954): 86–100.

———. *"Xinping xian Yi zu fangwen cailiao* [Materials from the Visitation with the Yi Minzu of Xinping County]." YNPA, Quanzong 2152, Index 3, File 19 (1954): 72–95.

———. *"Yingjiang xian Husa Lasa Achang zu gaikuang* [Situation of the Achang Minzu of Husalasa in Yingjiang County]." YNPA, Quanzong 2152, Index 3, File 65 (1954): 53–79.

———. *"Yongsheng di'er qu Lude xiang 'Liude' zu fangwen jilü* [Transcript of the Visitation with the 'Liude' Minzu of Lude Village in the Second Area of Yongsheng County]." YNPA, Quanzong 2152, Index 3, File 78 (September 1954): 88–97.

———. *"Yongsheng, Lijiang, Lanping, Ninglang xian dui 'Xifan' zu fangwen jilü* [Record of Interviews with the 'Xifan' Minzu of Yongsheng, Lijiang, Lanping, and Ninglang Counties]." YNPA, Quanzong 2152, Index 3, File 79 (1954): 29–75.

———. *"Yongsheng 'Luo' 'Shuitian' 'Zhili' 'Ziyi' 'Liming' shibie xiaojie* [Summary Report on the Classification of the 'Luo,' 'Shuitian,' 'Zhili,' 'Ziyi,' and 'Liming' of Yongsheng]." YNPA, Quanzong 2152, Index 3, File 78 (1954): 98–104.

———. *"Yongsheng 'Luo' zu he 'Shuitian' zu qingkuang diaocha* [Investigation into the Situation of the 'Luo' and 'Shuitian' Minzu of Yongsheng County]." YNPA, Quanzong 2152, Index 3, File 78 (1954): 42–57.

———. *"Yongsheng Shuitian, Luoluo, Zhili, Ziyi, Lang'e, Talu deng minzu de yuyan* [The Languages of the Shuitian, Luoluo, Zhili, Ziyi, Lang'e, and Talu Minzu of Yongsheng County]." YNPA, Quanzong 2152, Index 3, File 78 (October 1954): 74–77.

———. *"Yongsheng xian di'er qu 'Nazha' 'Talu' diaocha cailiao* [Materials from the Investigation of the 'Nazha' and 'Talu' of the Second Area of Yongsheng County]." YNPA, Quanzong 2152, Index 3, File 78 (1954): 117–31.

———. *"Yongsheng xian di'er qu 'Tagu' zu diaocha* [Investigation of the 'Tagu' Minzu of the Second Area of Yongsheng County]." YNPA, Quanzong 2152, Index 3, File 78 (1954): 18–25.

———. *"Yongsheng xian 'Lang'e' qingkuang diaocha* [Research into the Situation of the 'Lang'e' of Yongsheng County]." YNPA, Quanzong 2152, Index 3, File 78 (1954): 26–41.

———. *"Yongsheng xian 'Liming' zu qingkuang diaocha baogao* [Report on the Investigation into the Situation of the 'Liming' Minzu of Yongsheng County]." YNPA, Quanzong 2152, Index 3, File 78 (1954): 1–12.

———. *"Yongsheng 'Zhili' zu qingkuang diaocha fu Ziyi zu qingkuang* [Investigation into the Situation of the 'Zhili' Minzu of Yongsheng with an Addendum on the Situation of the 'Ziyi' Nationality]." YNPA, Quanzong 2152, Index 3, File 78 (1954): 58–73.

———. "*Yunnan sheng Jingdong xian 'Mili' zu qingkuang diaocha chubu zongjie* [Preliminary Summary of the Investigation into the Situation of the 'Mili' Minzu of Jingdong County in Yunnan Province]." YNPA 2152, Index 3, File 34 (1954): 1–13.

———. "*Yunnan sheng minzu shibie yanjiu di yi jieduan chubu zongjie* [Preliminary Summary of the First Phase of Ethnic Classification Research in Yunnan]." Kunming: Yunnan sheng minzu shibie yanjiuzu, 1954.

Yunnan sheng minzu shiwu weiyuanhui yanjiushi. "*Yunnan minzu shibie cankao ziliao* [Reference Materials for the Yunnan Ethnic Classification Project]." Kunming: Yunnan sheng minzu shiwu weiyuanhui yanjiushi, 1955.

Yunnan sheng renmin zhengfu minzu shiwu weiyuanhui yanjiushi. "*Yunnan shaoshu minzu renkou tongjibiao (xuanweihui cailiao)* [Population Chart for the Minority Nationalities of Yunnan (Electoral Commission Materials)]." YNPA, Quanzong 2152, Index 1, File 48 (August 25, 1954).

Yunnan sheng xuanju weiyuanhui. "*Yunnan sheng xuanju gongzuo baogao (chugao)* [Report on Election Work in Yunnan County (Draft)]." YNPA, Quanzong 2, Index 2114, File 84 (July 23, 1954).

Zhang Fengqi. "*Yunnan sheng minzu shibie zonghe baogao* [Summary Report on Ethnic Classification in Yunnan]." Kunming: Yunnan sheng minzu shibie yanjiuzu, 1960.

Zhang Junjun. *Zhongguo minzu de gaizao* [Reconstruction of the Chinese Race]. Shanghai: Zhonghua shuju, 1935.

Zhang Yanxiu. "*Zai lun Yi Han tongyuan* [Once More on the Common Origins of the Yi and Han]." *Xinan bianjiang* 6 (1939): 501–9.

"*Zhaodai Xizang zhijingtuan ji ge di minzu daibiao* [Receiving the Salutatory Envoy from Tibet and Minority Representatives from All Areas]." *Renmin ribao*, October 17, 1952.

"*Zhonggong zhongyang guanyu shaoshu minzu duli zizhu de yuanze de zhishi* [Central Party Directive on The Principles of Independence and Self-Rule among the National Minorities]." In *Minzu wenti wenxian huibian: 7/1921–9/1949* [Collection of Documents on the National Question, July 1921–September 1949]. Edited by Zhonggong zhongyang tongzhanbu. Beijing: Zhonggong zhongyang dangxiao chubanshe, 1991.

"*Zhonggong zhongyang xibei gongzuo weiyuanhui guanyu Huihui minzu wenti de tigang* [The Policy Outline of the Northwest Work Committee on the Question of the Hui Minzu]." In *Minzu wenti wenxian huibian: 7/1921–9/1949* [Collection of Documents on the National Question, July 1921–September 1949]. Edited by Zhonggong zhongyang tongzhanbu. Beijing: Zhonggong zhongyang dangxiao chubanshe, 1991.

"*Zhonggong zhongyang xibei gongzuo weiyuanhui guanyu kangzhan zhong Menggu minzu wenti tigang* [The Policy Outline of the Northwest Work Committee on the Question of the Mongol Minzu during the War of Resistance]." In *Minzu wenti wenxian huibian: 7/1921–9/1949* [Collection of Documents on the National Question, July 1921–September 1949]. Edited by Zhonggong zhongyang tongzhanbu. Beijing: Zhonggong zhongyang dangxiao chubanshe, 1991.

"*Zhongguo gong-nong hongjun zhengzhibu guanyu Miao-Yao minzu zhong gongzuo yuanze de zhishi* [Directive of the Political Department of the Worker-Peasant Red Army Regarding Work Principles among the Miao and Yao Minzu]." In *Minzu wenti wenxian hui-*

bian: 7/1921–9/1949 [Collection of Documents on the National Question, July 1921–September 1949]. Edited by Zhonggong zhongyang tongzhanbu. Beijing: Zhonggong zhongyang dangxiao chubanshe, 1991.

"*Zhongguo gong-nong hongjun zong zhengzhibu guanyu zhuyi zhengqu yimin de gongzuo* [Directive of the Central Political Department of the Worker-Peasant Red Army on Paying Attention to the Work of Winning over the Yi people]." In In *Minzu wenti wenxian huibian: 7/1921–9/1949* [Collection of Documents on the National Question, July 1921–September 1949]. Edited by Zhonggong zhongyang tongzhanbu. Beijing: Zhonggong zhongyang dangxiao chubanshe, 1991.

Zhonghua renmin gongheguo diyi jie quanguo renmin daibiao dahui diyi ci huiyi mishuchu, ed. *Zhonghua renmin gongheguo diyi jie quanguo renmin daibiao dahui diyi ci huiyi lukan* [Record of the First Meeting of the First Plenum of the All-Country National People's Congress of the People's Republic of China]. Beijing: Zhonghua renmin gongheguo diyi jie quanguo renmin daibiao dahui diyi ci huiyi mishuchu, 1955.

"*Zhonghua suweiai zhongyang zhengfu dui Huizu renmin de xuanyan* [The Declaration of the Central Government of the Chinese Soviet to the People of the Hui Nationality]." In *Minzu wenti wenxian huibian: 7/1921–9/1949* [Collection of Documents on the National Question, July 1921–September 1949]. Edited by Zhonggong zhongyang tongzhanbu. Beijing: Zhonggong zhongyang dangxiao chubanshe, 1991.

Zhongyang minzu xueyuan [Central Institute for Nationalities]. "*Yunnan Tujia zu diaocha cailiao* [Research materials on the Tujia of Yunnan]." Beijing: Central Institute for Nationalities, 1955.

Zhongyang renmin zhengfu minzu shiwu weiyuanhui [Central People's Government Nationalities Affairs Commission]. *Zhongguo shaoshu minzu jianbiao* [Simple Chart of the Minorities of China]. Beijing: Zhongyang renmin zhengfu minzu shiwu weiyuanhui, 1950.

Zhou Enlai. "Relations Among Nationalities (October 23, 1951)." In *Chinese Policies Towards Minorities: An Essay and Documents,* edited by Henry G. Schwarz. Bellingham: Western Washington State College Program in East Asian Studies, 1971.

SECONDARY SOURCES: BOOKS, ARTICLES, AND ESSAYS

Abramson, Marc. *Ethnic Identity in Tang China.* Philadelphia: University of Pennsylvania Press, 2008.

Aird, John S. *The Size, Composition, and Growth of the Population of Mainland China.* Washington, DC: U.S. Government Printing Office, 1961.

An Chunyang and Liu Bohua, eds. *Where the Dai People Live.* Beijing: Foreign Languages Press, 1985.

Anderson, Benedict. *Imagined Communities: Reflections on the Origin and Spread of Nationalism.* Rev. ed. New York: Verso, 1991.

Arkush, R. David. *Fei Xiaotong and Sociology in Revolutionary China.* Cambridge, MA: Council on East Asian Studies, Harvard University Press, 1981.

Atwill, David. *The Chinese Sultanate: Islam, Ethnicity, and the Panthay Rebellion in Southwest China, 1856–1873.* Stanford: Stanford University Press, 2005.

Avedon, John F. *In Exile in the Land of Snows.* New York: Knopf, 1984.

Bai Zhihong. "The Discourse of Tourism Development in the Construction of a Bai Cultural and Historical City." *Thai-Yunnan Project Bulletin* 2 (2001): 1–3.

Barth, Fredrik. "Introduction." In *Ethnic Groups and Boundaries,* edited by Fredrik Barth. Oslo: Universitetsforlaget, 1969.

Becker, Peter. "The Standardized Gaze: The Standardization of the Search Warrant in Nineteenth-Century Germany." In *Documenting Individual Identity: The Development of State Practices in the Modern World.,* edited by Jane Caplan and John Torpey, 139–63. Princeton: Princeton University Press, 2001.

Bello, David. "To Go Where No Han Could Go for Long: Malaria and the Qing Construction of Ethnic Administrative Space in Frontier Yunnan." *Modern China* 31, no. 3 (July 2005): 283–317.

Bieder, Robert E. *Science Encounters the Indian, 1820–1880: The Early Years of American Ethnology.* Norman: University of Oklahoma Press, 1986.

Blum, Susan D. *Portraits of 'Primitives': Ordering Human Kinds in the Chinese Nation.* Lanham, MD: Rowman and Littlefield, 2001.

———. "Margins and Centers: A Decade of Publishing on China's Ethnic Minorities." *Journal of Asian Studies* 61, no. 4 (November 2002): 1287–310.

Boorman, Howard, and Richard Howard, eds. *Biographical Dictionary of Republican China.* 4 vols. Columbia: Columbia University Press, 1967–1979.

Bowker, Geoffrey, and Susan Leigh Star. *Sorting Things Out: Classification and Its Consequences.* Cambridge, MA: MIT Press, 1999.

Bradley, David. "Language Policy for the Yi." In *Perspectives on the Yi of Southwest China,* edited by Stevan Harrell, 195–213. Berkeley: University of California Press, 2001.

Brown, Melissa J., ed. *Negotiating Ethnicities in China and Taiwan.* Berkeley: Institute of East Asian Studies, University of California, 1996.

———. "On Becoming Chinese." In *Negotiating Ethnicities in China and Taiwan,* edited by Melissa J. Brown, 37–74. Berkeley: Institute of East Asian Studies, University of California, 1997.

———. "Ethnic Classification and Culture: The Case of the Tujia in Hubei, China." *Asian Ethnicity* 2, no. 1 (2001): 55–72.

Bulag, Uradyn. *The Mongols at China's Edge: History and the Politics of National Unity.* New York: Rowman & Littlefield, 2002.

———. "The Yearning for 'Friendship': Revisting 'the Political' in Minority Revolutionary History in China." *Journal of Asian Studies* 65, no. 1 (Feburary 2006): 3–32.

Burrow, J. W. "The Uses of Philology in Victorian England." In *Ideas and Institutions of Victorian Britain,* edited by Robert Robson, 180–204. London: Bell and Sons, 1967.

Caffrey, Kevin. "Who 'Who' Is, and Other Poetics of National Policy: Yunnan *Minzu Shibie* and Hui in the Process." *China Information* 18, no. 2 (2004), 243–74.

Caplan, Jane, and John Torpey, eds. *Documenting Individual Identity: The Development of State Practices in the Modern World.* Princeton: Princeton University Press, 2001.

Carrère d'Encausse, Hélène. *The Great Challenge: Nationalities and the Bolshevik State, 1917–1930.* Translated by Nancy Festinger. New York: Holmes & Meier, 1992.

Chao, Emily. "Depictions of Difference: History, Gender, Ritual and State Discourse Among the Naxi of Southwest China." PhD Dissertation, University of Michigan, 1995.

———. "Hegemony, Agency, and Re-Presenting the Past." In *Negotiating Ethnicities in China and Taiwan*, edited by Melissa J. Brown, 208–39. Berkeley: Institute of East Asian Studies, University of California, 1996.

Chatterjee, Partha. "Whose Imagined Community?" In *Nationalism: Critical Concepts in Political Science*, vol. 3, edited by John Hutchinson and Anthony D. Smith, 940–45. London: Routledge, 2000.

Chen Guoqing. *Kemu yu yanjiu* [Research on the Kemu Language]. Beijing: Minzu chubanshe, 2002.

Chen Ta. "The Beginnings of Modern Demography." *American Journal of Sociology* 52 Supplement: Population in Modern China (1947): 7–16.

———. "New China's Population Census of 1953 and its Relations to National Reconstruction and Demographic Research." *Bulletin de l'Institut International de Statistique* 36, no. 2 (1957).

Cheng Zhifan and Li Antai, eds. *Yunnan minzu fushi* [The Clothes and Ornaments of Yunnan Ethnic Groups]. Kunming: Yunnan minzu chubanshe, 2000.

Cheung, Siu-woo. "Millenarianism, Christian Movements, and Ethnic Change among the Miao in Southwest China." In *Cultural Encounters on China's Ethnic Frontiers*, edited by Stevan Harrell, 217–47. Seattle: University of Washington Press, 1995.

———. "Representation and Negotiation of Ge Identities in Southeast Guizhou." In *Negotiating Ethnicities in China and Taiwan*, edited by Melissa J. Brown, 240–73. Berkeley: Institute for Asian Studies, University of California, 1996.

———. "Miao Identities, Indigenism and the Politics of Appropriation in Southwest China during the Republican Period." *Asian Ethnicity* 4, no. 1 (February 2003): 85–114.

Chia, Ning. "The Lifanyuan and the Inner Asian Rituals in the Early Qing (1644–1795)." *Late Imperial China* 14, no. 1 (June 1993): 60–92.

Chiang, Yung-chen. *Social Engineering and the Social Sciences in China, 1919–1949*. Cambridge: Cambridge University Press, 2001.

Ching, May-bo. "Classifying Peoples: Ethnic Politics in late Qing Native-Place Textbooks and Gazetteers." In *The Politics of Historical Production in Late Qing and Republican China*, ed. Tze-ki Hon and Robert Culp, 55–78. Leiden: Brill, 2007.

Chow, Kai-wing. "Imagining Boundaries of Blood: Zhang Bingling and the Invention of the Chinese Race in Modern China." In *Racial Identities in East Asia*, edited by Barry Sautman, 34–52. Hong Kong: Hong Kong University of Science and Technology, 1995.

———. "Narrating Nation, Race and National Culture: Imagining the Hanzu Identity in Modern China." In *Constructing Nationhood in Modern East Asia*, edited by Kai-wing Chow, Kevin Doak, and Poshek Fu, 47–83. Ann Arbor: University of Michigan Press, 2001.

Chow Tse-tsung. *The May Fourth Movement: Intellectual Revolution in Modern China*. Stanford: Stanford University Press, 1967.

Christian, John L. "Anglo-French Rivalry in Southeast Asia: Its Historical Geography and Diplomatic Climate." *Geographical Review* 31, no. 2 (April 1941), 272–82.

Clark, Paul. "Ethnic Minorities in Chinese Films: Cinema and the Exotic." *East-West Film Journal* 1, no. 2 (1987): 15–32.

Cohn, Bernard. "The Command of Language and the Language of Command." In *Subaltern Studies IV*, edited by Ranajit Guhat. Delhi: Oxford University Press, 1987.

———. *Colonialism and its Forms of Knowledge: The British in India*. Princeton: Princeton University Press, 1996.

Connor, Walker. *The National Question in Marxist-Leninist Theory and Strategy*. Princeton: Princeton University Press, 1984.

———. *Ethnonationalism: The Quest for Understanding*. Princeton: Princeton University Press, 1994.

Crossley, Pamela Kyle. *Orphan Warriors: Three Generations and the End of the Qing World*. Princeton: Princeton University Press, 1990.

———. "Thinking about Ethnicity in Early Modern China." *Late Imperial China* 11, no. 1 (1990): 1–35.

———. *A Translucent Mirror: History and Identity in Qing Imperial Ideology*. Berkeley: University of California Press, 1999.

———. "Nationality and Difference in China: The Post-Imperial Dilemma." In *The Teleology of the Modern Nation-State: Japan and China*, edited by Joshua Fogel, 138–58. Philadelphia: University of Pennsylvania Press, 2005.

Crossley, Pamela, Helen Siu, and Donald Sutton, eds. *Empire at the Margins: Culture, Ethnicity and Frontier in Early Modern China*. Berkeley: University of California Press, 2006.

Dai Qingxia. *Langsu yu yanjiu* [Research on the Langsu Language]. Beijing: Minzu chubanshe, 2005.

Dai, Yingcong. "The Rise of the Southwestern Frontier under the Qing, 1640–1800." PhD diss., University of Washington, 1996.

———. "A Disguised Defeat: The Myanmar Campaign of the Qing Dynasty." *Modern Asian Studies* 38, no. 1 (2004): 145–89.

Daston, Lorraine. "The Coming Into Being of Scientific Objects." In *Biographies of Scientific Objects*, edited by Lorraine Daston, 1–14. Chicago: Chicago University Press, 2000.

Davies, A. M. *Nineteenth-Century Linguistics*, vol. 4. London: Longman, 1998.

Davis, Sara. "Singers of Sipsongpanna: Folklore and Authenticity in Contemporary China." PhD diss., University of Pennsylvania, 1999.

———. "The Hawaiification of Xishuangbanna: Orality, Power, and Cultural Survival in Southwest China." *The Drama Review* 45, no. 4 (Winter 2001): 25–41.

Deal, David Michael. "National Minority Policy in Southwest China, 1911–1965." PhD diss., University of Washington, 1971.

De Bary, William Theodore, and Richard John Lufrano, eds. *Sources of Chinese Tradition: From 1600 through the Twentieth Century*. New York: Columbia University Press, 1999.

DeFrancis, John. "National and Minority Policies." *Annals of the American Academy of Political and Social Science* 277 (1951): 146–55.

Desrosières, Alain. "How to Make Things which Hold Together: Social Science, Statistics and the State." In *Discourses on Society: The Shaping of the Social Science Disciplines*, edited by Peter Wagner, 195–218. Dordrecht: Kluwer Academic Publishers, 1991.

Dessaint, Alain Y. *Minorities of Southwest China: An Introduction to the Yi (Lolo) and Related Peoples and an Annotated Bibliography*. New Haven, CT: HRAF Press, 1980.

Di Cosmo, Nicola. "Qing Colonial Administration in Inner Asia." *International Historical Review* 20, no. 2 (June 1998): 287–309.

Diamond, Norma. "Defining the Miao: Ming, Qing, and Contemporary Views." In *Cultural*

Encounters on China's Ethnic Frontiers, edited by Stevan Harrell, 92–116. Seattle: University of Washington Press, 1995.

———. "The Miao and Poison: Interactions on China's Southwest Frontier." *Ethnology* 27, no. 1 (1998): 1–25.

Diao, Richard. "The National Minorities of China and Their Relations with the Chinese Communist Regime." In *Southeast Asian Tribes, Minorities, and Nations,* edited by Peter Kunstadter, 169–201. Princeton: Woodrow Wilson School of Public and International Affairs, Center of International Studies, and American Anthropological Association, 1967.

Dikötter, Frank. *The Discourse of Race in Modern China.* London: Hurst, 1992.

———. "Culture, 'Race' and Nation: The Formation of National Identity in Twentieth Century China." *Journal of International Affairs* 49, no. 2 (1996): 590–605.

———. "Racial Discourse in China: Continuities and Permutations." In *The Construction of Racial Identities in China and Japan,* edited by Frank Dikötter, 12–33. Hong Kong: Hong Kong University Press, 1997.

Dirks, Nicholas B. *Castes of Mind: Colonialism and the Making of Modern India.* Princeton: Princeton University Press, 2001.

Dittmer, Lowell, and Samuel S. Kim, eds. *China's Quest for National Identity.* Ithaca: Cornell University Press, 1993.

Doak, Kevin M. "Building National Identity through Ethnicity: Ethnology in Wartime Japan and After." *Journal of Japanese Studies* 27, no. 1 (Winter 2001): 1–39.

Douglas, Mary. "Introduction." In *How Classification Works: Nelson Goodman Among the Social Sciences,* edited by Nelson Goodman, Mary Douglas, and David L. Hull. Edinburgh: Edinburgh University Press, 1992.

———. "Rightness of Categories." In *How Classification Works: Nelson Goodman Among the Social Sciences,* edited by Nelson Goodman, Mary Douglas, and David L. Hull, 239–71. Edinburgh: Edinburgh University Press, 1992.

Dowling, Linda. "Victorian Oxford and the Science of Language." *Publication of the Modern Language Association* 97, no. 2 (1982): 160–78.

Dreyer, June Teufel. "China's Minority Nationalities: Traditional and Party Elites." *Pacific Affairs* 43, no. 4 (1970): 506–30.

———. *China's Forty Millions: Minority Nationalities and National Integration in the People's Republic of China.* Cambridge, MA: Harvard University Press, 1976.

———. "Language Planning for China's Ethnic Minorities." *Pacific Affairs* 51, no. 3 (1978): 369–83.

Duara, Prasenjit. *Rescuing History from the Nation: Questioning Narratives of Modern China.* Chicago: University of Chicago Press, 1995.

———. "Ethnics (minzoku) and Ethnology (minzokushugi) in Manchukuo." Asia Research Institute Working Paper Series 74, September 2006.

Eberhard, Wolfram. *China's Minorities: Yesterday and Today.* Belmont, CA: Wadsworth, 1982.

Edgar, Adrienne Lynn. *Tribal Nation: The Making of Soviet Turkmenistan.* Princeton: Princeton University Press, 2006.

Elliott, Mark C. *The Manchu Way: The Eight Banners and Ethnic Identity in Late Imperial China.* Stanford: Stanford University Press, 2001.

———. "Ethnicity in the Qing Eight Banners." In *Empire at the Margins: Culture, Ethnicity, and Frontier in Early Modern China*, edited by Pamela Kyle Crossley, Helen F. Siu, and Donald S. Sutton, 27–57. Berkeley: University of California Press, 2006.

Eriksen, Thomas. *Ethnicity and Nationalism*. London: Pluto Press, 1993.

Esenbel, Selçuk. "Japan's Global Claim to Asia and the World of Islam: Transnational Nationalism and World Power, 1900–1945." *American Historical Review* 109, no. 4 (2004): 1140–70.

Esherick, Joseph W. "How the Qing Became China." In *Empire to Nation: Historical Perspectives on the Making of the Modern World*, edited by Joseph W. Esherick, Hasan Kayali, and Eric Van Young, 229–59. Lanham, MD: Rowman & Littlefield, 2006.

Fabian, Johannes. *Language and Colonial Power: The Appropriation of Swahili in the Former Belgian Congo, 1880–1938*. Berkeley: University of California Press, 1986.

Fang Fuqi. *Fang Guoyu zhuan* [Biography of Fang Guoyu]. Kunming: Yunnan daxue chubanshe, 2001.

Farquhar, David M. "Emperor as Bodhisattva in the Governance of the Ch'ing Empire." *Harvard Journal of Asiatic Studies* 38, no. 1 (June 1978): 5–34.

Fei Xiaotong. "Ethnic Identification in China." In *Toward a People's Anthropology*. Edited by Fei Xiaotong, 60–77. Beijing: New World Press, 1981.

———. *Toward a People's Anthropology*. Beijing: New World Press, 1981.

———. *Zhonghua minzu duoyuan yiti geju* [The Plurality and Organic Unity of the Zhonghua minzu]. Beijing: Zhongyang renmin xueyuan chubanshe, 1989.

Feyerabend, Paul K. *Against Method*. London: Verso, 1988.

Fiskesjö, Magnus. "Rescuing the Empire: Chinese Nation-Building in the Second Half of the Twentieth Century." *European Journal of East Asian Studies* 5, no. 1 (2006): 15–44.

Fitzgerald, John. "The Nationless State: The Search for a Nation in Modern Chinese Nationalism." *Australian Journal of Chinese Affairs* 33 (January 1995): 75–104.

Fogel, Joshua A. "Race and Class in Chinese Historiography: Divergent Interpretations of Zhang Bing-lin and Anti-Manchuism in the 1911 Revolution." *Modern China* 3, no. 3 (July 1977): 346–75.

———, ed. *The Teleology of the Modern Nation-State: Japan and China*. Philadelphia: University of Pennsylvania Press, 2005.

Foucault, Michel. *The Order of Things: An Archaeology of the Human Sciences*. New York: Vintage Books, 1970.

Furth, Charlotte. *Ting Wen-chiang: Science and China's New Culture*. Cambridge, MA: Harvard University Press, 1970.

Gellner, Ernest. *Nations and Nationalism*. Ithaca: Cornell University Press, 1983.

Giersch, C. Patterson. *Asian Borderlands: The Transformation of Qing China's Yunnan Frontier*. Cambridge, MA: Harvard University Press, 2006.

Gladney, Dru. *Muslim Chinese: Ethnic Nationalism in the People's Republic*. Cambridge, MA: Harvard University Press, 1991.

———. "Representing Nationality in China: Refiguring Majority/Minority Identities." *Journal of Asian Studies* 53, no. 1 (February 1994): 92–123.

———. *Ethnic Identity in China: The Making of a Muslim Minority Nationality*. Fort Worth, TX: Harcourt Brace, 1998.

Goldstein, Melvyn. *A History of Modern Tibet, 1913–1951: The Demise of the Lamaist State.* Berkeley: University of California Press, 1989.

Goodman, Nelson, Mary Douglas, and David L. Hull, eds. *How Classification Works: Nelson Goodman among the Social Sciences.* Edinburgh: Edinburgh University Press, 1992.

Grenoble, Lenore A., and Lindsay J. Whaley, eds. *Endangered Languages: Language Loss and Community Response.* Cambridge: Cambridge University Press, 1998.

Gros, Stéphane. "The Politics of Names: The Identification of the Dulong (Drung) of Northwest Yunnan." *China Information* 18, no. 2 (2004): 275–302.

Guldin, Gregory. "Anthropology by Other Names: The Impact of Sino-Soviet Friendship on the Anthropological Sciences." *Australian Journal of Chinese Affairs* 27 (1992): 133–49.

———. *The Saga of Anthropology in China: From Malinowski to Mao.* Armonk, NY: M. E. Sharpe, 1994.

Guo Hongsheng. *A Comparative Study of the National Question in China and the Former Soviet Union* [Zhongguo yu qian Sulian minzu wenti duibi yanjiu]. Beijing: Minzu Press, 1997.

Hacking, Ian. "Making Up People." In *The Science Studies Reader,* edited by Mario Biagiolo, 161–71. New York: Routledge, 1999.

Hamrin, Carol Lee, and Timothy Cheek, eds. *China's Establishment Intellectuals.* Armonk, NY: M. E. Sharpe, 1986.

Hansen, Mette. *Lessons in Being Chinese: Minority Education and Ethnic Identity in Southwest China.* Seattle: University of Washington Press, 1999.

Harrell, Stevan, ed. *Cultural Encounters on China's Ethnic Frontiers: Studies on Ethnic Groups in China.* Seattle: University of Washington Press, 1995.

———. "Ethnicity, Local Interest, and the State: Yi Communities in Southwest China." *Comparative Study in Society and History* 32, no. 3 (July 1990): 515–48.

———. "The History of the History of the Yi." In *Cultural Encounters on China's Ethnic Frontiers,* edited by Stevan Harrell, 63–91. Seattle: University of Washington Press, 1995.

———. "Languages Defining Ethnicity in Southwest China." In *Ethnic Identity: Creation, Conflict, and Accommodation,* edited by Lola Romanucci-Ross and George DeVos, 97–114. Walnut Creek, CA: Altamira Press, 1995.

———. "Introduction." In *Negotiating Ethnicities in China and Taiwan,* edited by Melissa J. Brown, 1–10. Berkeley: Institute for East Asian Studies, University of California, 1996.

———. "The Nationalities Question and the Prmi Prblem." In *Negotiating Ethnicities in China and Taiwan,* edited by Melissa J. Brown, 274–96. Berkeley: Institute for East Asian Studies, University of California, 1996.

———, ed. *Perspectives on the Yi of Southwest China.* Berkeley: University of California Press, 2001.

———. *Ways of Being Ethnic in Southwest China.* Seattle: University of Washington Press, 2001.

Hattaway, Paul. *Operation China: Introducing All the Peoples of China.* Carlisle, UK: Piquant, 2000.

Heberer, Thomas. "Nationalities, Conflict and Ethnicity in the People's Republic of China, with Special Reference to the Yi in the Liangshan Yi Autonomous Prefecture." In *Perspectives on the Yi of Southwest China,* edited by Stevan Harrell, 214–37. Berkeley: University of California Press, 2001.

Henson, Hilary. *British Social Anthropologists and Language: A History of Separate Development.* Oxford: Clarendon, 1974.

Herman, John E. "Empire in the Southwest: Early Qing Reforms to the Native Chieftain System." *Journal of Asian Studies* 56, no. 1 (Feb. 1997): 47–74.

———. "The Cant of Conquest: Tsui Offices and China's Political Incorporation of the Southwestern Frontier." In *Empire at the Margins: Culture, Ethnicity, and Frontier in Early Modern China,* edited by Pamela Kyle Crossley, Helen F. Siu, and Donald S. Sutton, 135–70. Berkeley: University of California Press, 2006.

Hill, Ann Maxwell. "Captives, Kin, and Slaves in Xiao Liangshan." *Journal of Asian Studies* 60, no. 4 (Nov. 2001): 1033–49.

Hirsch, Francine. *Empire of Nations: Ethnographic Knowledge and the Making of the Soviet Union.* Ithaca: Cornell University Press, 2005.

Ho, Ping-ti. *Studies on the Population of China, 1368–1953.* Cambridge, MA: Harvard University Press, 1959.

———. "In Defense of Sinicization: A Rebuttal of Evelyn Rawski's 'Reenvisioning the Qing.'" *Journal of Asian Studies* 57, no. 1 (February 1998): 123–55.

Hobsbawm, Eric. *Nations and Nationalism: Programme, Myth, Reality.* Cambridge: Cambridge University Press, 1992.

Hobsbawm, Eric, and Terence Ranger, eds. *The Invention of Tradition.* Cambridge: Cambridge University Press, 1983.

Hoenigswald, Henry M. "On the History of the Comparative Method." *Anthropological Linguistics* 5, no. 1 (1963): 1–11.

Honig, Emily. *Creating Chinese Ethnicity: Subei People in Shanghai, 1850–1980.* New Haven: Yale University Press, 1992.

Hostetler, Laura. *Qing Colonial Enterprise: Ethnography and Cartography in Early Modern China.* Chicago: University of Chicago Press, 2001.

Hsieh, Shi-chung. "On Three Definitions of the Han Ren: Images of Majority People in Taiwan." In *Making Majorities: Constituting the Nation in Japan, Korea, China, Malaysia,* edited by Dru C. Gladney, 95–105. Stanford: Stanford University Press, 1998.

Huang Guangxue, ed. *Dangdai Zhongguo de minzu gongzuo (shang)* [Ethnicity Work in Contemporary China, volume 1]. Beijing: Dangdai zhongguo congshu bianji weiyuanhui, 1993.

———. *Zhongguo de minzu shibie* [Ethnic Classification in China]. Beijing: Minzu chubanshe, 1995.

Hung, Chang-tai. *Going to the People: Chinese Intellectuals and Folk Literature, 1918–1937.* Cambridge, MA: Harvard University Press, 1985.

Hyde, Sandra. "Sex Tourism Practices on the Periphery: Eroticizing Ethnicity and Pathologizing Sex on the Lancang." In *China Urban: Ethnographies of Contemporary Culture,* edited by Nancy Chen, 143–64. Durham: Duke University Press, 2001.

Hymes, Dell. "Notes Toward a History of Linguistic Anthropology." *Anthropological Linguistics* 5, no. 1 (January 1963): 59–103.

———, ed. *Studies in the History of Linguistics: Traditions and Paradigms.* Bloomington: Indiana University Press, 1974.

———. *Essays in the History of Linguistic Anthropology: Amsterdam Studies in the Theory and History of Linguistic Science III.* Amsterdam: John Benjamin, 1983.

Ishikawa, Yoshihiro. *Racialism during the Revolution of 1911 and the Rise of Chinese Anthopology*. Beijing: Central Literature Press, 2002.

———. "Anti-Manchu Racism and the Rise of Anthropology in Early 20th Century China." *Sino-Japanese Studies* 15 (April 2003): 19–26.

Israel, John. "Southwest Associated University: Preservation as an Ultimate Value." In *Nationalist China during the Sino-Japanese War, 1937–1945*, edited by Paul K. T. Sih. Hicksville, NY: Exposition Press, 1977.

Jaschok, Maria, and Shui Jingjun. *The History of Women's Mosques in Chinese Islam*. Surrey: Curzon Press, 2000.

Jenks, Robert D. *Insurgency and Social Disorder in Guizhou: The 'Miao' Rebellion, 1854–1873*. Honolulu: University of Hawai'i Press, 1994.

Jespersen, Otto. *Language: Its Nature, Development and Origin*, London: Allen & Unwin, 1922.

Jin Binghao, ed. *Minzu gangling zhengce wenxian xuanbian, 1921–2005* [Selected Key Policies on Minority Affairs, 1921–2005]. Beijing: Central University for Nationalities Press, 2006.

Jin Xinghua, ed. *Zhongguo minzu yuwen gongzuo* [Minorty Language Work in China]. Beijing: Minzu chubanshe, 2005.

Jing, Q. C. "Development of Psychology in China." *International Journal of Psychology* 29, no. 6 (1994): 667–75.

Kauko, Laitinen. *Chinese Nationalism in the Late Qing Dynasty: Zhang Binglin as an Anti-Manchu Propagandist*. London: Curzon Press, 1990.

Kaup, Katherine Palmer. *Creating the Zhuang: Ethnic Politics in China*. Boulder, CO: Lynne Rienner Publishers, 2000.

Kertzer, David I., and Dominique Arel. "Censuses, Identity Formation, and the Struggle for Political Power." In *Census and Identity. The Politics of Race, Ethnicity, and Language in National Censuses*, edited by David I. Kertzer and Dominique Arel. Cambridge: Cambridge University Press, 2002.

Keyes, Charles. "Towards a New Formulation of the Concept of Ethnic Group." *Ethnicity* 3 (1976): 202–13.

———. "Presidential Address: 'The Peoples of Asia'—Science and Politics in the Classification of Ethnic Groups in Thailand, China, and Vietnam." *Journal of Asian Studies* 61, no. 4 (2002): 1163–203.

Khan, Almaz. "Who are the Mongols? State, Ethnicity, and the Politics of Representation in the PRC." In *Negotiating Ethnicities in China and Taiwan*, edited by Melissa J. Brown, 125–59. Berkeley: Institute for East Asian Studies, University of California, 1996.

Khan, Harold L. *Monarchy in the Emperor's Eyes: Image and Reality in the Ch'ien-lung Reign*. Cambridge, MA: Harvard University Press, 1971.

King, Ambrose Yeo-Chi, and Wang Tse-Sang. "The Development and Death of Chinese Academic Sociology: A Chapter in the Sociology of Sociology." *Modern Asian Studies* 12, no. 1 (1978): 37–58.

Klein, Donald and Anne B. Clark, ed. *Biographical Dictionary of Chinese Communism, 1921–1965*, 2 vols. Cambridge, MA: Harvard University Press, 1971.

Knorr Cetina, Karen. *Epistemic Cultures: How the Sciences Make Knowledge*. Cambridge, MA: Harvard University Press, 1999.

Koerner, E. F. K. "Towards a Historiography of Linguistics: 19th and 20th Century Paradigm."

In *History of Linguistic Thought and Contemporary Linguistics*, edited by Herman Parret, 685–718. Berlin: Walter de Gruyter, 1976.

Krader, Lawrence, and John Aird. "Sources of Demographic Data on Mainland China." *American Sociological Review* 24, no. 5 (October 1959): 623–30.

Kuhn, Thomas S. *The Structure of Scientific Revolutions*. Chicago: University of Chicago Press, 1962.

"La Recensement de la Chine. Méthodes et Principaux Resultats." *Population* 11, no. 4 (October–December 1956).

Lacoupérie, Albert Terrien de. *Western Origin of the Early Chinese Civilisation from 2,300 B.C. to 200 A.D.* Osnabrück: Otto Zeller, 1966.

———. *The Languages of China Before the Chinese*. Osnabrück: Otto Zeller, 1969.

Latour, Bruno. *Science in Action: How to Follow Scientists and Engineers through Society*. Cambridge, MA: Harvard University Press, 1987.

———. "On the Partial Existence of Existing and Nonexisting Objects." In *Biographies of Scientific Objects*, edited by Lorraine Daston, 247–69. Chicago: University of Chicago Press, 2000.

Lattimore, Owen. "The Frontier in History." In *Studies in Frontier History*. Oxford: Oxford University Press, 1962.

Legendre, A. F. *Au Yunnan et dans le Massif du Kin-ho*. Paris: Fleuve d'or, 1913.

Leibold, James. "Competing Narratives of Racial Writing in Republican China: From the Yellow Emperor to Peking Man." *Modern China* 32, no. 2 (2006): 181–220.

———. *Reconfiguring Chinese Nationalism: How the Qing Frontier and Its Indigenes Became Chinese*. New York: Palgrave Macmillian, 2007.

Lelyveld, David. "Colonial Knowledge and the Fate of Hindustani." *Comparative Studies in Society and History* 35, no. 4 (October 1993): 665–82.

Li Ji. *The Formation of the Chinese People. An Anthropological Inquiry*. New York: Russell and Russell, 1967.

Li Qiao. *Yizu jiang Zhang Chong zhuanji* [A Biography of the Yi General Zhang Chong]. Chengdu: Sichuan wenyi chubanshe, 1989.

Li Qunjie. "*Tigong wo sheng jige ge gezu ge cheng de zhengming chubu yijian de baogao.*" YNPA, Quanzong 2152, Index 1, File 44: 74–78.

———. "*Yunnan sheng shaoshu minzu shibie yanjiuzu chengli huishang de baogao.*" YNPA, Quanzong 2152, Index 1, File 44: 11–15.

Li Yunbing. *Laji yu yanjiu* [Research on the Laji Language]. Beijing: Minzu chubanshe, 2000.

Lieu, D. K. "The 1912 Census of China." *Bulletin de l'Institut International de Statistique* 26, no.2 (1931): 85–109.

Lin Hsiao-ting, *Tibet and Nationalist China's Frontier: Intrigues and Ethnopolitics, 1928–49*. Vancouver: University of British Columbia Press, 2006.

Lipman, Jonathan. *Familiar Strangers: A History of Muslims in Northwest China*. Seattle: University of Washington Press, 1997.

———. "How Many Minzu in a Nation? Modern Travelers Meet China's Frontier Peoples." *Inner Asia* 4 (2002): 113–30.

Litzinger, Ralph. "Memory Work: Reconstituting the Ethnic in Post-Mao China." *Cultural Anthropology* 13, no. 2 (May 1998): 224–55.

———. *Other Chinas: The Yao and the Politics of National Belonging.* Durham: Duke University Press, 2000.

Liu, Xiaoyuan. *Frontier Passages: Ethnopolitics and the Rise of Chinese Communism, 1921–1945.* Stanford: Stanford University Press, 2004.

Ma Yin, ed. *China's Minority Nationalities.* Beijing: Foreign Languages Press, 1989.

MacFarquhar, Roderick, and Michael Schoenhals. *Mao's Last Revolution.* Cambridge, MA: Harvard University Press, 2006.

Mackerras, Colin. *China's Minorities: Integration and Modernization in the Twentieth Century.* Hong Kong: Oxford University Press, 1994.

———. *China's Minority Cultures: Identities and Integration Since 1912.* New York: St. Martin's Press, 1995.

Maher, John Peter. "More on the History of the Comparative Methods: The Tradition of Darwinism in August Schleicher's work" *Anthropological Linguistics* 8 (1966): 1–12.

Makley, Charlene E. "The Meaning of Liberation: Representations of Tibetan Women." *Tibet Journal* 22, no. 2 (1997): 4–29.

———. "Gendered Practices and the Inner Sanctum: The Reconstruction of Tibetan Sacred Space in 'China's Tibet.'" In *Sacred Spaces and Powerful Places in Tibetan Culture: A Collection of Essays,* edited by Toni Huber, 343–66. Dharamsala, India: Library of Tibetan Works and Archives, 1999.

———. "On the Edge of Respectability: Sexual Politics in China's Tibet." *positions* 10, no. 3 (2002): 575–630.

Martin, Terry. *The Affirmative Action Empire: Nations and Nationalism in the Soviet Union, 1923–1939.* Cornell: Cornell University Press, 2001.

Matsumoto Masumi. *Chūgoku minzoku seisaku no kenkyū: Shinmatsu kara 1945-nen made no 'minzokuron' o chūshin ni* [A Study of the Ethnic Policies of China: Focusing on "Ethnic Theories" from the Late Qing until 1945]. Tokyo: Taga Shuppan, 1999.

McKhann, Charles F. "Fleshing Out the Bones: Kinship and Cosmology in Naxi Religion." PhD diss., University of Chicago, 1992.

———. "The Naxi and the Nationalities Question." In *Cultural Encounters on China's Ethnic Frontiers,* edited by Stevan Harrell, 39–62. Seattle: University of Washington Press, 1995.

Millward, James. "The Qing Frontier." In *Remapping China: Fissures in Historical Terrain,* edited by Gail Hershatter. Stanford: Stanford University Press, 1996.

———. *Beyond the Pass: Economy, Ethnicity, and Empire in Qing Central Asia, 1759–1864.* Stanford: Stanford University Press, 1998.

Mitchell, Timothy. *Colonising Egypt.* Berkeley: University of California Press, 1991.

———. *Rule of Experts: Egypt, Techno-Politics, Modernity.* Berkeley: University of California Berkeley, 2002.

Moerman, Michael. "Ethnic Identification in a Complex Civilization: Who Are the Lue?" *American Anthropologist* 67, no. 5 (1965): 1215–30.

Moseley, George. *The Consolidation of the South China Frontier.* Berkeley: University of California Press, 1973.

Mueggler, Erik. *The Age of Wild Ghosts: Memory, Violence, and Place in Southwest China.* Berkeley: University of California Press, 2001.

Mullaney, Thomas S. "Coming to Terms with the Nation: Towards a History of the Ethnic

Classification Project (*minzu shibie*)." Paper Presented at the Fifty-Fourth Annual Meeting of the Association for Asian Studies, Washington, DC, April 2002.

———. "55 + 1 = 1 or the Strange Calculus of Chinese Nationhood." *China Information* 18, no. 2 (July 2004): 197–205.

———. "Ethnic Classification Writ Large: The 1954 Yunnan Province Ethnic Classification Project and its Foundations in Republican-Era Taxonomic Thought." *China Information* 18, no. 2 (July 2004): 207–41.

———. "Coming to Terms with the Nation: Ethnic Classification and Scientific Statecraft in Modern China, 1928–1954." PhD diss., Columbia University, 2006.

Nationality Work Editorial Board, ed. *Minzu gongzuo shouce* [Handbook for Nationality Work]. Kunming: Yunnan People's Press, 1985.

Newmeyer, F. J. *The Politics of Linguistics*. Chicago: University of Chicago Press, 1986.

Notar, Beth Ellen. "Wild Histories: Popular Culture, Place, and the Past in Southwest China." PhD diss., University of Michigan, 1999.

Oakes, Timothy S. "Ethnic Tourism in Rural Guizhou: Sense of Place and the Commerce of Authenticity." In *Tourism, Ethnicity, and the State in Asian and Pacific Societies*, edited by Michel Picard and Robert E. Wood, 35–70. Honolulu: University of Hawai'i Press, 1997.

———. *Tourism and Modernity in China*. London: Routledge, 1998.

Ou, Tsuin-chen. "Education in Wartime China." In *Nationalist China during the Sino-Japanese War, 1937–1945*, edited by Paul K. T. Sih, 89–123. Hicksville, NY: Exposition Press, 1977.

Pang, Keng-Fong. "Being Hui, Huan-nang, and Utsat Simultaneously: Contextualizing History and Identities of the Austronesian-Speaking Hainan Muslims." In *Negotiating Ethnicities in China and Taiwan*, edited by Melissa J. Brown. Berkeley: Institute of East Asian Studies, University of California, 1997.

Pelkey, Jamin R. "Initial Investigative Report on the Yi Peoples of Honghe Prefecture." N.d. Unpublished manuscript provided by the author.

———. "Yunnan's Myriad 'Yi': Profiles on the Peoples Classified as 'Yi' in Yunnan Province." 1999. Unpublished manuscript provided by the author.

Peng Yingming. "*Guanyu wo guo minzu gainian lishi de chubu kaocha* [Preliminary Research on the History of the Concept of minzu in China]." *Minzu yanjiu* 2 (1985): 5–11.

Penner, Peter. *Robert Needham Cust, 1821–1909: A Personal Biography*. New Delhi: Chanakya Publications, 1987.

Perdue, Peter. "Empire and Nation in Comparative Perspective: Frontier Administration in Eighteenth-Century China." *Journal of Early Modern History* 5, no. 4 (November 2001): 282–304.

———. *China Marches West: The Qing Conquest of Central Eurasia*. Cambridge, MA: Harvard University Press, 2005.

Pusey, James Reeve. *China and Charles Darwin*. Cambridge, MA: Harvard University Press, 1983.

Qian Liquan, ed. *Minzu gongzuo daquan*. Beijing: Guoji jingji chubanshe, 1994.

Rawski, Evelyn S. "Presidential Address: Reenvisioning the Qing: The Significance of the Qing Period in Chinese History." *Journal of Asian Studies* 55, no. 4 (November 1996): 829–50.

———. *The Last Emperors: A Social History of Qing Imperial Institutions*. Berkeley: University of California Press, 1998.

Rhoads, Edward J. M. *Manchus and Han: Ethnic Relations and Political Power in Late Qing and Early Republican China, 1861–1928*. Seattle: University of Washington Press, 2000.

Robins, R. H. *A Short History of Linguistics*. Bloomington: Indiana University Press, 1967.

Rossabi, Morris, ed. *Governing China's Multiethnic Frontiers*. Seattle: University of Washington Press, 2004.

Salisbury, Harrison E. *The Long March*. New York: Harper and Row, 1985.

Sampson, Geoffrey. *Schools of Linguistics*. Stanford: Stanford University Press, 1980.

Saussure, Ferdinand de. *Course in General Linguistics*. LaSalle, IL: Open Court, 1986.

Sautman, Barry. "Myths of descent, racial nationalism and ethnic minorities in the People's Republic of China." In *The Construction of Racial Identities in China and Japan*, edited by Frank Diköktter, 75–95. Hong Kong: Hong Kong University Press, 1997.

Schein, Louisa. "Gender and Internal Orientalism in China." *Modern China* 23, no. 1 (January 1997): 69–98.

———. *Minority Rules: The Miao and the Feminine in China's Cultural Politics*. Durham: Duke University Press, 2000.

Schutz, A.J. *The Voices of Eden: A History of Hawaiian Language Studies*. Honolulu: University of Hawai'i Press, 1994.

Schwarcz, Vera. *The Chinese Enlightenment: Intellectuals and the Legacy of the May Fourth Movement of 1919*. Berkeley: California University Press, 1986.

Schwarz, Henry G. *Chinese Policies towards Minorities: An Essay and Documents*. Bellingham: Western Washington State College Program in East Asian Studies, 1971.

———. "Ethnic Minorities and Ethnic Policies in China." In *The Background of Ethnic Conflict*, edited by William Petersen, 137–50. Leiden: E. J. Brill, 1978.

Scott, James C. *Seeing Like a State: How Certain Schemes to Improve the Human Condition Have Failed*. New Haven: Yale University Press, 1998.

Sen, Sudipta. "The New Frontiers of Manchu China and the Historiography of Asian Empires: A Review Essay." *Journal of Asian Studies* 61, no. 1 (2002): 165–77.

Sha Like. "'Zuqun' yu 'minzu' de guoji duihua [The International Dialogue about 'Zuqun' and 'Minzu']." *Minzu wenti yanjiu* 12, no. 7 (2001).

Shabad, Theodore. "Counting 600 Million Chinese." *Far Eastern Survey* (April 1956): 60–61.

She Yize. *Zhongguo tusi zhidu* [China's Native Chieftain System]. Chongqing: Zhengzhong shuju, 1944.

Shih, Chuan-kang. "The Yongning Moso: Sexual Union, Household Organization, Gender, and Ethnicity in a Matrilineal Duolocal Society in Southwest China." PhD diss., Stanford University, 1993.

———. "Genesis of Marriage among the Moso and Empire-Building in Late Imperial China." *Journal of Asian Studies* 60, no. 2 (2001): 381–412

Shin, Leo K. *The Making of the Chinese State: Ethnicity and Expansion on the Ming Borderlands*. Cambridge: Cambridge University Press, 2006.

Silverstein, M. "Encountering Language and Languages of Encounter in North American Ethnohistory." *Journal of Linguistic Anthropology* 6, no. 2 (1997): 126–44.

Sohn, I. G. "Taxonomic Synonymy, What Is It And Why?" *Journal of Paleontology* 68, no. 3 (1994): 669–70.

Solinger, Dorothy J. "Minority Nationalities in China's Yunnan Province: Assimilation, Power, and Policy in a Socialist State." *World Politics* 30, no. 1 (October 1977): 1–23.

———. *Regional Government and Political Integration in Southwest China, 1949–1954: A Case Study*. Berkeley: University of California Press, 1977.

Star, Susan Leigh, ed. *Ecologies of Knowledge: Work and Politics in Science and Technology*. Albany: SUNY Press, 1995.

———. "Introduction." In *Ecologies of Knowledge: Work and Politics in Science and Technology*, edited by Susan Leigh Star, 1–38. Albany: SUNY Press, 1995.

Stocking, George. *Race, Culture, and Evolution: Essays in the History of Anthropology*. Chicago: University of Chicago Press, 1982.

Stranahan, Patricia. *Underground: The Shanghai Communist Party and the Politics of Survival, 1927–1937*. Lanham, MD: Rowman and Littlefield, 1998.

Suny, Ronald Grigor, and Terry Martin, eds. *A State of Nations: Empire and Nation-Making in the Age of Lenin and Stalin*. Oxford: Oxford University Press, 2001.

Sutton, Donald S. "Violence and Ethnicity on a Qing Colonial Frontier." *Modern Asian Studies* 37, no. 1 (2003): 41–80.

———. "Ethnicity and the Miao Frontier in the Eighteenth Century." In *Empire at the Margins*, edited by Pamela Crossley, Helen Siu, and Donald Sutton, 190–228. Berkeley: Univeristy of California Press, 2006.

Swain, Margaret Byrne. "Pere Vial and the Gni-P'a. Orientalist Scholarship and the Christian Project." In *Cultural Encounters on China's Ethnic Frontiers*, edited by Stevan Harrell, 140–85. Seattle: University of Washington Press, 1995.

Tam Siu-mi and David Y. H. Wu. "Minority Policy in China: Its Implications in Southeast Asia." *Southeast Asian Journal of Social Sciences* 16, no. 2 (1988): 78–95.

Tapp, Nicholas. "In Defense of the Archaic: A Reconsideration of the 1950s Ethnic Classification Project in China." *Asian Ethnicity* 3, no. 1 (2002): 63–84.

Taub, Lisa. "Evolutionary Ideas and 'Empirical' Methods: The Analogy between Language and Species in Works by Lyell and Schleicher." *British Journal for the History of Science* 26, no. 2 (June 1993): 171–93.

Thierry, Francois. "Empire and Minority in China." In *Minority Peoples in the Age of Nation-States*, edited by Gérard Ghaliand, 76–99. Paris: Pluto, 1989.

Thongchai, Winichakul. *Siam Mapped: A History of the Geo-Body of a Nation*. Honolulu: University of Hawai'i Press, 1994.

Thoraval, Joël. "Le Concept Chinois de Nation est-il 'Obscur'? À Propos du Débat sur la Notion de minzu dans les Années 1980." *Bulletin de sinologie* 65 (1990): 24–41.

Tillman, Hoyt. "Proto-Nationalism in Twelfth-Century China? The Case of Ch'en Liang." *Harvard Journal of Asiatic Studies* 39, no. 2 (1979): 403–28.

Townsend, James. "Chinese Nationalism." In *Chinese Nationalism*, edited by Jonathan Unger, 1–30. New York: M. E. Sharpe, 1996.

Trask, R. L. *The Dictionary of Historical and Comparative Linguistics*. Edinburgh: Edinburgh University Press, 2000.

Trouillot, Michel-Rolph. *Silencing the Past: Power and the Production of History*. Boston: Beacon Press, 1995.

Tufte, Edward R. *Envisioning Information. The Visual Display of Quantitative Information.* Chesire, CT: Graphics Press, 1990.

Unger, Jonathan, ed. *Chinese Nationalism.* Armonk: M. E. Sharpe, 1996.

Wang Jianmin. *Zhongguo minzuxue shi: Shang, 1903-1949* [The History of Ethnology in China: Part 1, 1903-1949]. Kunming: Jiaoyu chubanshe, 1997.

Wang Jianmin, Zhang Haiyang, and Hu Hongbao. *Zhongguo minzuxue shi: Xia, 1950-1997* [The History of Ethnology in China: Part 2, 1950-1997]. Kunming: Jiaoyu chubanshe, 1999.

Wang Mingming. "The Third Eye: Towards a Critique of 'Nativist Anthropology.'" *Critique of Anthropology* 22 (2002).

Waterman, John. *Perspectives in Linguistics.* Chicago: University of Chicago Press, 1970.

White, Sydney. "Medical Discourses, Naxi Identities, and the State: Transformations in Socialist China." PhD diss., University of California Berkeley, 1993.

———. "State Discourses, Minority Policies, and the Politics of Identity in the Lijiang Naxi Peoples' Autonomous County." In *Nationalism and Ethnoregional Identities in China,* edited by William Safran, 9-27. London: Frank Cass, 1998.

Wiens, Herold J. *China's March toward the Tropics: A Discussion of the Southward Penetration of China's Culture, Peoples, and Political Control in Relation to the Non-Han-Chinese Peoples of South China and in the Perspective of Historical and Cultural Geography.* Hamden, CT: Shoe String Press, 1954.

Wolf, Arthur P., and Chieh-shan Huang. *Marriage and Adoption in China, 1845-1945.* Stanford: Stanford University Press, 1980.

Wong, Siu-lun. *Sociology and Socialism in Contemporary China.* London: Routledge and K. Paul, 1979.

Wu, David Y. H. "Chinese Minority Policy and the Meaning of Minority Culture: The Example of Bai in Yunnan, China." *Human Organization* 49, no. 1 (1990): 1-13.

———. "The Construction of Chinese and Non-Chinese Identities." *Daedalus* 120, no. 2 (1991): 159-79.

Xie Benshu. *Zhang Chong zhuan 1901-1980* [A Biography of Zhang Chong, 1901-1980]. Chengdu: Sichuan renmin chubanshe, 1993.

Xu Lin. "*Cangshan erhai lian yulong xueshan qing.*" *Dali wenhua* 1 (1992).

Yong, Young-tsu. *Search for Modern Nationalism: Zhang Binglin and Revolutionary China, 1869-1936.* Oxford: Oxford University Press, 1989.

You Zhong. *Yunnan minzu shi* [History of the Nationalities in Yunnan]. Kunming: Yunnan daxue chubanshe, 2005.

Zarrow, Peter. "Historical Trauma: Anti-Manchuism and Memories of Atrocity in Late Qing China." *History and Memory* 16, no. 2 (Fall/Winter 2004): 67-107.

Zhang Haiyang. *Zhongguo de duoyuan wenhua yu Zhongguoren de rentong.* Beijing: Minzu chubanshe, 2006.

Zhao, Gang. "Reinventing China: Imperial Qing Ideology and the Rise of Modern Chinese National Identity in the Early Twentieth Century." *Modern China* 32, no. 1 (2006): 3-30.

Zhaona Situ and Li Hengpu. *Dangdai Zhongguo minzu yuyanxuejia* [Contemporary Chinese Minority Linguists]. Xining: Qinghai renmin chubanshe, 1989.

Zhonggong zhongyang wenxian yanjiushi, ed., *Mao Zedong nianpu* [Chronological Biography of Mao Zedong, vol. 2]. Beijing: Renmin chubanshe, 1993.

Zhou Minglang. *Multilingualism in China: The Politics of Writing Reforms for Minority Languages, 1949–2002*. Berlin: Mouton de Gruyter, 2003.

Zhou Minglang and Sun Hongkai, eds. *Language Policy in the People's Republic of China: Theory and Practice since 1949*. Boston: Kluwer Academic Publishers, 2004.

Zhou Xiyin. "Hongjun Changzheng yu dang de minzu, tongxian he zongjiao zhengce [The Red Army's Long March and the Party's Nationality, United Front and Religion Policy]." In *Changzheng dashidian*, ed. Changzheng dashidian bianweihui, vol. 2. Guiyang: Guizhou renmin chubanshe, 1996.

INDEX

Italicized page numbers refer to maps, figures, and tables.

217

TEXT
10/12.5 Minion Pro

DISPLAY
Minion Pro (Open Type)

COMPOSITOR
Integrated Composition Systems

CARTOGRAPHER
Bill Nelson

INDEXER
Sharon Sweeney

Printed in the USA
CPSIA information can be obtained
at www.ICGtesting.com
JSHW021754050324
58636JS00002B/142

9 780520 272743